Understanding Financial Statements

UNDERSTANDING FINANCIAL STATEMENTS

Vern Krishna

CM, QC, FRSC, FCGA
BCom (Manchester), MBA, LLB (Alberta)
DCL (Cambridge), LLM (Harvard)

University of Ottawa (Common Law)
Barrister at Law, Borden Ladner Gervais, LLP

IRWIN
LAW

Published in 2013 by

Irwin Law Inc.
14 Duncan Street
Suite 206
Toronto, ON
M5H 3G8

www.irwinlaw.com

ISBN: 978-1-55221-324-7
e-book ISBN: 978-1-55221-325-4

Library and Archives Canada Cataloguing in Publication

Krishna, Vern
    Understanding financial statements / Vern Krishna.

Includes bibliographical references and index.
Issued also in electronic format.
ISBN 978-1-55221-324-7

    1. Financial statements — Canada. I. Title.

HF5681.B2K75 2013   657'.30971   C2013-901409-8

The publisher acknowledges the financial support of the Government of Canada through the Canada Book Fund for its publishing activities.

We acknowledge the assistance of the OMDC Book Fund, an initiative of Ontario Media Development Corporation.

Printed and bound in Canada.

1 2 3 4 5   17 16 15 14 13

To Savitri, Linda, Nicola, Sacha, Vivian, and Biggie

Summary Table of Contents

Detailed Table of Contents

Chapter III: Generally Accepted Accounting Principles and Reporting Standards *48*

Preface

All commercial legal arrangements have financial and accounting implications. Similarly, all financial statements reflect relationships from consummated and, sometimes, potential, commercial transactions. Hence, the inextricable link between law and accounting requires lawyers, directors, managers, and investors to have an understanding of financial statements.

The purpose of this primer is to educate users, and potential users, in the art of reading and understanding financial statements after they have been prepared by accountants. This is not a text on preparing financial statements.

The events of the past decade illustrate the central role of properly measuring and recording financial information in both private and public corporations. Events such as Livent, Enron, Hollinger, WorldCom, Tyco, and, most recently, Nortel, are graphic examples of the need to understand financial statements in the regulation and management of corporations. In each of the above events, accountants and management played the central role in preparing financial statements. However, it was left to others — lawyers, investors, and directors — to interpret the results and make decisions. Users who are untrained in reading financial statements are vulnerable.

Lawyers and directors interact with other professions in interpreting, drafting, and litigating issues involving financial information. Although there are many textbooks on accounting and preparation of statements, there are no easy-to-read texts aimed specifically at non-technical users of financial information. This text is intended to fill that void and provide users with an understanding of financial statements and reporting standards so that they can better appreciate the nuances, meaning, pitfalls, and limitations of financial information.

The text is a primer, not an encyclopedia. It covers the following aspects of financial information:

- Explanation of each of the financial statements and their components;
- Basic concepts and unwritten conventions of accounting;
- Generally accepted accounting principles (GAAP) and International Financial Reporting Standards (IFRS);
- Role of auditors and liability for audits;
- Interpretation of financial statements; and
- Legal clauses in corporate and business agreements.

Thus, we emphasize understanding, rather than preparing, financial statements that have been prepared by accountants for legal and business purposes.

I am acutely aware of the elevation in blood pressure that some people experience when they see numbers. Hence, I have deliberately used simple and plain English to describe the meaning of financial statements. This may be disappointing for accountants and MBAs but will, I hope, make the subject less intimidating for "non-numerical" people. I also include a brief discussion of the time value of money, which is the single most important concept underlying finance and valuation.

A significant change in the landscape of Canadian accounting occurred on 1 January 2013. Effective that date, Canadian public (and some private) entities must apply International Financial Reporting Standards (IFRS) to financial statements. Some of these standards (for example, IFRS 13) concern new methodologies in measuring "fair value" and disclosure. The text refers to some of the salient IFRS in understanding financial statements.

I welcome constructive comments for further improvement: Vkrishna@blg.com.

The text is current as of 1 April 2013.

Acknowledgment

I acknowledge the generous assistance of the fellows and life fellows of the Foundation for Legal Research in the preparation of this text.

Chapter I: Introduction

Accounting is the language of business and government. Lawyers, directors, businesspeople, creditors, and investors should understand the language so that they can evaluate the results of operations and the status of the corporation. Financial meltdowns at Lehman Brothers, Enron, WorldCom Inc, Nortel, and Madoff teach us that law and accounting are intertwined and permeate all commercial transactions and investment decisions. Bad accounting is the stepping stone to financial disaster.

A. BUSINESS CYCLES

The business cycle of a manufacturing or production business generally comprises seven stages:

1) Injection of cash;
2) Purchase of raw materials for cash or credit;
3) Production of raw materials into work in progress (WIP);
4) Completion of finished goods or products for sale;
5) Sales for cash or on account;
6) Collection of accounts receivable from customers; and
7) Return of cash and payment of accounts payable to creditors.

At any point, there are multiple and overlapping cycles. The length of the cycle depends upon the nature of the business. The cycle may be extremely short — for example, a fast-food business catering to customers in a downtown business area. On the other hand, the cycle can be extremely long — for example, a company producing scotch whisky that matures for thirty years before bringing it onto the market.

B. WHAT IS ACCOUNTING?

Businesses record transactions at each stage of the business cycle to determine the profitability of the enterprise, track cash flows, and determine what it owns and owes. At the end of the enterprise's fiscal year, accounting statements will summarize the transactions and present a snapshot of its year-end status, and its profitability for the year.

There are three distinct elements of accounting: identification, measurement, and communication. It is the third element (communication) of accounting information that is of greatest interest to lawyers, directors, and other users of financial statements. Hence, this text focuses on *understanding* financial statements and not on preparing them. Too much information about the preparation of accounting statements is unproductive. However, to understand what is being communicated in the financial statements, users should have at least a modest understanding of the general principles and concepts underlying their preparation.

Lawyers draw on financial information in many areas of practice. For many lawyers, however, the world of financial accounting is a mystery involving numbers and, as such, best left to accountants. The accounting profession welcomes the lawyer's aversion to numbers because it allows them to benefit from the mysterious "science" of numbers.

Accountants use arcane terms and opaque language and speak an obscure language that few translate for the world at large. That, however, should neither surprise nor disappoint lawyers. Every profession seeks to ring fence its monopolistic territory. It is not entirely an accident that lawyers in medieval England drafted their pleadings in Latin and argued in the courts in Norman French, thereby excluding most of the population from understanding their "science."

It is difficult, however, to conceive of lawyers who act in business, commercial, or financial transactions not getting involved with numbers at one level or another. Lawyers deal with businesses, shareholders, creditors, debtors, governments, and regulatory bodies. They arrange real estate deals and engage in family transactions.

Most civil litigation is a fight for money. Whether in contract, tort, securities, insolvency, corporate, or family law, litigation inevitably draws upon accounting, finance, and tax law in calculating damages or providing a civil remedy.

If accounting is the language of business, lawyers who deal with commercial issues should understand the rudimentary concepts of the discipline. The professional obligation to be "competent" requires commercial lawyers to have at least a modest understanding of the principles of accounting and finance. Would a lawyer who wants to practise Canadian law be professionally responsible if he or she did not have a basic understanding of the English language?

Lawyers encounter accounting issues and terminology in a variety of negotiated agreements. Even a simple bonus contract that promises an executive a percentage of "net profit" involves subtle issues, many of which end up in litigation. Of course, lawyers must also be sensitive to the possibility that an enterprise has engaged in, or been a victim of, financial fraud, which, almost inevitably, involves financial statements.

Law students, lawyers, and judges fear financial statements. The mere mention of numbers elevates blood pressure and causes numbness in critical nerve centres. Legal minds suffer hyper-anxiety when presented with financial information that requires an understanding of the four basic functions of arithmetic. The stress is entirely understandable. Law schools attract many students from the arts, humanities, social sciences, and philosophy, which, generally, are non-quantitative disciplines.

To be sure, accounting has become more complex in response to the needs of modern business. As we shall see, there is a shift from the historical cost of accounting model towards a mixed-attribute model that relies increasingly on reporting transactions at their fair value. At the same time, there is continuing division between accounting standards setting bodies. The International Accounting Standards Board (IASB) and the American Financial Accounting Standards Board (FASB) have not yet managed to agree (as of November 2012) on accounting principles in financial reporting. Absent some consensus between standards-setting bodies, there will continue to be reduced comparability between international financial statements.

Lawyers must also pay attention to the various standards in drafting agreements. Canada has adopted International Financial Reporting Standards (IFRS) issued by IASB and has converted its Generally Accepted Accounting Principles (GAAP) to harmonize with the European Union. The conversion became effective for Canadian public companies after 1 January 2011. Equally significant, for American publicly traded companies, the *Sarbanes-Oxley Act* (SOX) of 2002 — the most significant piece of accounting legislation since the enactment of the *Securities Act* in 1933 — adds a new level of complexity (and cost) for listed companies in the United States.

We recognize that there are fundamental differences in the culture of lawyers and accountants. Lawyers rely heavily upon the form of their transactions for legal effect. For example, a 999-year lease is just what it says — a "lease" without transfer of legal title. Accountants often rely on economic substance in characterizing transactions for financial statement purposes. In economic substance, a 999-year lease is the financial equivalent of an absolute transfer in fee simple title. Unfortunately, proving this proposition requires familiarity with the time value of money and net present value concepts.

The form versus substance approach is particularly relevant in timing recognition of revenue in financial statements. Transfers of property with side agreements can raise subtle issues as to whether or not there has been a "true sale" involving a transfer of the risks and rewards of ownership.[1] Enron, for example, recognized

---

1   Canadian Institute of Chartered Accountants, *CICA Handbook — Accounting*, loose-leaf (Toronto: Canadian Institute of Chartered Accountants, 2010), section 3400 [*CICA Handbook*].

revenues on its books after transferring certain assets to special purpose entities. The various side agreements resulted in the company retaining all the risks of ownership after the transfers. In fact, Enron did not really "earn" the revenues that it reported on its financial statements, which ultimately led to its downfall. Investors, pension funds, and employees discovered this in the litigation that followed, but by then they were fighting over the company's carcass. Closer attention by lawyers to the red flags of accounting would have saved a lot of people grief in their retirement.

Users of financial information should also understand the principles and judgment that accountants apply in preparing financial statements according to international and domestic standards. Accounting involves estimates and forecasting. Lawyers must deal with accounting problems in the same way they address other issues, with judgment and analysis. This means that lawyers need to understand accounting to draft financial clauses in contracts, structure negotiated settlements, advocate in litigation, plan for tax, and negotiate damage awards.

Users do not need to understand the detailed processes of identification and recording—the debits and credits of bookkeeping—of financial information. That is the job of accountants and bookkeepers. Nevertheless, the end user of financial statements should have a general understanding of the principal assumptions—the rules of grammar of financial language—that accountants use in preparing statements.

It is easy to build the case for corporate lawyers to understand the language of accounting and finance. Corporate lawyers deal every day with corporations, banks, financial statements, shareholder rights, partnership agreements, insolvency and bankruptcy trustees, mergers and acquisitions. Every one of these areas involves digesting financial information—sometimes fairly simple; other times, complex and sophisticated—and crafting it into legal documents.

Commercial lawyers should understand the handling of securitization and other financial transactions that rely on the value of assets and the impact of their transactions on client financial statements. Commercial litigators often retain forensic accounting experts to testify in court in fraud cases and valuation experts to assess economic damages. They can be helpful in litigation. The key is to find one who can speak plain English to the lawyer, judge, and jury.

Hence, it is virtually impossible for business lawyers to avoid accounting concepts, such as "net income," "profit," "net book value," "net worth," assets and Generally Accepted Accounting Principles (GAAP). Contracts — for example, employment contracts, union contracts, lending agreements, buy-sell agreements — all refer to material related to financial statements and concepts. Even a simple contract that provides a manager with a bonus equal to 10 percent of his division's "net income" for the year is implicitly engaging a financial accounting concept that someone must interpret. All too often, however, lawyers run for the escape hatch by simply referring to GAAP, but without any clear understanding of what GAAP is or which GAAP — Canadian, US, or International — apply to the particular agreement. Call the accountant when trouble occurs and the matter is in litigation. At that time, the accountant can give the lawyer an intensive course on the particular GAAP that are the subject of the litigation.

Family lawyers handling divorce, separation, and custody proceedings must also wrestle with financial statements in the division of family assets, and understand the nuances of the statements and the financial and tax implications of property and pension divisions. Of course, family lawyers handling support agreements must understand not only the legal, but also the financial, character of "income" for family law and tax purposes.

Estate planners think about death. They take into account not only the net wealth of their clients' estate, but also the financial and tax impact of property distributions to beneficiaries, who may be individuals, foundations, corporations, or charities.

Even criminal lawyers should understand financial statements, particularly if they prosecute or defend white-collar crime. The Madoff Ponzi scheme — the largest in history — netted the mastermind (Mr Bernie Madoff) nearly $50 billion (US). As the scheme unravelled, it became clear that for twenty-five years he had sucked some very sophisticated investors as enthusiastic disciples into his grand plan. The criminal trial of three senior executives at Nortel in 2012 focused almost exclusively on accounting entries and the impact of using reserves on income.

Insider trading, stock market manipulation, stock option price fixing, and even old-fashioned looting of corporate assets all impact financial statements. Prosecuting and defence counsel in such cases must manoeuvre through dense financial data in long trials purportedly assisted by the dense testimony of "forensic" accountants. In these cases, the fraudster does not use accounting for the purpose of communication. Quite the contrary, the fraudster (with the aid of his financial advisors) uses accounting to cloud the financial picture in order to continue his wrongdoing.

C. EVOLUTION OF ACCOUNTING

Given the long history of business — the Greeks were trading in India in 400 BC — it is surprising that modern-day accounting begins only in 1494, when an Italian monk, Luca Pacioli, published a book on double-entry record keeping. Pacioli was not a businessman, but an academic mathematician who was trying to find uses for the new (in Europe) mystery of numbers. Pacioli, the father of accounting, was born in Borgo San Sepolcro, a small city east of Florence in Tuscany. San Sepolcro is famous for at least three things: 1) tasty dried mushrooms; 2) the *Resurrection of Piero della Francesca*, one of the world's great paintings; and 3) the statue of Luca Pacioli. He wrote his treatise (his *Summa*) at the height of the Italian Renaissance.

It took another 500 years for the next major developments in accounting following the great boom in capital formation that followed the American Civil War. This time the protagonists were mostly Scotsmen — the contributors of whisky, golf, and accountants. Today they have expanded into the largest purveyors of legal services.[2]

---

2   Pacioli's text, *Everything About Arithmetic, Geometry and Proportion*, is the first organized treatise on double-entry bookkeeping.

Accounting is the orderly assimilation of numbers for the purposes of preparing financial statements and communicating with users of such statements. As ownership of capital separated from management of capital, the need for accounting to the owners of capital (the stewardship function) became more important. "Public" accountants — that is, accountants from outside the business — were needed to audit and certify financial statements and render an opinion on them. In England and Canada, such accountants are known as "licensed public accountants"; in the United States they are called "certified public accountants."

Accounting has two distinct roles: reporting financial statements that focus on stewardship of corporate assets; and providing financial information for decision making. Both roles, however, rely on historical data. The stewardship aspect of accounting in reporting to the owners of capital remains an important function in the development of the modern corporation and the raising of capital in the public markets. As public financial markets opened and expanded, however, investors and their advisors came to rely on financial information to evaluate public companies. Thus, public agencies — such as the Ontario Securities Commission (OSC) in Canada and the Securities & Exchange Commission (SEC) in the United States — play an important role in the development and dissemination of financial information to investors.

Traditionally, financial statements focused primarily on their stewardship function. Management is the steward of capital supplied by the owners (shareholders) and creditors who contribute or lend money to the business. The key aspect of stewardship reporting is on the measurement of historical "profits" or "net income."

In the past fifty years, however, the perspective of accounting has shifted from economic income measurement to an informational approach. The objective of the informational approach is to facilitate decision making by investors. Informational reporting also allows other users — such as creditors and contracting parties — to structure their contracts by reference to financial reporting data. For example, management bonuses and incentive contracts often rely upon the accounting entity's "net income" or the "profit" of a division of the entity. Similarly, holders of stock options in corporations are keenly interested in its "net income," which will drive the market price of the stock and, therefore, determine the value of their options. Thus, accounting has evolved from its initial role of stewardship reporting to providing information to existing and potential investors in the capital markets.

D. FINANCE

Corporate finance is the study of how businesses value and raise and use capital. Hence, finance is a mode of analysis to value assets and businesses. Financial accounting provides information that analysts use in business valuations.

Since all value depends upon time of payment or receipt of funds, the "time value of money" is the single most important concept in finance. For example, how do we value a bond, preferred share, or common share of a going concern business? Finance deals with such questions, which require reliable information from accountants on the "profit," "income," "net income," "earnings," and assets of the enterprise. Thus, finance relies upon accounting information. As we read our daily papers, we see how unreliable accounting information can lead to financial disasters and severe loses for investors in the capital markets.

E. THE REGULATORS

Regulators are concerned with businesses that sell securities (stocks, bonds, and derivatives) to the public. The primary focus of securities regulation is on common stockholders. Creditors and labour unions are also interested in financial information, but such groups are not the primary focus of securities regulators and legislation.

Canada also has thirteen securities regulators, one for each province and territory. The Ontario Securities Commission is by far the largest in size and volume of transactions. The fragmentation of securities regulation results in a proliferation of administrative rules and dilution of expertise. In 2012, the Supreme Court of

Canada turned back an attempt by the federal government to form a unified National Securities Regulator.[3] In doing so, the Court underestimated the increasing internationalization of capital markets and the risks inherent in fragmented securities regulation. Instead, it emphasized the constitutional division of powers between federal and provincial (territorial) governments rather than on the economic substance of the "trade and commerce" power.

In the United States, the SEC is an independent agency created under the authority of the *Securities Acts* of 1933 and 1934. The role of the SEC is to ensure "full and fair" disclosure by corporations and issuers of securities to the public.

Accountants are also regulators concerned with the preparation of financial statements. The Canadian Institute of Chartered Accountants (CICA) has the primary responsibility for the development of accounting principles, which it publishes in its "Handbook" as Generally Accepted Accounting Principles (GAAP) and IFRS. Canadian corporate statutes recognize the CICA as the authoritative source of accounting principles for public and private corporations.[4]

The US accounting profession created the Financial Accounting Standards Board (FASB) in 1973 as a separate, permanent independent entity designed to regulate accounting principles. It comprises seven members: three from private accounting, two from industry, and one from government and academia. FASB members work exclusively for FASB during their five-year terms. The board issues Statements of Financial Accounting Standards (SFAS), which are the highest authority of the accounting profession on accounting principles.

Although organizations such as the CICA and FASB play an important role in the development of accounting standards and principles, there is also some development of accounting by businesses. As businesses enter into new transactions, they must develop methods for recording the transactions on their books. Absent specific

---

3   *Reference re Securities Act*, 2011 SCC 66, [2011] 3 SCR 837.
4   See CBCA.

guidance from the regulatory and supervisory authorities, businesses must make their own decisions about the appropriate method for recording such transactions. The businesses' auditors must then determine whether the new reporting method is appropriate and one on which they can express a favourable opinion. As more businesses employ the same method of reporting similar transactions, the method used becomes "generally accepted" for future transactions.

F. THE THREE Cs OF ACCOUNTING

Accounting concerns three Cs:

- Characterization;
- Classification; and
- Communication.

Characterization is the proper identification of revenues and expenses and their relationship to financial reporting periods. Improper characterization can seriously distort financial results. For example, we must decide whether inflows should be considered revenues in the current fiscal period or deferred sales in a subsequent period. Similarly, we must characterize expenditures as being current costs or future costs. Current costs would be expenses relevant to the current financial reporting period; future costs would be capital costs relevant to future time periods. Ultimately, the income statement must match current revenues against current costs in order to determine net income in the current period.

Having characterized a transaction properly, the next step is to classify it into its appropriate category. For example, an expenditure on account of assets must be further classified into whether the asset is a current or a long-term asset and, then, into the particular type of long-term asset, such as tangible or intangible. Misclassifications can distort financial ratios, which may affect financial covenants in contracts.

Classification means pigeonholing the particular financial item into its appropriate slot. Thus, we must ask questions such as:

- Where does the item belong?
- In which entity do we put the item?
- In which division within the entity should we classify the item?
- In which department within the division should we classify the item?
- Where should we allocate overhead cost?

We characterize transactions according to their fundamental nature. For example, a business must characterize its expenditures as expenses relevant to the current financial year or as capital outlays that pertain to future financial periods. Characterization errors result in misleading financial statements. In 2002, for example, WorldCom Inc characterized $8 billion of its expenses as assets in order to inflate its income, resulting in a massive fraud and the largest bankruptcy protection in US history.

Finally, having characterized and classified accounting information into a manageable form, we must communicate the information to potential users, which is the ultimate purpose of all financial statements. Effective communication requires full, fair, and clear disclosure of all relevant and material items for decision making. Thus, financial statements should use such form and terminology that significant information is readily understandable.[5]

Information must be relevant for decision making in allocating resources and investments. Investors, creditors, members, partners, government, and regulatory bodies all use information to make their decisions. To be sure, each of these users has a different focus and requires varying degrees of detail. For example, a tax authority requires much more detailed information than that released in public filings. Information for tax purposes is strictly confidential whereas public filings are intended for a wide audience. Nevertheless, there is a substantial degree of commonality between user needs. The principal difference between users is the degree of detail in the financial statements.

---

5   *CICA Handbook*, section 1400, para 06.

As in all communication, language is susceptible to linguistic error. Thus, we should not blindly believe everything we read or hear in the media. Phrases in financial statements may have subtle undertones. For example, on 30 December 2002, Tyco International filed a report with the Securities & Exchange Commission in the United States in which it said it was reducing previously reported earnings. Its auditors, PricewaterhouseCoopers, approved the financial disclosures at Tyco, despite the company's use of "aggressive accounting that, even when not erroneous, was undertaken with the purpose and effect of increasing reported results above what they would have been if more conservative methods were used"! What was PWC telling its audience of readers?

Obfuscation is an art. Politicians, lobbyists, and communications consultants practise it routinely. But so can business and accountants. For example, Research in Motion Ltd (RIM) suffered a disastrous year in 2011. The company introduced underwhelming products, and had service disruptions and blackouts of services. The company's stock fell 78 percent and the shares closed at $13.97 on Friday, 16 December 2011, a level not seen since 2004. In the face of such performance, the company issued the following statement:

> While we have remained solidly profitable and delivered significant unit volume during this transition, we recognize that our shareholders may feel that we have fallen short in terms of product execution, market share and financial performance. [Mr Balsillie, Co-chairman, in a conference call with investors.]

RIM closed at $7.59 on 23 October 2012 or 46 percent lower!

G. WHAT IS USEFUL INFORMATION?

Useful financial information in a commercial context concerns:

- Economic resources (assets): What does a business own?
- Obligations (liabilities): What does a business owe?
- Owners' investments (equity): What is the owner's investment?

- Changes in the preceding over time (income statement): How did a business perform?
- Solvency (cash flows): How much cash did a business generate?
- Economic performance (financial ratios): How do we measure performance?

The answers to these questions must be understandable, relevant, reliable, comparable, and timely. Only then can they be useful. We examine each of these aspects of financial information in the following chapters.

Chapter II: Fundamental Financial Concepts

Finance comprises a spectrum of accounting and financial principles, concepts, conventions, postulates, and axioms that, collectively, provide the reference points by which accounting bodies, regulatory agencies, and academics set new standards. Hence, we need to understand the fundamental concepts and their limitations.[1] We examine these concepts in this chapter as a stepping stone to discussing financial statements in later chapters.

A. MONETARY MEASUREMENT

Financial statements record only facts that we can express in monetary terms. They do not record other information that may be highly relevant in determining the viability or success of an enterprise. For example, a law firm's balance sheet will show only how much property the firm owns as assets: cash, receivables, work in process, investments, computers, furniture, art, land and buildings. The firm's

---

1   See, generally, Canadian Institute of Chartered Accountants, *CICA Handbook — Accounting*, loose-leaf (Toronto: Canadian Institute of Chartered Accountants, 2010), Part II, section 1000 [*CICA Handbook*]. The Financial Accounting Standards Board (FASB) in the United States has issued various *Statements of Financial Accounting Concepts* that address some of these fundamental issues, such as the purpose of financial statements, the nature of assets and liabilities, and the kind of information useful for users of financial statements.

balance sheet will not disclose anything about its "real," and most valuable, assets: the talent pool of its lawyers and staff—the assets that give it value and generate its revenues.

The following example shows three estimates of brand size and diversity of brand values for some of America's largest corporations in 2011.

Example Company	Interbrand	Millward Brown	Brand Finance
		(US$ billion)	
Coca-Cola	71.86		
IBM	69.91	100.85	36.16
Microsoft	59.09	78.24	42.81
Google	55.32	111.50	44.29
GE	42.81		
Apple		153.29	
McDonald's		81.02	
Walmart			36.22
Vodafone			30.67

Therefore, in analyzing an entity, we need to be mindful of the limits of financial statements and evaluate both its financial and non-financial assets.

1) Constant Dollars

Another aspect of money measurement is that conventional financial statements assume that all dollars are equal and have constant values. For example, if a business bought 10 acres of land in downtown Toronto in 1950 for $1 million and purchased one acre of adjacent land in 2012 for $1 million, the asset (land) on its balance sheet will show at a cost of $2 million. Thus, for accounting purposes, the 1950s dollar is assumed to be the same as the 2012 dollar. However, recent developments in International Financial Reporting Standards (IFRS) require disclosure of market values for certain assets.

As a matter of empirical evidence, we know that the assumption of constant dollars is not accurate. In interpreting assets on the balance sheet we must be sensitive to their nature and the mixing of dollars. It does not matter much if we mix assets such as accounts receivable because of their short life. A March accounts receivable mixed with a July accounts receivable does not distort the financial statements because the change in value, assuming normal inflation, is slight. The issue is important, however, when we mix capital assets (such as land) that are on the books for many years, sometimes decades or even centuries.

2) Historical Costs

Subject to IFRS requirements, the convention is that financial statements are prepared primarily based on the historical cost of assets at the time that the business acquires them.[2] Thereafter, the asset may appreciate or depreciate in value. With certain exceptions for diminution in value of property, plant, and equipment, for example, subsequent changes do not usually show up in the balance sheet. Financial statements do not generally reflect the market value of a business or its assets.

Example

If a company acquires a building for $10 million, the asset is on the balance sheet at that cost (value). The company will depreciate the building over its useful life by allocating the cost of the asset to several accounting periods. For example, if the building has an estimated useful life (with zero residual value) of fifty years, it may allocate $200,000 per year for depreciation. If the building appreciates in value to $80 million in thirty years, the balance sheet will still reflect its original cost less accumulated depreciation. Unless revalued, the potential gain of $70 million will not show on a conventional balance sheet prepared on the basis of historical costs.

The historical cost model can produce hysterical results. For example, the Disney company carries all the land on its books at their

---

2   *CICA Handbook*, Part II, section 1000, para 48.

1930s costs. This information may be highly objective, but is of limited use to a reader of the company's financial statements. Similarly, the company has no cost on its books for all of its "classic" animated features released over the past sixty years. The costs related to these classics have been written off. Hence, the company clearly has very valuable "hidden assets" that comply fully with GAAP.

The moral of the story is that asset values on a balance sheet become increasingly dated the further one moves out in time. Hence, we must read the balance sheet with the historical cost assumption in mind. A balance sheet prepared according to conventional accounting principles for fiduciary reporting to shareholders does not help us in valuing the business for the purposes of obtaining loan financing or in issuing its securities in a public offering.

The traditional argument in favour of historical cost accounting is that costs are objectively determinable based upon consummated transactions and actual values at the time that the asset is purchased. To be sure, historical cost statements are objective and more readily verifiable. Thus, they serve a useful purpose for fiduciary reporting duties by custodians of assets. Historical cost statements, however, are largely irrelevant in the context of fixed asset valuations for other purposes, such as financing, securitization, and purchase and sale of businesses.

There are exceptions to the use of historical cost depending upon the type of asset and the type of business. For example, GAAP requires that inventory should be valued at the lower of cost or market value. This rule reflects another fundamental assumption of accounting — conservatism. Hence, a company may use replacement cost to measure "market value." Similarly, a company may use the discounted present value of future expected cash flows to measure pension liabilities. Recently, there has been a shift towards "fair value" accounting, particularly by the International Accounting Standards Board (IASB), which developed IFRS.

On the other hand, certain businesses — for example, a mutual fund — will report their investment portfolios at current market values and not at cost. This is clearly necessary for the holder of mutual fund units who will want to transact in them at their current values.

B. GOING CONCERN

The general assumption in preparing an enterprise's financial statements is that the entity will continue as a "going concern" and viable operation for the foreseeable future. Management must prepare financial statements on a going concern basis unless it intends to liquidate the entity or there is no realistic alternative but to do so.[3] The going concern and historical cost assumptions are connected. If the company is a going concern into the indefinite future, we can record its assets at cost and allocate the costs over their useful life on the assumption that the entity will continue for the foreseeable future and will be able to realize assets and discharge liabilities.[4]

Where, however, a business is to be liquidated, we value its assets according to their liquidation values, which, in turn, will depend upon whether the liquidation is voluntary and orderly or involuntary and compelled. For example, a "fire sale" liquidation will produce lower values than an ordinary liquidation.

Similarly, we value inventory at the lower of cost or market value. If the entity is a going concern into the indefinite future, it matters little in the measurement of net income in a year. The market value of the inventory will show up in the selling price that the company charges for its products.

The valuation of goodwill also depends on the going concern assumption. Purchased goodwill is the difference between the fair market value of shares purchased and the price that the purchaser pays for them. Goodwill is, in effect, the premium that a purchaser pays for a business over and above the monetary fair market value of the assets or shares purchased. In 2011, for example, Interbrand estimated Coca-Cola's brand value at approximately $72 billion, which will contribute to its goodwill if the company is sold. The value of goodwill relies on the assumption that the business will continue and that the goodwill will serve to attract customers and enhance sales in the future. No one would be willing to pay a premium for a business if it were about to be liquidated.

---

3   *CICA Handbook*, section 1400, para .07.
4   *Ibid*, section 1000, para 58.

Thus, unless stated otherwise, all financial statements are assumed to be prepared on the basis of the going concern assumption. Indeed, the auditor of financial statements must satisfy himself or herself that the assumption is appropriate and applies to the business on which he or she expresses an opinion. Financial statements prepared for the purposes of liquidation should clearly say so in order to alert the reader that the going concern assumption does not apply in the particular circumstances.

C. ANNUAL REPORTING

The essence of accounting is to produce financial reports on a regular basis. The regularity of the reporting process depends upon the intended audience. For external reporting purposes, public companies will produce annual audited financial statements for shareholders and reporting to regulatory bodies. Companies may, however, also file interim financials (unaudited) with regulators, such as securities commissions.

The thorniest problems in accounting concern allocation of revenues and costs to the appropriate financial time period. This problem results directly from the annual reporting requirement for financial statements. Current costs and expenses are allocated to the income statement and deducted from revenues earned during the same period in computing net income. Costs that will benefit future operations are allocated to the balance sheet, where they will appear as assets to be assigned (with the exception of land) to future time periods.

Thus, the shorter the financial reporting period, the more difficult it is to make accurate allocations. For example, in an annual financial report covering the calendar year, it does not matter very much whether we allocate expenses to June or July or August of the year. In each case, the expenses will be in the appropriate calendar year. In preparing monthly financial statements, however, the allocation of expenses between the three months is more important as there will be three separate reporting periods.

We could dispense with allocation problems, if we measured the income of an entity only over its entire life. If the only reporting was at the beginning and at the end of the life of the business, the process is quite simple. To measure the income of the business over its entire life, we would look at the initial investment of cash into the business (stage 1 of the business cycle) and compare it to the ultimate distribution of cash to the owners (stage 7 of the business cycle) when it is liquidated.[5] The excess amount — with appropriate adjustments for interim distributions or additional contributions of cash — would be the income of the business.

D. TIME & ALLOCATION

Financial statements have meaning only if they are considered in the context of time and allocation. There are three concepts of timing in accounting and finance:

- Cash;
- Accrual; and
- Net present value.

The cash concept concerns recording transactions when the enterprise receives or disburses cash. There is no requirement for matching and the process of income measurement under this concept is quite straightforward. Receipt and disbursement of cash is easy to identify and measure with certainty. As we shall see, we use this concept in the cash flow statement.[6]

The accrual concept requires a matching of revenue and expenses according to when the business *earns* its revenues and recognizes expenses that it incurs to earn the revenues, regardless of when it collects or dispenses cash. The accrual concept is more complicated because it requires judgmental decisions and estimates as to when the business should recognize its revenues and identify the appropriate expenses to match with those revenues. Misallocating revenues and expenses distorts annual financial results. For example, a company that earns $30 million in Year 1, but assigns its expenses

---

5   See Chapter 1, Section A.
6   See, generally, *CICA Handbook*, Part II, section 1540.

of $20 million incurred to earn the revenue to Year 2, will over-state net income by $10 million in the first year and understate it in the following year. The income statement will understate expenses by $20 million in Year 1 and the balance sheet overstates assets by an equal amount. Although the amounts will balance out over two years, the annual results will be distorted.

Notwithstanding the difficulties that annual (or regular) re-porting creates, it is the most defensible system of financial re-porting. Financial reports must be timely in order to be relevant for decision makers. Annual reporting and all of its associated prob-lems are the price that we pay for making information relevant for decision makers.

We use the net present value of time only very rarely in conven-tional financial statements. The net present value concept discounts future earnings and expenses to their present value according to a formula that is based on the timing of the estimated receipts and the relevant discount factor, which is usually linked to interest rates. The concept underlies the discipline of finance and is relevant in determining the value of assets, shares, bonds, and long-term lia-bilities, such as future pension benefits for retirees.

E. CONSERVATISM

It is not entirely coincidental that accountants have a reputation for being conservative. Conservatism is in fact one of the basic concepts underlying financial statements. The concept is a core ac-counting value and a fundamental principle of valuation and in-come measurement.

Conservatism basically means that where there is uncertainty about recording a transaction or the value that one should attach to an asset, we should resolve the uncertainty with a "bias" in favour of understating income or assets. Stated another way, one should not anticipate gains, but one may anticipate losses.

For example, we value inventory at the lower of cost or market. Assume, for example, that a business purchased products at a cost of $10 per unit. The business has 10,000 units on hand at the end of the year with a total cost of $100,000. Due to market conditions, the unit cost of the product has fallen to $7 per unit as at the year-end. In these circumstances, it will be appropriate for the business to write-down its ending inventory to $70,000 on the balance sheet by charging $30,000 to the income statement as an expense. The replacement value of the inventory is less than its historical cost. Thus, by being conservative, we reduce net income by $30,000 and the inventory on the balance sheet by an equivalent amount.

Similarly, this occurs with fixed assets subject to depreciation. The following example illustrates the effect of a change in estimate of the useful life of a capital asset from twelve to ten years.

Example

Fixed Asset Account

	A	B
Capital Cost (Year 1)	$100,000	$100,000
Estimate Life in Years	10	12
Annual Equal Depreciation	$10,000	$8,333
Net Book Value (after depreciation)	$90,000	$91,667

If we estimate the useful life of the asset to be twelve years, the annual equal (straight line) depreciation charge would be $8,333 (assuming no residual value). We are uncertain, however, as to the useful life of the asset. The accountant might obtain a second opinion on the useful life of the asset and reduce it to ten years. In this case (option A), the annual charge for depreciation is $10,000 and the net book value of the asset after depreciation of the asset at the end of Year 1 drops from $91,667 to $90,000. Thus, both the asset value and net income are reduced by $1,167.

Similarly, with accounts receivable:

Accounts Receivable Account

	A	B
Accounts Receivable	$200,000	$200,000
Estimate of Doubtful Accounts	15,000	10,000
Net Book Value	$185,000	$190,000

We see what happens to accounts receivable if the business estimates that $15,000 of its receivables (Option A) will not likely be collected or $10,000 (Option B) will default. The difference of $5,000 in the estimate of doubtful accounts shows in the net book value of accounts receivable. The difference of $5,000 will also show up in the income statement. Under Option A, net income will be $5,000 lower than under Option B.

The preceding examples also explain a salient feature of our tax laws. Clearly, if the tax laws left everything up to accountants to determine write-offs and write-downs of asset values and charges to the income statement, there might be a tendency to be overly conservative — nay, even downright pessimistic. The more conservative the estimate, the lower the net income figure and the lower the taxes payable. We should not be entirely surprised that income tax laws generally control the amount that can be written off for tax purposes, regardless of the amount that the business deducts for financial statement purposes. For example, the Canadian *Income Tax Act* controls the annual depreciation charge on capital assets through a structured (and rigid) system known as "capital cost allowance," which mathematically dictates the maximum amount that a business can claim in any year. Hence, net income for financial statement purposes can differ from income for tax purposes, which, in turn, can lead to deferred assets and liabilities on the books.

Is it good to be conservative in preparing financial statements? The answer depends, in part, upon the purpose for which one prepares the financial statements. Bankers prefer to have financial statements prepared using conservative values because they are concerned with the amount of security behind a loan. The more conservative the value of the asset, the greater the security of the loan.

Conservatism in asset valuation, however, has a cost for investors who hold shares in publicly listed companies. Conservative valuation leads to lower net income, which, in turn, leads to lower earnings-per-share, a key figure that financial analysts use in valuing the market price of shares. Excessive conservatism means that a person selling his or her shares in the market may not get their "real value" because the earnings numbers have been depressed through pessimistic valuations.

Excessive conservatism can also lead to "hidden reserves." As noted earlier, the Disney company, for example, carries its "classic" animated features at zero. If assets are deliberately undervalued because of conservative estimates — such as depreciation and the allowance for doubtful accounts — the real value of the business is higher than its stated value. Thus, the real value of the assets is hidden because they are understated. Of course, on the sale of a business, the vendor will insist upon the full value of the business and will not be satisfied with accepting an amount based solely on book values.

Conservatism also affects the income statement and net income. The general tenet of conservatism is to recognize revenues only when the business is reasonably certain that it has earned them and has realized the revenue. Hence the maxim is: delay revenue recognition until there is substantial certainty; recognize expenses as soon as reasonably possible.

F. REVENUE RECOGNITION

Having determined that it is useful to have financial statements prepared at least annually, we must devise methods to allocate revenues to their appropriate financial periods. The revenue recognition principle requires us to allocate and assign revenues to financial periods and to match those revenues against the costs that the business incurs to earn the revenues. Thus, revenue recognition and the matching principle are the heart of income measurement.

An aspect of conservatism is the timing of revenues for income statement purposes. As a general rule, we recognize revenues only when the business is reasonably certain of the amount to be realized and the collectability of the consideration.[7]

An important correlative aspect of revenue recognition is that we should recognize expenses and match them with the revenues for which the business incurred them. Revenues and expenses arising from the same event or transactions should be recorded in the same time period.

---

7   *CICA Handbook*, Part II, section 1000, para 42.

Thus, the conservatism and matching principles allow management and accountants considerable latitude in exercising judgment on timing of revenue recognition and appropriate matching. The following illustrates the latitude that accountants have in applying the matching principle.

Example
Company buys intangible assets on purchase of business

Cost of intangible:	$10,000,000
40-year amortization:	$250,000
10-year amortization:	$1,000,000

Management can manage its net income by deciding to lengthen or shorten the amortization period. If we assume a forty-year amortization, the annual charge is $250,000. If we assume ten years, the annual charge is $1 million. This flexibility in estimating the life of the asset can lead to "earnings management."

G. CONSISTENCY

The concept of consistency in financial statements is important if we use them to compare numbers over time. Consistency requires one to prepare financial statements using the same method of accounting between different time periods, unless there is a sound reason for change. Consistency facilitates comparability. We want to compare apples with apples. Where there is a change in the method applied in valuing assets or determining income between two time periods, the change should be fully explained in the Notes to the financial statements.

H. MATERIALITY

The concept of materiality is a principle that overrides all technical rules and principles of accounting. Materiality is one of those obscure concepts that is difficult to define with precision. Thus, management, the accountant, and the auditor must determine whether an item is material or not in each case where the issue arises.

The theory of materiality is simple enough: the financial statements should disclose all significant information and disregard insignificant events or amounts. There is, however, no bright line test of "materiality." The *CICA Handbook* describes materiality as follows:[8]

> Materiality is the term used to describe the significance of financial statement information to decision makers. An item of information, or an aggregate of items, is material if it is probable that its omission or misstatement would influence or change a decision. Materiality is a matter of professional judgment in the particular circumstances.[9]

The *CICA Handbook* describes *grey area* as follows:

> Materiality is not a fine line where one dollar less is not material or one dollar more is material. It represents a gray area between what is very likely not material and what is very unlikely material.[10]

There are two aspects to materiality: subjective and objective. The subjective aspect is that an item should be considered to be material if knowledge of the item would have an effect on the decision process of a reader or user of the financial statements. This is a difficult test to apply because one can never be certain of the audience of potential users of financial statements. At best, one might say that an item is material if a reasonable person's decision might be affected by knowledge of the particular item.

Given the difficulty of applying the subjective test, many accountants tend towards a mathematical solution, where one measures the particular item being considered for materiality against a base figure or reference number. For example, an item may be considered material if it is more than 1 percent of net income or 5 percent of assets.

Relying on such mathematical relationships gives the accountant a sense of greater certainty, but the method is fraught with traps.

---

8   See section 1000.17.
9   *Ibid*
10   See section 5130.06.

Even if a particular item is below the mathematical threshold (say 1 percent of net income), it is important to determine the cumulative effect of all other immaterial items to see if their total exceeds the threshold. For example, if there are ten items that are being considered for materiality and each of them represents 0.8 percent of net income, the cumulative effect of all ten (assuming they all pull in the same direction) might be 8 percent of net income.

Hence, regardless whether the accountant uses a subjective or objective method of resolving materiality, he or she must exercise judgment. We can see how it is quite easy for three accountants reviewing the same information to arrive at three different conclusions on the financial statements.

There are certain items that are material, regardless of the amount and its relationship to net income or net assets. For example, transactions between related parties must be disclosed, regardless of the amounts involved. Similarly, bribes that contravene statutes, such as the *Corruption of Foreign Officials Act*, must be disclosed regardless of the amount paid. The uncertainty with bribes, however, is distinguishing them from facilitation or "grease" payments, which are legal.

Finally, an enterprise should disclose uncertainties that relate to events or conditions that cast doubt upon its ability to continue as a going concern.[11]

I.   MISCONCEPTIONS ABOUT ACCOUNTING

There are various misconceptions about accounting that we need to identify and keep in mind. For example:

1) All dollars are equal
   No, costs are historical costs and co-mingled
2) Accounting reflects values
   Not usually — accounting measures flow of costs
3) Balance Sheet numbers represent market values
   No, only unallocated costs

---

11   *CICA Handbook*, section 1400, para 8A.

4) "Net Worth" really means net worth
   No, it is merely a residual figure, the difference between assets and liabilities
5) Incurring expense is the same as paying for expense
   No, there are timing differences
6) Earning revenues is the same as getting paid
   No
7) Depreciation is a cash expense
   No, it is a cost allocation
8) EBIDA is a more accurate measure of income and performance
   Not always — it is a measure of operating income, not net income

J. THE TIME VALUE OF MONEY

Time has monetary value. The value is the effect of time on invested money. There are two dimensions to value: future and present. Given a sum of money, we can determine its value at some future date if we know the interest rate at which we can invest the money. Conversely, if we know that we are to receive a sum of money in the future, we can determine its value today if we know the rate at which it is, or can be, invested. Thus, all money has "time value."

To determine the value of money we need information about interest rates, the principal sum, and the time horizon. *All* assets, tangible and intangible, can be expressed in terms of their future or present value if we can determine the rate at which the asset is invested or discounted. The appropriate rate is usually the market-determined interest or investment rate.

In economic terms, "interest" is the rental cost of borrowing money. As with all rentals, the cost of renting money may be fixed in advance, determinable at a future time, or variable according to specified conditions. Thus, interest and time are inextricably related. An interest rate is relevant if, and only if, it is specified in relation to time.

Although most of us are familiar with the calculation of simple and compound interest, we are less intuitive about the concept of the discounted value of future sums of money. This is because we are taught to think intuitively of investing for the future but not of the present value of future sums. Yet, mathematically speaking, future value and present value are mirror images of each other looked at from different perspectives. The primary purpose of determining future and present values is to measure money in comparable terms across time periods by translating future dollars into economically equivalent current dollars, and *vice versa*.

The concept of the time value of money is relevant in finance, accounting, and law. Lawyers deal with assets that have a "time value" in virtually all aspects of commercial practice. For example, suppose that a plaintiff's lawyer is offered a choice between a cash settlement of $500,000 or six successive payments of $100,000 payable at the end of each year. Should the lawyer accept the lump-sum settlement or pursue the extended payment plan? Ignoring questions of risk and insolvency, the answer depends upon the prevailing interest rate and income tax considerations associated with the two alternatives. At an interest rate of 10 percent, the six payments of $100,000 have a present value of only $435,300. Hence, the plaintiff would be better off with the nominally lower lump-sum settlement. If the interest (discount) rate was 4 percent, however, the six payments would have a net present value of $524,000 (see Table 2-3, below in this chapter).

We can arrive at this answer in two ways. We can add the present values of each of the payments for six years at 10 percent. The present values of $1 would be (see Table 2-2 at the end of this chapter):

Year		
	1	0.909
	2	0.826
	3	0.751
	4	0.683
	5	0.620
	6	0.564
		4.353

Hence, the present value of $100,000 payable in six instalments would be $435,300.

Alternatively, we arrive at the same answer by looking at Table 2-3. Reading down the 10 percent column and across the six-year row, we see that the present value of an annuity of $1 payable at the end of each year is $4.35. Hence, the present value of a $100,000 annuity would be $435,000 (rounded). At 4 percent it would be $524,000.

Similarly, the defendant in a lawsuit involving future lost profits of a business enterprise may ask the court to reduce the size of any lump-sum award to the plaintiff to take into account the accelerated value of receiving the money today rather than over an extended period of time. For example, if one can establish that the defendant's actions will cause the plaintiff a loss of $100,000 of business profits annually for a period of five years, should the defendant be required to pay the nominal amount of the damages ($500,000) up front or some lesser discounted amount because of the time value of money? At an interest rate of 12 percent the annual loss of $100,000 spread over five years is worth only $360,000 today if the payments are receivable at the end of each year (see Table 2-3, below in this chapter). Ignoring the time value of money would penalize the defendant and provide the plaintiff with a windfall gain. Thus, time value considerations should be taken into account in structuring damage settlements to account for the net present value of related tax costs and savings.

1) Future Value

We determine the future value of money by reference to the effect of interest rates on a principal sum. There are two forms of interest, simple and compound. We refer to interest paid only on the amount originally invested, but not on any interest that accrues subsequently, as simple interest. Simple interest is a function of the principal sum (P) multiplied by rate (R) multiplied by time (n):

Thus: Interest = $P \times R \times n$

For example, if one deposits $10,000 in a guaranteed investment certificate (GIC) for a period of one year at 6 percent, the GIC will be worth $10,600 at the end of the year. The interest earned is $600, or 6 percent of the principal amount for one year.

Hence, in four years the total sum will equal $12,400.

In contrast, compound interest refers to the process whereby interest is earned not only on the amount originally invested but also on subsequently accrued interest. Compound interest starts out with exactly the same formula as simple interest but extends it to account for the reinvested interest. Thus, the interest on the second and subsequent time periods is calculated not only on the initial principal amount, but also on any interest accumulated in preceding time periods.

For example, if one invests $10,000 in a GIC at 8 percent compounded annually for two years, the GIC is worth $11,664 at the end of the second year. At the end of the first year the principal and the interest are $10,800 (the same as with simple interest). But the interest for the second year is calculated as 8 percent of $10,800, which is $864.

We arrive at the same result by looking at Table 2-1 (below in this chapter), where we see that the future value of $1 invested at 8 percent for two years is $1.17 (rounded). In contrast, simple interest for both years would have produced only $11,600. The incremental $64 is due entirely to the fact that the interest in the second year is calculated not only on the initial principal amount, but also on the reinvested interest. The $64 is the premium for the compounding of interest — the interest on earlier interest.

To generalize, a future amount is determined by the formula:

$$F = P(1 + R) n$$

Where:

F = the future value of money;
P = the present sum of money;
R = net interest rate over a period of time; and
n = the number of periods of time.

The formula demonstrates that the longer the time horizon for investment and the more frequent the compounding intervals, the greater the future value of a present sum of money. For example, the future value of $1 invested at 8 percent at the end of years 1 through to 5 is as follows:

Year	1	$1.080
	2	$1.166
	3	$1.260
	4	$1.360
	5	$1.469

If, instead, we compound $10,000 over a period of eight quarters at 2 percent per quarter (which nominally appears to be the same thing as 8 percent per year), we get a future value of $11,717, or $53 more than in the previous example of compounding only once per year. Using these numbers, on a $100 million transaction the difference between annual and quarterly compounding is $530,000.

The lesson is simple: a lender will benefit from compounding interest as frequently as possible and the borrower will pay more for frequent compounding. Thus, in an open and competitive market, the borrower and the lender must negotiate both the interest rate and the frequency of compounding intervals.

There is no such negotiation, however, in tax law. The CRA compounds interest on a *daily* basis on outstanding amounts of taxes payable. In the above example, if the $10,000 was the outstanding amount of a tax assessment, daily compounding of the amount at an equivalent of 8 percent per year would increase the tax payable at the end of two years to $11,735. Hence, it is almost always to a taxpayer's advantage to pay his assessment and then challenge its validity at a later date. It is virtually impossible for a taxpayer to obtain an alternative investment that will yield an equivalent amount of interest for the same risk. Since tax disputes can continue for eight to ten years, the daily compounding effect has an enormous impact on the ultimate amount payable if the taxpayer ultimately loses the appeal. For example, an outstanding assessment of $10,000 if compounded at 8 percent daily will grow to $22,240 in ten years.

Compounding of interest allows us to determine the economic equivalence of money across different time periods. For example, if the market rate of interest is 8 percent, we should be indifferent between paying $1,000 today and $1,469 five years from now because we could invest the $1,000 at 8 percent today and it would grow to $1,469 in five years on a pre-tax basis. The two sums, $1,000 today and $1,469 in five years, are equivalent returns in economic terms if the prevailing rate of interest is 8 percent (see Table 2-1).

2) The Rule of 72

The Rule of 72 allows us to calculate the approximate length of time or interest rate that it will take to double an investment using compound interest. For example, assuming a compound interest rate of 8 percent, it will take approximately nine years (72 divided by 8) to double an investment. We can confirm this in Table 2-1, which shows that $1 will be equal to $2 in nine years if invested at 8 percent compounded.

Similarly, we can estimate the rate of interest required to double money in a specified number of years. For example, given an interest rate of 6 percent, it will take twelve years (72 divided by 6) to double an investment (see Table 2-1).

The Rule of 72 illustrates the power of compounding interest in planning for retirement, paying off debt, and investing for the long run.

3) Taxes

Taxes play a significant role in determining future values. Taxes payable on a current basis reduce the amount of interest available for reinvestment (the "R" in the formula) and, hence, reduce the compounding effect on the principal sum. For example, assume that Nicola invests $10,000 in a tax-sheltered investment that earns 10 percent compounded annually for ten years. At the end of ten years, the future value of the investment will be $25,937 (see Table 2-1). The accumulated gain of $15,937 represents the gross compound interest over a period of ten years. Thus, the money will more than double in ten years.

In contrast, if Nicola pays tax at 40 percent on her earned interest on a current basis, she will have only 6 percent to reinvest each year. The future value of $10,000 invested at 6 percent (net) will be $17,908 at the end of ten years. Thus, the ultimate value of the currently taxed investment is $8,029 or 31 percent less than the value of the tax-sheltered investment — hence, the attraction of tax shelters and the benefits of tax deferral.

Since taxes decrease the amount that can be reinvested, it generally pays to delay (defer) the payment of taxes (the longer, the better) provided that the CRA is not levying interest on the outstanding amount at the same time. For example, a $1,000 investment compounding at 20 percent in a tax shelter is worth $1.4 million after forty years. If the investment is taxed annually at 25 percent, the net return is 15 percent and the investment is worth approximately $267,000 in forty years. If taxed at 40 percent, the net return is 12 percent and the investment is worth only $93,000 after forty years (see Table 2-1).

The Rule of 72 also illustrates the impact of taxes on investments. We saw earlier that investment at 6 percent will double in twelve years. Table 1-1 tells us that each $1 would be worth $2.01 at the end of 12 years. If taxes reduce the reinvestment rate by 40 percent to 3.6 percent, it will take 20 years for the money to double. Thus, reinvestment gross of tax is always preferable to reinvestment net of tax. Compounding for long periods, even at modest rates, leads to explosive growth. At 3 percent, for example, $1 will grow to $6,874,000,000,000 in 1,000 years!

4) Present Value

We evaluate the time value of money in two ways: the future value of a present sum of money or the present value of a future sum. Although this may seem obtuse, both values are in fact merely different ways of looking at the same thing. The future value is the sum to which an amount, or a series of periodic and equal amounts, will grow at the end of a certain amount of time if compounded at a particular interest rate. The present value is the discounted value at a particular rate of interest of a sum of money to be received in the future. Thus, we can restate the compound interest formula as follows:

$$P = \frac{F}{(1 + R)n}$$

where:

F = the future value of money;
P = the present sum of money;
R = net interest rate over a period of time; and
n = the number of periods of time.

The more distant the time when an amount has to be paid on account of tax, the lower its present value. Hence, it pays to delay or defer the payment of taxes as long as possible so as to minimize the present value of the obligation today.

For example, the present value of $1 invested at 8 percent at the end of years 1 through 5 is as follows:[12]

Year		
	1	$0.926
	2	$0.857
	3	$0.794
	4	$0.735
	5	$0.681

When we say that the interest rate is 8 percent per year, we mean that we should be able to exchange 93 cents today in return for $1 a year from now and 86 cents in return for $1 two years from now, and so on. Hence, if we can defer the obligation to pay $1,000 in taxes today for five years, the present value of the liability to pay is only $681. Although the face amount of the legal obligation to pay remains the same, namely, $1,000 in five years, its economic value varies depending upon when it is paid. The economic value is only $681 if paid today, $735 if paid a year from now, $794 if paid

---

12   See Table 2-2.

two years from now, and so on. Stated another way, if we invested $681 in a deposit that compounded tax free at a rate of 8 percent, we would accumulate $1,000 at the end of five years with which to pay the tax liability. By deferring the tax payable for five years we reduce the tax liability by $319.

To continue with the same example: let us assume that we can defer the tax payable for a period of fifty years. The present value of $1,000 payable in fifty years at a discount rate of 8 percent is $21. In other words, if we invest $21 today and compound it for fifty years net 8 percent annually, we will have $1,000 at the end of the investment period. The discounted amount shrinks as a function of two factors: time (n) and the discount rate (R). The longer the period of deferral and the higher the interest rate, the lower the discounted present value. Hence, $1,000 payable in fifty years and discounted at 20 percent has a present value today of (effectively) zero.

In determining present and future values, we must be clear about the assumptions underlying the mathematical calculations. Since time value calculations require an interest rate, an error in estimating the rate can significantly distort results. There is no easy way to minimize this risk other than to rely upon responsible predictions. For example, if one earns 10 percent (instead of 12 percent) over ten years, $10,000 invested in an RRSP would grow to only $25,900 instead of $31,100. The 2 percent difference in interest rates reduces the investment return by $5,200, a reduction of 16.5 percent over ten years.

The longer the investment horizon, the greater the risk that inaccurate assumptions will creep into the reinvestment formula. Hence, long-term retirement plans should be based on conservative estimates of future reinvestment rates. It is also important in time value calculations to consider the income tax effect of payments. As noted above, reinvestment rates can vary substantially depending upon whether the funds are invested in a tax shelter or in a currently taxable investment. With marginal tax rates of 45 percent, ignoring taxes can be even more significant than the miscalculation of anticipated inflation.

5) Nominal and Effective Interest Rates

When we speak of interest rates, we must distinguish between "nominal" and "effective" rates. The difference between the two depends upon the method of calculation and the frequency of the compounding period. For example, when we say that a person has a bank loan at 10 percent annual rate of interest, we mean that is the nominal rate. The effective rate of interest will also be 10 percent, but only if interest is calculated at year-end. If the compounding period is more frequent, the effective rate of interest increases. This is important with credit cards that disclose an annual percentage rate (APR). If the APR is 18 percent annually, the monthly charge rate is 1.5 percent, which makes the effective rate of interest 19.56 percent.

Section 347 of the *Criminal Code* of Canada[13] makes it a criminal offence to charge usurious interest rates, which is defined as annual interest that exceeds 60 percent. The purpose of the provision is to deal with "loan sharks." In fact, the provision is rarely applied against such persons, who use unorthodox collection methods. Instead, the provision is more often used against legitimate commercial lenders. In *Garland v Consumers' Gas Co*, for example, the defendant gas company sold its gas to consumers under a sales agreement that contained a late penalty payment (LPP) clause that required customers to pay a charge of 5 percent on monthly unpaid bills if payment was not made within sixteen days. On an annual basis, the LPP violated Section 347 of the *Criminal Code* if a customer paid within thirty-seven days, but not if a customer paid after that period. Applying a "wait-and-see" approach, which determines the effective rate of interest when payment is *actually* made, the Supreme Court of Canada held that the LPPs violated the *Criminal Code*.

6) Annuities

An annuity is a series of equal payments — for example, regular payments on a mortgage. The present value of an annuity is equal to the sum of the present values of each payment discounted at the

---

13   RSC 1985, c C-46.

appropriate rate of interest. We can also think of the present value as a lump-sum amount that must be invested now at compound interest, which will permit a series of equal withdrawals at regular intervals, and end up with nothing after the final withdrawal.

Example

Assume a simple annuity pays $1,000 per year at year-end for each of ten years. If the compound rate of interest is 10 percent per year, we can discount the series of $1,000 payments to their present value by adding the present values of each payment from Table 2-2 as follows:

Payment at End of Year	Present Value of Payment of $1.00 (to two decimals)
1	.91
2	.83
3	.75
4	.68
5	.62
6	.56
7	.51
8	.47
9	.42
10	.39
TOTAL	$6.14

Thus, the present value of the ten equal payments of $1,000 is $6,140.

We arrive at the same conclusion by looking at Table 2-3 to determine the present value of an annuity of $1 received at the end of ten years. Looking at the 10 percent column and reading down to year 10, we see that the present value of a $1 annuity is 6.14. Hence, the present value of a $1,000 annuity is $6,140.

We can also check our calculation using arithmetic.

Example

Assume that we deposit $6,140 in a savings account that pays 10 percent per year and we make $1,000 withdrawals at the end of each year. The ten-year profile of the account would be as follows:

Example

Year	Opening Balance	Annual Interest	Withdrawals	Closing Balance
1	$6,140	$614	$1,000	$5,754
2	$5,754	$575	$1,000	$5,329
3	$5,329	$533	$1,000	$4,862
4	$4,862	$486	$1,000	$4,348
5	$4,348	$435	$1,000	$3,783
6	$3,783	$378	$1,000	$3,161
7	$3,161	$316	$1,000	$2,477
8	$2,477	$248	$1,000	$1,725
9	$1,725	$173	$1,000	$898
10	$898	$90	$1,000	$0 (rounded)*

* The closing balance of $0 is rounded because we are working with only two decimal places.

7) Perpetuities

A perpetuity is a promise to pay a certain periodic sum forever. A pure perpetuity is a theoretical ideal that is useful in valuing a business. The closest thing to a perpetuity in reality is land because it offers a perpetual potential income stream.

Under a discounted present value model, a perpetuity has finite value because the payments that will be made far in the future have such miniscule values that their sum is considered finite. For example, look at the value of $1 at 20 percent in fifty years in Table 2-2. A dollar receivable in fifty years is worth only .000109 today. Working with two decimal places, a dollar is worth zero today — hence, the paradox of the tired walker who gets halfway to his ultimate destination each hour. He never overshoots his destination, no matter how long he walks, even though he makes real progress each hour.

The present value of a perpetuity is the amount of money that one would pay lump sum today in order to produce an annual yield equal to the appropriate rate of interest. For example, in order to obtain a dollar in perpetuity at an interest rate of 10 percent, we would need to put $10 on deposit to produce the requisite flow of income if payments were made at the end of each year. Thus, the present value of a $1 a year perpetuity is worth $10 today. To generalize:

Value (V) × R = PMT
Thus, V = PMT/R.

Where V = Value of a perpetuity
R = Market rate of interest
PMT = Perpetual payment

K. BOND VALUATION

Using present value principles, we can value a bond if we know the market rate of interest, the term of the bond, the nominal rate of interest payable on the bond and its face (principal) amount. For example, assume that a bond pays 10 percent on its principal ($10,000) at the end of each of five years and repays its face amount at the end of the fifth year. Thus, the bond comprises four annual payments of $1,000 at the end of each of the first four years and $11,000 ($1,000 interest plus $10,000 principal) at the end of the fifth year. Using Table 2-2, we calculate the present value of each of these payments as follows:

Year	Payment	Present Value @ 10 %
1	$1,000	$909
2	$1,000	$826
3	$1,000	$751
4	$1,000	$683
5	$11,000	$6,820
TOTAL		$10,000 (rounded)

As one might expect, the bond is worth its face amount of $10,000, because its nominal rate of interest is equal to the market rate. If the market rate of interest rises to 12 percent, the value of the bond will fall to $9,274. We can check this by using Table 2-2 as follows:

Year	Payment	Present Value @ 12 %
1	$1,000	$893
2	$1,000	$797
3	$1,000	$711
4	$1,000	$636
5	$11,000	$6,237
TOTAL		$9,274

Conversely, if the market rate of interest falls to 6 percent, the value of the bond will rise to $11,681.

Year	Payment	Present Value @ 6 %
1	$1,000	$943
2	$1,000	$890
3	$1,000	$839
4	$1,000	$792
5	$11,000	$8,217
TOTAL		$11,681

Thus, bond prices move inversely to interest rates. This effect is more pronounced the longer the remaining life of the bond. Hence, for example, the value of a thirty-year Treasury Bill will fluctuate more than the value of a ten-year bill in response to movements in market rates of interest. Similarly, a ten-year bond will be more volatile in response to changes in the market rate of interest than a two-year bond of equal risk.

L. THE POWER OF COMPOUNDING

We see the dramatic power of compounding in a recently reported incident in the sleepy hamlet of Mittenwalde in Eastern Germany. According to a Reuters,[14] the town historian (Vera Schmidt) uncovered a centuries-old debt slip dating back to 1562 in the archives where it had been filed. Mittenwalde apparently lent Berlin 400

---

14   See *Law Times*, "Bizarre Briefs" (6 August 2012) at 16.

Guilders on 28 May 1562 which was to be repaid with 6 percent interest per year. According to Radio Berlin Brandenburg, adjusting the debt for compound interest and inflation, the total debt now lies in the trillions. Apparently, the Mayor of Mittenwalde and his predecessors have asked Berlin for the return of their money and have made such a request every fifty-five years since 1820, but always to no avail. Mittenwalde, which had a population in 2012 of 8,800 people, would benefit enormously from repayment. Berlin, however, is not playing along. Why?

M. BUSINESS VALUATION

A business is the sum of the values of all of its net assets, which can be more or less than the value of its net assets as shown on its balance sheet. Finance values businesses as a whole, generally by valuing the stock of the enterprise and does not try to attribute that value to its underlying business assets. Finance values businesses by analyzing them to a perpetuity. The theoretical analogy is useful if the business will create a fairly constant level of cash flows indefinitely. However, in any other case, the analogy becomes troublesome.

In the abstract, one might suggest that the total value of a company's stock should be equal to the value of the company's total net assets. A share of stock should be equal to its proportionate share of the total stock value. In fact, there are many reasons why this is not so. First, there may be hidden and undisclosed assets, such as goodwill and reputation associated with the company's corporate brand. Second, it is usually the case that a large block of stock will be worth more proportionately than the sum of the values of the component shares because of the premium that attaches to control of the corporation. Third, there may be significant income tax considerations embedded in the asset values that may not be readily seen.

We refer to the discounted present value of a stream of future payments as the "capitalized" value and the interest rate used in capitalizing the future payments as the "capitalization rate" or "cap rate." For example, as we saw above, the perpetuity valuation model is:

Value = PMP/R(Cap Rate).
Therefore, Cap Rate equals PMP/Value.

In the simplest case, a share that provides the shareholder with $1 a year in (year-end) dividends for ever (and no other return) resembles a perpetuity. Assuming a 10 percent annual yield, the share is worth $10, which is PMP/R (the formula for valuing a perpetuity).

We refer to the ratio of the capitalized value to annual future payments as the "multiple," that is, the amount one multiplies the future payments by in order to determine the capitalized value. Thus, multiple is equal to 1/Cap Rate. For example, with a 10 percent annual yield the multiple is 10; with a 5 percent annual yield the multiple is 20. Stated another way, with a 10 percent yield, it would take ten years to recover one's investment; with a 5 percent yield, it would take twenty years to recover the investment.

As noted earlier, the simple perpetuity valuation method requires only two numbers: the Cap Rate and the Expected Payment. Cap Rate is a function of risk. The Expected Payment schedule is where finance and accounting intersect because both business valuations use "profit," "income," or "earnings" to measure expected cash flows — hence, the relationship between accounting and finance. Finance needs information to value businesses. Accounting provides the information. Thus, finance is an important consumer of accounting information.

There is, however, tension between finance and accounting. Finance looks to the future and focuses on valuation based on prospective cash flows. The past is irrelevant except to the extent that it provides information about the future. In contrast, accounting looks exclusively to the past in measuring the performance of the enterprise. This explains why stocks can go up even when profits go down and go down even when profits go up. An enterprise may report lower earnings and see its stock go up because finance values future earnings and stock values depend upon expectations about the future. When expectations disappoint, stock values can go down even when reported profits go up. Conversely, when a company exceeds expectations, stocks can go up even if reported profits have fallen.

N. TABLES

Table 2-1

Compound Amount of $1: Amount to Which $1 Now Will Grow by End of Specified Year at Compounded Interest

Year	3%	4%	5%	6%	7%	8%	10%	12%	15%	20%
1	1.03	1.04	1.05	1.06	1.07	1.08	1.10	1.12	1.15	1.20
2	1.06	1.08	1.10	1.12	1.14	1.17	1.21	1.25	1.32	1.44
3	1.09	1.12	1.16	1.19	1.23	1.26	1.33	1.40	1.52	1.73
4	1.13	1.17	1.22	1.26	1.31	1.36	1.46	1.57	1.74	2.07
5	1.16	1.22	1.28	1.34	1.40	1.47	1.61	1.76	2.01	2.49
6	1.19	1.27	1.34	1.41	1.50	1.59	1.77	1.97	2.31	2.99
7	1.23	1.32	1.41	1.50	1.61	1.71	1.94	2.21	2.66	3.58
8	1.27	1.37	1.48	1.59	1.72	1.85	2.14	2.48	3.05	4.30
9	1.30	1.42	1.55	1.68	1.84	2.00	2.35	2.77	3.52	5.16
10	1.34	1.48	1.63	1.79	1.97	2.16	2.59	3.11	4.05	6.19
11	1.38	1.54	1.71	1.89	2.10	2.33	2.85	3.48	4.66	7.43
12	1.43	1.60	1.80	2.01	2.25	2.52	3.13	3.90	5.30	8.92
13	1.47	1.67	1.89	2.13	2.41	2.72	3.45	4.36	6.10	10.7
14	1.51	1.73	1.98	2.26	2.58	2.94	3.79	4.89	7.00	12.8
15	1.56	1.80	2.08	2.39	2.76	3.17	4.17	5.47	8.13	15.4
16	1.60	1.87	2.18	2.54	2.95	3.43	4.59	6.13	9.40	18.5
17	1.65	1.95	2.29	2.69	3.16	3.70	5.05	6.87	10.6	22.2
18	1.70	2.03	2.41	2.85	3.38	4.00	5.55	7.70	12.5	26.6
19	1.75	2.11	2.53	3.02	3.62	4.32	6.11	8.61	14.0	31.9
20	1.81	2.19	2.65	3.20	3.87	4.66	6.72	9.65	16.1	38.3
25	2.09	2.67	3.39	4.29	5.43	6.85	10.8	17.0	32.9	95.4
30	2.43	3.24	4.32	5.74	7.61	10.0	17.4	30.0	66.2	237
40	3.26	4.80	7.04	10.3	15.0	21.7	45.3	93.1	267.0	1470
50	4.38	7.11	11.5	18.4	29.5	46.9	117	289	1080	9100

To read this table, determine the compounding rate for the applicable number of compounding periods. For example, each dollar invested at 8 percent for five years yields $1.47 if compounding occurs annually at the end of each year. Compounding semi-annually at 4 percent for ten time periods yields $1.48.

Table 2-2

Present Value of $1: What a Dollar at End of Specified Future Year Is Worth Today

Year	3%	4%	5%	6%	7%	8%	10%	12%	15%	20%
1	.971	.962	.952	.943	.935	.926	.909	.893	.870	.833
2	.943	.925	.907	.890	.873	.857	.826	.797	.756	.694
3	.915	.890	.864	.839	.816	.794	.751	.711	.658	.578
4	.889	.855	.823	.792	.763	.735	.683	.636	.572	.482
5	.863	.823	.784	.747	.713	.681	.620	.567	.497	.402
6	.838	.790	.746	.705	.666	.630	.564	.507	.432	.335
7	.813	.760	.711	.665	.623	.583	.513	.452	.376	.279
8	.789	.731	.677	.627	.582	.540	.466	.404	.326	.233
9	.766	.703	.645	.591	.544	.500	.424	.360	.284	.194
10	.744	.676	.614	.558	.508	.463	.385	.322	.247	.162
11	.722	.650	.585	.526	.475	.429	.350	.287	.215	.134
12	.701	.625	.557	.497	.444	.397	.318	.257	.187	.112
13	.681	.601	.530	.468	.415	.368	.289	.229	.162	.0935
14	.661	.577	.505	.442	.388	.340	.263	.204	.141	.0779
15	.642	.555	.481	.417	.362	.315	.239	.183	.122	.0649
16	.623	.534	.458	.393	.339	.292	.217	.163	.107	.0541
17	.605	.513	.436	.371	.317	.270	.197	.146	.093	.0451
18	.587	.494	.416	.350	.296	.250	.179	.130	.0808	.0376
19	.570	.475	.396	.330	.277	.232	.163	.116	.0703	.0313
20	.554	.456	.377	.311	.258	.215	.148	.104	.0611	.0261
25	.478	.375	.295	.232	.184	.146	.0923	.0588	.0304	.0105
30	.412	.308	.231	.174	.131	.0994	.0573	.0334	.0151	.00421
40	.307	.208	.142	.0972	.067	.0460	.0221	.0107	.00373	.000680
50	.228	.141	.087	.0543	.034	.0213	.00852	.00346	.000922	.000109

To read this table, determine the discount rate for the applicable number of discounting periods. For example, each dollar receivable in five years is worth only 68 cents today if the discount rate is 8 percent. If the discount rate is 4 percent semi-annually, the value of each dollar falls to 67 cents.

Table 2-3

Present Value of Annuity of $1, Received at End of Each Year

Year	3%	4%	5%	6%	7%	8%	10%	12%	15%	20%
1	0.971	0.960	0.952	0.943	0.935	0.926	0.909	0.890	0.870	0.833
2	1.91	1.89	1.86	1.83	1.81	1.78	1.73	1.69	1.63	1.53
3	2.53	2.78	2.72	2.67	2.62	2.58	2.45	2.40	2.28	2.11
4	3.72	3.63	3.55	3.46	3.39	3.31	3.16	3.04	2.86	2.59
5	4.58	4.45	4.33	4.21	4.10	3.99	3.79	3.60	3.35	2.99
6	5.42	5.24	5.08	4.91	4.77	4.62	4.35	4.11	3.78	3.33
7	6.23	6.00	5.79	5.58	5.39	5.21	4.89	4.56	4.16	3.60
8	7.02	6.73	6.46	6.20	5.97	5.75	5.33	4.97	4.49	3.84
9	7.79	7.44	7.11	6.80	6.52	6.25	5.75	5.33	4.78	4.03
10	8.53	8.11	7.72	7.36	7.02	6.71	6.14	5.65	5.02	4.19
11	9.25	8.76	8.31	7.88	7.50	7.14	6.49	5.94	5.23	4.33
12	9.95	9.39	8.86	8.38	7.94	7.54	6.81	6.19	5.41	4.44
13	10.6	9.99	9.39	8.85	8.36	7.90	7.10	6.42	5.65	4.53
14	11.3	10.6	9.90	9.29	8.75	8.24	7.36	6.63	5.76	4.61
15	11.9	11.1	10.4	9.71	9.11	8.56	7.60	6.81	5.87	4.68
16	12.6	11.6	10.8	10.1	9.45	8.85	7.82	6.97	5.96	4.73
17	13.2	12.2	11.3	10.4	9.76	9.12	8.02	7.12	6.03	4.77
18	13.8	12.7	11.7	10.8	10.1	9.37	8.20	7.25	6.10	4.81
19	14.3	13.1	12.1	11.1	10.3	9.60	8.36	7.37	6.17	4.84
20	14.9	13.6	12.5	11.4	10.6	9.82	8.51	7.47	6.23	4.87
25	17.4	15.6	14.1	12.8	11.7	10.7	9.08	7.84	6.46	4.95
30	19.6	17.3	15.4	13.5	12.4	11.3	9.43	8.06	6.57	4.98
40	23.1	19.8	17.2	15.0	13.3	11.9	9.78	8.24	6.64	5.00
50	25.7	21.5	18.3	15.8	13.8	12.2	9.91	8.30	6.66	5.00

This table is a shorthand extension of Table 2-2. It shows the cumulative present value of an annual series of equal payments received at the end of each year. For example, the present value of three annual payments of $1 invested at 8 percent is equal to $2.58 today. We can arrive at the same result from Table 2-2 by adding together 0.926, 0.857, and 0.794.

Chapter III: Generally Accepted Accounting Principles and Reporting Standards

The phrase "generally accepted accounting principles" (GAAP) is an intrinsic and fundamental component of financial language. The auditor's report refers specifically in its opinion to GAAP. The auditor's report for Duggan Inc, for example, states that the company's financial statements for the years ended 20-2 and 20-1 were prepared in accordance with Canadian generally accepted accounting principles. Since 1 January 2011, public companies must also report using International Financial Reporting Standards (IFRS).

GAAP and IFRS refer to broad principles and conventions that apply generally in accounting. They also refer to specific rules to determine accounting practices at particular times. In Canada, the authoritative source of GAAP and IFRS is the *Handbook* of the Canadian Institute of Chartered Accountants, which states (at para 1000.60):

> GAAPs encompass not only specific rules, practices and procedures relating to particular circumstances but also broad principles and conventions of general application.

However, GAAPs are not universal and identical. The United States has its own set of GAAPs. The International Accounting Standards Board (IASB) has other GAAPs. Canada has adopted international GAAPs as articulated by the IASB, and known as IFRS, for public companies.

A. WHERE DO GAAPs AND IFRS COME FROM?

GAAPs and IFRS are *generally accepted* principles developed by accounting bodies after study and research in consultation with academics, business, and government. Accounting bodies develop GAAPs and IFRS by exercising professional judgment and analyzing the advantages and disadvantages of alternative methods of accounting and reporting. Since accounting does not produce precise answers to every question, GAAPs and IFRS provide rules and guidelines that are generally acceptable. GAAPs and IFRS may offer choices between allowable alternatives or may be entirely silent on the particular point.

GAAPs and IFRS also have an important role in the calculation and disclosure of net income for income tax purposes. However, they are not determinative. Ultimately, the *Income Tax Act* of Canada is the principal source of law for tax purposes and it will, in many cases, specify methods that do not necessarily comply with commercial GAAPs.

Legal contracts often refer to GAAPs in the preparation of financial statements. For example, contracts that contain negative covenants relating to financial status or ratios, such as working capital or debt/equity ratios, frequently state that the relevant financial statements must be prepared in accordance with GAAP. In these circumstances, it is best to specify which GAAP — Canadian, American, or International — should apply to the particular contract.

B. THE HIERARCHY OF GAAP SOURCES

There are various sources for GAAP. At the top of the hierarchy, however, are the official statements from organizations that the accounting profession designates as the official body to determine appropriate accounting treatment for financial transactions. In Canada, the Institute of Chartered Accountants of Canada is the official source of GAAP, which are discussed in its *Handbook*.

In the United States, the official body for determining the appropriate accounting treatment of transactions is the Financial Accounting Standards Board (FASB), an independent body created to establish and improve standards for financial accounting and reporting. It is made up of a cross-section of accountants, academics, and users of financial statements. In order to enhance the independence of the board, the seven members of FASB cannot hold private employment during their tenure of service on the board.

Lawyers should be familiar with GAAP and IFRS but need not have technical expertise. Lawyers can rely upon professional accountants to explain the technical details of particular principles. For example, in a lawsuit involving the appropriate accounting treatment of inventory valuation, lawyers can rely on professional opinions on the appropriate principles to apply.

In the United States, the Securities and Exchange Commission (SEC) regulates the sale of securities and securities markets. Therefore, publicly listed companies must file regular financial statements according to specified criteria with the SEC.

The SEC does not routinely develop accounting principles, but leaves the development of such principles to the independent accounting bodies, such as FASB. Nevertheless, the SEC will, on some occasions, promulgate accounting principles if it is of the opinion that the accounting profession or bodies are not acting fast enough on their own.

C. GAAP & TAX LAW

Tax accounting is quite different from financial statement accounting because the objectives of the two processes are quite different.[1] The policies and objectives of an income tax system are quite different from the policies that underlie the preparation of general purpose financial statements. To be sure, both tax accounting and general financial accounting share a common overarching objective: the preparation of financial statements that produce a meaningful and fair measure of net income for the taxpayer or accounting entity. Hence, they start from the same premise that "net income" is the base upon which one should pay income taxes.

---

1   See Chapter 1 for fuller discussion.

However, tax law also has other policy objectives — social, cultural, political, and economic — that can distort the accounting measure of net income. For example, the tax system generally requires an entity to include unearned revenues in income. For accounting purposes, unearned revenues would not be included in the current year's net income, but would show as deferred liabilities revenue on the balance sheet until the entity earns the revenue. The government, however, prefers to tax receipts sooner rather than later and taxes the unearned revenue because the taxpayer has use of the money.

Similarly, although a Canadian business can use the last-in, first-out (LIFO) system of accounting for inventories, it cannot use LIFO for income tax purposes. In the United States, a slightly different rule applies: if a business elects to use LIFO for income tax purposes, it must also use the same method for its financial statement reporting to shareholders. IFRS does not approve of LIFO for income measurement.

D. AUDITING & PROFESSIONAL STANDARDS

Before the *Sarbanes-Oxley Act* (SOX) (2002), the American Institute of Certified Public Accountants (AICPA) used to set auditing and professional standards. Since SOX, however, the Public Company Accounting Oversight Board (PCAOB) is responsible for setting standards for public companies and the AICPA for private companies. Similarly, in Canada, IFRS applies to public companies and Canadian GAAP for private companies.

E. ROLE OF MANAGEMENT IN SELECTING GAAPs

Management has a key role in determining the nature, format, and underlying principles of its financial statements. Indeed, the Representation Letter that corporate management must submit to its auditors will usually state in the first paragraph:

> We are responsible for the fair presentation in the financial statements of financial position, results of operations and changes

in financial position in conformity with generally accepted accounting principles.

To discharge its responsibility, management must select accounting principles; determine asset life; and decide reporting policy if there is no existing principle.

The interaction between management and the corporation's auditors is delicate and, sometimes, tense. Accounting firms are first and foremost businesses that value client retention. They realize, however, that corporations can "opinion shop" if the audit firm is being difficult in respect of particular items on the financial statements — hence, the tension between client retention and proper disclosure. Thus, at the very least, a lawyer who uses financial statements should have a general understanding of GAAP and IFRS that the audit opinion addresses. The Notes to the financial statements will set out the corporation's selection of GAAP and IFRS and their impact on the financial statements.

F.   IS GAAP GOOD FOR YOU?

GAAP and IFRS are rules of content that deal with compiling and disclosing information in the financial statements. The first item in the Notes to the financial statements will describe the principles that the particular enterprise applies in the preparation of its financial statements. GAAP and IFRS provide considered and properly researched principles that accountants can adhere to and readers can use with reasonable confidence in understanding financial statements. They also make financial statements more comparable if the underlying GAAP are the same for all statements.

There are, however, some limiting aspects of GAAP. We have seen, for example, that conservatism is one of the basic underlying concepts of accounting, which generally tends to understate income and understate assets. Although this may be a desirable aspect of stewardship accounting, conservatism can lead to conservative valuations, which can mislead investors.

Given the variety of GAAPs that one may apply to measure or

report upon the same situation, we can have many net income figures, each of which is equally valid and according to GAAP. This is an important consideration in drafting legal agreements. In a sense, consistent application is just as important as the particular GAAP that one applies in a contract. Thus, in many situations, cash flow is a much more reliable figure because it eliminates the need to select between alternative accounting principles. Ultimately cash is king!

G. ACCOUNTING STANDARDS

The two key accounting standards–setting bodies in the world are the International Accounting Standards Board (IASB) and the Financial Accounting Standards Board (FASB) of the United States. The two bodies do not have identical standards. Indeed, they differ quite significantly in some areas such as "fair value" accounting.

Broadly speaking, fair value accounting standards value a firm's assets and liabilities based upon market value rather than historical cost. The difference is particularly important in the valuation of financial instruments and property, plant, and equipment on the balance sheet.

Canada adopted International Financial Reporting Standards (IFRS) for public companies in 2011 even though our economy is more closely linked to the United States, which primarily uses FASB.

H. FRAMEWORK OF IFRS

IFRS refers to the body of authoritative literature of the International Accounting Standards Board (IASB) designed principally for use by profit-oriented entities. The IFRS Foundation oversees the IASB. The IASB developed a *Conceptual Framework* for the development of IFRS and for guidance to accountants in preparing public entity financial statements. The objective of the IASB is to narrow the differences among accounting standards, procedures, and regulations that apply in the preparation of financial statements in different countries. Harmonization will facilitate economic decision making and international comparisons of companies. Reporting entities must comply with all of the standards and interpretations (including disclosure requirements) and make a positive statement of explicit and unreserved compliance in the audit opinion.

The framework recognizes that the overall objective of general purpose financial reporting is to provide financial information about the reporting entity that is useful to existing and potential investors, lenders and other creditors in making decisions about providing resources to the entity.[2] General purpose financial reports are not designed to show the value of a reporting entity. However, they provide useful information to help existing and potential investors, lenders, financial analysts, and other creditors to estimate the value of the reporting entity.

Financial statements prepared according to IFRS involve:

- Accounting policy choices;
- Professional judgment in making estimates;
- Fair value measures in the financial statements; and
- Disclosures in the Notes.

The overall objective of IFRS is fair presentation in the financial statements. In this aspect, there is no underlying difference in principle between IFRS and Canadian GAAP. However, absent specific prohibition, IFRS admits deviation and provides for a "true and fair" override if complying with IFRS would produce misleading information. In contrast, there is no such concept of a true and fair view override in Canadian GAAP.

Financial reports are based on estimates, judgments, and models rather than exact depictions. The Conceptual Framework of IFRS establishes the concepts that underline those estimates, judgments, and models.[3] The fundamental qualitative characteristics of useful financial information are relevance and faithful representation.[4]

---

2   Canadian Institute of Chartered Accountants, *CICA Handbook — Accounting*, loose-leaf (Toronto: Canadian Institute of Chartered Accountants, 2010), Part I (2012) OB 2 [*CICA Handbook*].
3   *Ibid*, OB 11.
4   See *ibid*, QC 5.

Financial statements, *per se*, are not predictions or forecasts. However, relevant and faithful representation of material financial information are the foundation for making predictions and forecasts by investors, management, and financial analysts. Thus, accounting is a stepping stone to financial valuation.

Faithful representation does not imply perfect accuracy in all respects, but the information should be relevant and faithfully represented. Financial information in reports should be material. Materiality means that omission or misstatement of the information could influence decisions that users make based on the information about a specific reporting entity.

Materiality is an entity-specific aspect of relevance based on the nature or magnitude, or both, of the items to which the information relates in the context of its financial report. The IASB does not specify a uniform quantitative threshold for materiality.[5] Whether an item is material or not is a matter of professional judgment in the circumstances of the entity's financial information.

Both IFRS and Canadian GAAP rely on a conceptual framework of accounting standards, which preparers of financial statements can refer to in the absence of specific guidance. IFRS states that it does not apply to items that are "immaterial." Although Canadian GAAP does not contain a similar explicit statement, that, in practice, is how accountants apply GAAP.

I.   WHO IS AFFECTED BY IFRS?

The underlining objective of the IFRSs is to produce global accounting standards that are transparent and provide comparable information on financial statements. By having a single set of global standards, public corporations can eliminate multiple GAAP reconciliations between countries.

Both IFRS and Canadian GAAP are comprehensive sets of principles-based standards that have a similar form and structure and share similar basic concepts of income recognition and measure-

---

5   *Ibid*, QC 11.

ment principles. However, IFRS requires more professional judgment and a greater volume of disclosures.

Canadian Accounting Standards are simpler to apply and, therefore, less costly. They also have fewer disclosure requirements than IFRS. However, Canada adopted IFRS for "publicly accountable enterprises" (PAE), which include "profit-oriented" enterprises with publicly issued securities and enterprises that hold assets in a fiduciary capacity for a broad group of outsiders. PAE also includes government business enterprises, such as the Ontario Securities Commission. Not-for-profits are not required to adopt IFRS.

Part I of the *CICA Handbook* deals with IFRS. Entities that prepare their financial statements in accordance with the part must state in their audit opinion that they have been prepared in accordance with IFRS. Such entities may also state that its financial statements are in accordance with Canadian GAAP.

IFRS and Canadian GAAP require that management account for financial transactions based upon their substance, rather than their legal form. Thus, accountants should recognize transactions with shareholders in their capacity as shareholders directly in the equity portion of the financial statements rather than through the income statement.

However, there are differences between IFRS and Canadian GAAP. Generally, there are fewer bright lines and rules in IFRS. Hence, there are more accounting policy choices and fewer interpretative matters. In particular, there are substantial differences in valuation and disclosure of impaired assets and securitizations.

J. IFRS AND US GAAP

In Canada, IFRS affects large multinational public companies and small private corporations differently. The big four Canadian accounting firms and their multinational corporate clients like IFRS because it simplifies transnational accounting and makes it easier for them to raise corporate capital in international markets. On the other hand, IFRS is more complex and expensive to administer and, therefore, not particularly attractive to smaller companies that operate only in Canada.

The United States Securities and Exchange Commission continues to study the implications for US companies. As of December 2012, the SEC could not recommend any final plan for the application of IFRS in the United States. It appears, however, that the United States will not adopt a full-blown changeover to IFRS because of the cost and burden of any such change. Instead, the United States may, like Canada, adopt a compromised "endorsement" model that would gradually incorporate IFRS into the US system of rules, while maintaining the United States' authority to modify or reject any international rules if it saw fit.

K. FAIR VALUE MEASUREMENT

Most items are disclosed in the financial statements based on their historical costs. In some circumstances (such as, inventories), historical cost may be reduced to reflect a loss if fair market value is less than cost (International Accounting Standard (IAS) 2). In other cases, such as property, plant, and equipment, an entity may reduce or increase amounts to reflect their fair value (IAS 16). IFRS 13 defines fair value and has a framework for measuring and disclosing it in the financials.

Fair value is the price that an entity would receive if it sold an asset or paid to transfer a liability in an orderly transaction between market participants as at the measurement date. Thus, fair value is a market-based measurement, not an entity-specific measurement. When measuring fair value, an entity uses the assumptions that market participants would use to price the asset or liability under current market conditions. As such, the entity's intention to hold the asset is not relevant when measuring fair value. The measure is what the buyer will pay for the benefit that it expects to generate from the use (or sale) of the assets, regardless of the entity's actual intentions.

An entity measuring fair value must determine:

- The particular asset or liability that is to be measured;
- For a non-financial asset, the highest and best use of the asset and whether it will be used in combination with other assets or on a stand-alone basis;

- The market in which the orderly transaction would take place for the asset or liability; and
- The appropriate valuation technique to use.

To increase consistency and comparability in the fair value measurements, IFRS 13 establishes a fair value hierarchy that categorizes the inputs used in valuation techniques.

- Level 1 inputs are quoted prices in active markets for identical assets or liabilities that the entity can access at the measurement date.
- Level 2 inputs are inputs (other than quoted prices included within Level 1) that are observable for the asset or liability, either directly or indirectly.
- Level 3 inputs are non-observable inputs for the asset or liability. Such inputs must reflect the assumption that market participants will use when pricing the asset or liability, including assumptions about risk.

In order to measure fair value, management must identify the characteristics of an asset or liability that market participants will take into account when pricing that asset or liability. They must also determine whether a principal market for an asset or liability exists and whether the entity has access to that market. In the absence of a principal market, it will be necessary to identify the most advantageous market for the asset or liability, which is likely to be that which maximizes the amount that would be received to sell the asset or minimize the amount that would be paid to transfer the liability.

For non-financial assets, management must determine the highest and best use of the asset from the perspective of market participants. This is so even if the entity intends to use the asset for a different purpose. Management must exercise judgment in determining the appropriate valuation technique to measure fair value.

The rationale of the input disclosures is to provide users with information so they may assess the valuation techniques and inputs used to develop fair value measurements, their effect on profit or loss or on other comprehensive income for the period.

Chapter IV: Overview of Financial Statements

A. OVERVIEW

Accounting is concerned with the assimilation and dissemination of financial information. The term "financial statement" encompasses the presentation of financial data, including accompanying Notes, derived from accounting records and intended to communicate an entity's economic resources and sources of financing at a point in time, or changes thereto for a period of time, in conformity with generally accepted principles, conventions, and assumptions. There are five components in a set of financial statements:

1) The Balance Sheet;
2) The Income Statement (and Statement of Comprehensive Income);
3) The Statement of Cash Flows;
4) The Statement of Shareholders' Equity; and
5) Notes to the Statements.

Each component discloses financial information about the business or entity from a different perspective. Collectively, however, they provide a composite that facilitates financial analysis and decision making.

The fundamental principles underlying these statements are reasonably uniform between entities and industries. Thus, when reduced to a common size, they permit one to apply similar techniques of interpretation and analysis, regardless of the size of the entity, the nature of its business, or its location.

The five key concepts underlying financial statements are:

- Assets are resources with monetary value.
- Liabilities are creditors' monetary claims on assets.
- Owners' equity represents the owners' or stockholders' claims against assets (net of liabilities).
- Revenues are sales and income from other sources.
- Expenses are the costs that an entity incurs in order to generate revenues and its income.

Each financial statement paints a part of the picture, but collectively they tell us of the entity's overall financial performance. Specifically, the financial statements tell us of the entity's economic resources; sources of financing from creditors and owners; ability to generate future income and cash flows; and solvency.

B. ILLUSTRATIVE FINANCIAL STATEMENTS

The following are illustrative (and simplified) comparative financial statements of a company, Duggan Inc:[1]

Balance Sheets as at 30 September (in thousands of dollars)	20-2	20-1
	$	$
Assets		
Current Assets:		
Cash	268	561
Cash equivalents	713	702
Marketable securities	1,100	1,000
Accounts receivable	5,835	5,621
Allowance for doubtful accounts	(467)	(430)
Inventories	4,031	4,164
Deferred tax assets	755	662
Prepaid expenses	216	86
Total Current Assets	12,451	12,366

1   For a comprehensive set of financial statements, see, for example, BCE Inc's

Capital Assets:		
Land	406	405
Buildings	10,657	10,212
Machinery and equipment	28,576	26,294
Leasehold improvements	3,086	3,026
Accumulated depreciation	(15,041)	(13,310)
Capital Assets (net)	27,684	26,627
Intangible Assets:	1,287	533
Other Assets:		
Accrued benefits	949	624
Total Assets	42,371	40,150

	20-2	20-1
Liabilities	$	$
Current Liabilities:		
Current portion of long-term debt	210	157
Notes payable	3,672	1,962
Accounts payable	3,088	3,138
Accrued liabilities:		
Income taxes	659	1,041
Salaries and wages	765	780
Advertising and promotion	2,338	2,280
Deferred revenue	1,414	1,352
Current Liabilities	12,146	10,710
Long-term liabilities	5,216	3,149
Non-pension postretirement benefits	4,509	4,076
Deferred income taxes	1,889	1,846
Capital leases	1,477	917
Long-term liabilities	13,091	9,988
Total Liabilities	25,237	20,698

2011 financial statement, online: www.bce.ca/assets/Uploads/Documents/
archivesAnnualReport/BCE/2011/BCEAR2011EN.pdf at 70–127.

Shareholders' Equity

Class A shares:

Authorized – unlimited

Issued and outstanding	1,496	1,467
Retained earnings	34,094	30,339
Treasury shares, at cost	(18,456)	(12,354)
Total shareholders' equity	17,134	19,452
Total Liabilities and Shareholders' Equity	42,371	40,150

Income Statements for years ended 30 September (in thousands of dollars)

	20-2	20-1
	$	$
Net sales	62,954	61,906
Cost of goods sold	29,890	29,877
Gross margin	33,064	32,029
Selling and administrative expenses	20,225	19,401
Other expenses	15	(368)
Research and development costs	2,150	2,000
Income from operations	10,674	10,996
Interest expense	333	292
Earnings before income taxes	10,341	10,704
Income taxes	3,534	3,876
Earnings before extraordinary items	6,807	6,828
Extraordinary items (net of tax benefits)	0	(2,516)
Net Income	6,807	4,312

Retained Earnings for years ended September 30 (in thousands of dollars)

	20-2	20-1
Retained earnings beginning of year	30,339	28,891
Net income	6,807	4,312
Dividends, declared and paid	(3,052)	(2,864)
Retained earnings end of year	34,094	30,339

Cash Flows for the year ended 30 September (in thousands of dollars)

	20-2
	$
Operating Activities	
Net income	6,807
Add items not affecting cash	
Depreciation	1,731
Future income taxes	43
	8,581
Accounts receivable	(177)
Inventories	133
Prepaids and other assets	(10)
Accounts payable and accrued liabilities	170
Income taxes	(575)
	8,122
Investing Activities	
Capital asset additions	(3,542)
Proceeds on disposal of capital assets	0
	(3,542)
Financing Activities	
Long-term debt	2,120
Notes payable	1,710
Issuance of common shares	29
Purchase of treasury shares	(6,102)
Cash dividends	(3,052)
Non-pension benefits	433
	(4,862)
Decrease in cash and cash equivalents	(282)
Cash and cash equivalents, beginning of year	1,263
Cash and cash equivalents, end of year	981
Cash and cash equivalents represented by:	
Cash	268
Short-term investments, at cost, which approximates market	
Commercial paper	713
	981

C. NOTES TO THE FINANCIAL STATEMENTS (CONDENSED)

1) Basis of Preparation and Significant Accounting Policies

These financial statements have been prepared in accordance with Canadian generally accepted accounting principles as set out in the *Handbook* of the Canadian Institute of Chartered Accountants ("*CICA Handbook*"). In 2010, the CICA Handbook was revised to incorporate International Financial Reporting Standards ("IFRS"), as issued by the International Accounting Standards Board ("IASB") and require publicly accountable enterprises to issue financial reports based on such standards effective for fiscal periods beginning on or after 1 January 2011.

The significant accounting policies used in the preparation of these financial statements are summarized below. These accounting policies conform, in all material respects, to IFRS.

a) Basis of Measurement

The financial statements have been prepared under the historical cost accounting convention, except for the revaluation of certain financial instruments to fair value, including cash, cash equivalents, and investments.

b) Use of Estimates and Judgments Made by Management

The preparation of financial statements requires management to make estimates and assumptions that affect the reported amounts of assets and liabilities and disclosure of contingent assets and liabilities at the date of the financial statements and the reported amounts of revenues and expenses during the reporting period. Actual results could differ from these estimates and changes in estimates are recorded in the reporting period in which they are determined.

Key areas where management has made difficult, complex, or subjective judgments in the process of applying the Company's accounting policies, often as a result of matters that are inherently uncertain, include: investment impairment; valuation techniques for fair value measurements of investments; and income taxes.

c) Financial Instruments — Recognition and Measurement

The Company's financial assets and liabilities are measured on the statement of financial position at fair value on initial recognition and are subsequently measured at fair value or amortized cost depending on their classification. Fair values of financial instruments are based where available on quoted market prices in active markets using bid prices for financial assets *and* ask prices for financial liabilities, and where needed on valuations utilizing market inputs.

Cash and cash equivalents consist of cash on deposit and short-term investments that mature in three months or less from the date of acquisition. The net gain or loss recognized incorporates any dividend or interest earned on the financial asset.

d) Foreign Currency Translation

The Canadian dollar is the functional and presentation currency of the Company. Transactions in foreign currencies are translated into Canadian dollars at rates of exchange at the time of such transactions. Monetary assets and liabilities are translated at current rates of exchange, with all translation differences recognized in investment income in the current period. Non-monetary assets and liabilities are translated at the date the fair value is determined.

e) Property and Equipment

Property and equipment are recorded in the statement of financial position at cost less accumulated amortization. Amortization is charged to operating expense on a straight-line basis over the estimated useful lives of the assets as follows:

Furniture and fixtures	5 years
Computer equipment	3 years
Computer software	1 to 3 years
Leasehold improvements	Term of lease

Property and equipment and other non-financial assets are reviewed for impairment losses whenever events or changes in circumstances indicate that the carrying amount may not be recoverable.

An impairment loss is recognized for the amount by which the carrying amount of the asset exceeds its recoverable amount.

f) Income Taxes

Income tax expense is recognized in the statement of income and the statement of comprehensive income. Current tax is based on taxable income, which differs from net income as reported in the statement of income and statement of comprehensive income because of items of income or expense that are taxable or deductible in other years and items that are never taxable or deductible. Current tax includes any adjustments in respect of prior years.

Deferred tax assets are generally recognized for all deductible temporary income tax differences to the extent that it is probable that taxable profits will be available against which those deductible temporary differences can be utilized.

Deferred tax liabilities are generally recognized for all taxable temporary differences.

Deferred tax assets and liabilities are determined based on the enacted or substantively enacted tax laws and rates that are anticipated to apply in the period of realization. The measurement of deferred tax assets and liabilities utilizes the liability method, reflecting the tax consequences that would follow from the manner in which the Company expects to recover or settle the carrying amount of the related assets and liabilities.

The carrying amount of the deferred tax asset is reduced to the extent that it is no longer probable that sufficient taxable profits will be available to allow all or part of the asset to be recovered.

Income tax assets and liabilities are offset when the income taxes are levied by the same taxation authority and there is a legally enforceable right to offset current tax assets with current tax liabilities.

2) Fair Value Measurements

The Company is responsible for determining the value of its financial assets and liabilities carried at fair value. The Company considers fair value to represent the amount of consideration that would be agreed upon in an arm's length transaction between knowledgeable, willing parties who are under no compulsion to act. The valuation process includes utilizing market-driven fair value measurements from active markets where available, considering other observable and unobservable inputs and employing valuation techniques which make use of current market data. Considerable judgment may be required in interpreting market data used to develop the estimates of fair value. Accordingly, the estimates presented in these financial statements are not necessarily indicative of the amounts that would be realized in a current market exchange.

3) Income Taxes

a) Income Tax Expense Recognized in the Statement of Income

The total income tax expense recognized in the statement of income is comprised as follows:

	20-2	20-1
Current tax		
Expensed (recovered) during the year	3,752	3,923
Prior year adjustments	(12)	8
Total current tax expense	3,740	3,931
Deferred tax		
Origination and reversal of temporary differences	(333)	(214)
Changes in statutory tax rates	127	159
Total deferred tax expense	(206)	(55)
Total income tax expense	3,534	3,876
(Explanations omitted)		

b) Net Deferred Income Tax Asset

The Company's net deferred income tax asset is the result of temporary differences between the carrying amounts of assets and liabilities for financial reporting purposes and the amounts used for income tax purposes. The sources of these temporary differences and the tax effects are as follows:

	20-2	20-1
Deferred tax assets		
Property and equipment	755	622
	755	622
Deferred tax liabilities		
Investments	1,889	1,846

4) Capital Stock and Retained Earnings

Capital stock of the Company represents:

14,960 Class A Shares npv – authorized, issued, and paid.

The Balance Sheet shows an accounting entity's resources and its sources of financing — that is, what it owns, what it owes to creditors, and the owners' interest. It is a snapshot of the entity at a particular point in time.

The income statement shows how much income or loss a company makes over a period of time, typically, a year.

The cash flow statement shows how much cash — as opposed to "income" — the company received and paid out in the same period as the income statement.

The statement of retained earnings shows changes in the owners' interest in the company over the same periods as the income and cash flow statements.

Notes describe the principles and methods applied in preparing the financial statements.

D. THE BALANCE SHEET

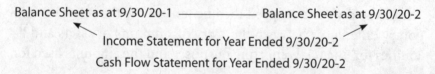

Balance Sheet as at 9/30/20-1 ——————— Balance Sheet as at 9/30/20-2

Income Statement for Year Ended 9/30/20-2

Cash Flow Statement for Year Ended 9/30/20-2

A balance sheet is a point in time statement — a snapshot of an enterprise as at one moment. Thus, a balance sheet should always identify the entity and time to which it applies. For example, Duggan's balance sheet states:

Duggan Inc
"Balance sheet *as at* 30 September 20-2 and 20-1"

1) Components

A fundamental premise of the balance sheet is that an entity's resources must equal its sources of financing. This is an immutable law: all resources, which we refer to as "assets" must be financed either by creditors ("liabilities") or the owners ("equity") of the business. As its name implies, a balance sheet "balances" assets (A), liabilities (L), and owners' equity (E). Thus, the fundamental balance sheet equation is:

$$A = L + E$$

The equation states the financial position of an enterprise at a point in time.

Assets are resources that represent future benefits from past transactions and that are under the control of the entity.

Liabilities are legal obligations that result from past transactions and that the entity has no discretion to avoid.

Equity is the company's *net* assets. Equity represents the excess of assets over liabilities. A deficit would represent the excess of liabilities over assets. Thus, we can restate the basic balance sheet equation as follows:

$$E = A - L$$

Corporate equity (E) has two components: contributed capital and retained earnings. Contributed capital is the investment of shareholders in the stock of the company. Retained earnings are, as its name implies, earnings that the company retains in the entity and does not distribute to shareholders. Transactions with shareholders are usually reflected in the equity account. Together, contributed capital and retained earnings represent the owners' interest in the enterprise.

There is really no mystery about why a balance sheet balances. After all, a balance sheet tells us what assets the entity owns and how it financed the assets. Since we finance everything that we own, either with debt (liabilities) or our own money (owners' equity), the relationship must always be in balance. It is metaphysically impossible for a properly prepared balance sheet not to balance.

2) Only Monetary Values

An essential element of the balance sheet is that it shows only assets (resources) that have a monetary value. For example, a law firm's balance sheet will show its assets — cash, receivables, work in progress, computer hardware, furniture, and equipment, etc. — but will not show its principal and most valued resource — its reputation for service, the ability of its lawyers and its "brand" recognition. Thus, a balance sheet does not reflect an entity's "value" for sale purposes. A high rating in a legal directory — for example, Martindale Hubbell — is a valuable "asset" to the lawyer and his or her law firm. For accounting purposes, however, the rating is not an asset because we cannot accurately measure its monetary value.

To summarize inelegantly: a balance sheet is a What got? How got? statement. It tells you what the entity has in the way of measurable monetary assets and how it acquired or financed those assets from external borrowing or equity. Assets do the entity's work; liabilities and equity facilitate the work.

Duggan Inc has total assets of $42,371,000 as at the end of the financial year (20-2). It financed its assets by borrowing $25,237,000. In addition, the shareholders provided financing of $17,134,000. The total financing is $42,371,000, which is exactly equal to the company's assets.

3) Categories

Assets are classified into subcategories — typically current assets, capital assets,[2] intangible assets, and other assets. For example, as at 30 September 20-2, Duggan Inc's total assets of $42,371,000 are subdivided into current assets of $12,451,000; capital assets of $27,684,000; intangible assets of $1,287,000; and other assets of $949,000.

Similarly, liabilities are subdivided into categories — current liabilities, long-term liabilities, and other liabilities. As at 30 September 20-2, Duggan Inc has current liabilities of $12,146,000 and long-term obligations of $13,091,000. The total is $25,237,000.

Classifying assets and liabilities into categories allows one to analyze financial statements in a more meaningful way than if we simply had one aggregate figure for all assets and liabilities. The extent of detail must be meaningful and appropriate. The depth of detail depends upon the purpose for which the reader will use the financial statements. For example, current assets are a useful measure of an entity's ability to pay its current debts as they are due. Thus, loan contracts often stipulate the minimum ratio of current assets to current liabilities.

Financial statements for public dissemination are relatively sparse and show only a few categories. They must balance the need for disclosure against the protection of confidential information. Too much detail would disclose the company's proprietary information to competitors. Financial statements prepared for management, however, are more detailed because management uses the information to make its operational and financing decisions.

Although the balance sheet gives us a lot of information about monetary assets and liabilities, costs, investments, obligations, and owners' equity (both initial and retained), it has limitations. For example, a balance sheet does *not* disclose the value of:

- Long-term contracts;
- Intrinsic goodwill and brand loyalty; or

---

2   Also referred to as fixed assets.

- Stock options that can dilute shareholder value.

Some of this information may be in other parts of the financial statements — for example, the notes, which are integral to the proper communication of financial information. The notes are also where management buries its financial skeletons.

Equity represents the residual claim that the owners of a company have against its assets after it satisfies all of its obligations to creditors. It is equally important to understand what equity is not. It is not a measure of:

- The market value of the entity;
- What the owners will receive if the entity is liquidated; or
- Future dividends.

The term "net worth," often used to describe owners' equity, is an unfortunate choice because it conveys the impression that it represents the "value" or worth of the company. In fact, net worth is nothing more than assets minus liabilities (NW = A – L). The term "net assets," that is, assets minus liabilities — is a more accurate description.

Since the balance sheet is a point in time statement, its utility diminishes as time passes and the information in it becomes stale. Thus, the balance sheet of an enterprise that is older than four to six months is of limited value for making decisions. Management would not use such stale-dated financial statements for its decisions.

Nevertheless, the statement is valuable for the purposes of historical reporting and stewardship accounting. For example, public companies are required to distribute their financial statements to shareholders annually and file the statements with regulatory agencies. The purpose of annual financial statements is to report on management's past stewardship of the company.

E. THE INCOME STATEMENT

The income statement measures revenues (R) and expenses (E) over a period of time. Revenues represent increases in net assets from normal operations and sales. Typically, revenues do not include extraordinary gains, which are reported elsewhere.[3]

The income statement tells us how much revenue (R) an entity earned and the expenses (E) that it incurred in order to earn its income. Thus, the formula for the income statement is simple:

Net Income = R – E.

The income statement links successive balance sheets and explains how the company's equity changed between. For example, Duggan's balance sheet tells us where it stood at a point in time — 30 September 20-2 — and the income statement tells us how the company moved from its financial status at the end of 20-1 to its position at the end of 20-2. Net income is the amount by which revenues exceed expenses for the period. For the year ended 30 September 20-2, Duggan Inc had net income of $6,807,000 — that is, its net sales of $62,954,000 exceeded its total expenses of $56,147,000. The summary of net changes is recorded in the statement of retained earnings.

The revenue that a company earns is a significant figure in determining bottom-line net income, which affects the stock price of publicly listed corporations. Hence, investment analysts and market watchers look for trends in top-line revenue in trying to predict the future of the company's stock price.

Comparative income statements provide a useful trend to show the historical performance of an enterprise. The income statement is a bridge between successive balance sheets. As a company does well and earns profits, its balance sheet will reflect the improvement in its resources/assets and owners' equity.

Expenses are decreases in net assets from normal operations and expired costs. Unexpired costs are assets that will be allocated against revenues in the future. Thus, the essential difference between capital assets and expenses is time. For example, if a business purchases a machine for $100,000 that it will use for ten years, it is

---

3   These are reported sometimes as a separate item on the income statement
     and sometimes in the statement of retained earnings.

reasonable to consider $10,000 as an expense in the first year and $90,000 as an asset or unexpired cost (assuming it is purchased on 1 January).

An income statement allocates costs that have been utilized in a particular time period in order to earn revenues that the entity earns in the same period. In essence, then, the income statement matches revenues and related expenses in a specified period. Thus, over time, all assets (except land) ultimately expire and become expenses.

The allocation of revenues and expenses to time periods raises important questions as to when we recognize revenues and charge expenses against those revenues. The matching process involves professional judgment. History teaches us that many accounting frauds involved a deliberate mismatching of revenues and expenses, usually to increase net income and, hence, stock prices. WorldCom in the 1990s, for example, treated $8 billion (US) of expenses as capital assets, thereby overstating net income in the current year by an equivalent amount. The stock shot up and management got rich.

We can now show the relationship between the income statement and the balance sheet in the accounting equation:

A = L + E
A = L + [Capital + RE]
A = L + Capital + [Opening RE + Net Income]
A = L + Capital + Opening RE + [R – E]

The income statement starts with sales on the top line — that is, income that an enterprise derives from the product or services that it sells in order to earn income. Net sales means gross sales minus any returns of product sold.

The next major item on the income statement is usually the cost of goods or services sold. This number represents the expense that is *directly* associated with creating the product or the service that the entity sells to its customers. The difference between net sales and cost of goods sold is gross income or gross profit.

Next, we deduct from the gross income all of the other expenses that an enterprise incurs to earn its income. Typically, there will be operating expenses — such as selling and administrative expenses, salaries, benefits, rent, etc. In published financial statements, such as those of Duggan Inc, all of these expenses are grouped together under one title, "Selling and Administrative Expenses." The aggregation of all of these different operating expenses into one number is acceptable for public reporting purposes because companies do not want to disclose sensitive confidential information. However, management will have a much more detailed breakdown of each component for their analysis.[4]

Duggan Inc had net sales of $62,954,000 for the year ended 30 September 20-2. In order to earn that income, Duggan incurred various expenses. The first expense is its cost in purchasing merchandise that it sold. The cost of goods sold was $29,890,000, which left Duggan Inc with a gross margin of $33,064,000. The gross margin percentage was 52.5 percent. As we shall see, this is an important number in financial statement analysis.

In addition to the cost of goods sold, Duggan also incurred various other expenses in its business. It had operating expenses (O) as follows:

Selling and administrative expenses	$20,225,000
Other expenses	$15,000
Research and development costs	$2,150,000
Total operating expenses (O)	$22,390,000

Duggan Inc also had financing expenses (F) and taxes (T) as follows:

Interest expense (F)	$333,000
Income taxes (T)	$3,534,000
Total	$3,867,000

Subtracting the operating, financing, and tax expenses from the gross margin left Duggan with a net profit of $6,807,000 for the year ended 30 September 20-2.

---

4   See Chapter 8.

It is premature at this point to say whether the net profit of $6,807,000 was a satisfactory return for Duggan Inc. We shall return later to the analysis of the financials to determine the components and adequacy of an entity's return on equity (ROE). The return must be evaluated in the context of industry norms and competitive companies.

When the cost of sales, and O, F & T expenses are less than sales, we have net income or net profit. When the cost of sales, and O, F & T expenses exceeds net sales, we have a net loss. The net income or net loss is added to the opening balance of retained earnings to determine how much better off an entity is at the end of a year as compared to the beginning. We see this in the statement of retained earnings of Duggan Inc, where the Net Income of $6,807,000 is added to the opening retained earnings balance of $30,339,000.

From the net income figure, we can also determine the earnings per share (EPS) of publicly listed operations. EPS, an important determinant in stock market prices, tells us how much each share of stock earned during the year. Some companies also use it to determine executive bonuses and in setting stock option prices for management and employees. Hence, once again, we recognize the temptation that management endures to boost EPS by overstating revenues or understating expenses. Accounting is the apple in the garden of business.

F. STATEMENT OF COMPREHENSIVE INCOME

"Income" in IFRS is a "comprehensive" concept that differs from the traditional concept of income. Under IFRS, a correct measure of periodic income should include items that are charged to reserves, gains, and losses on securities that are available-for-sale,[5] foreign exchange gains and losses, and certain revaluation adjustments to property, plant and equipment.[6]

---

5   IAS 39.
6   IAS 16.

The underlying concept is that these items, although different from traditional income statement items, are appropriately characterized as "income" in a broad sense. For example, the aggregate periodic amount charged to, or released from reserves, are included along with "conventional" net income to arrive at "comprehensive income." Similarly, expenditures that are periodically charged to reserves are elements of income for the period even if they are of a different nature from conventional income. Thus, the theory is that an analysis of the results of the entity should include changes in such reserves.

As a minimum, the income statement should disclose as line items the following amounts:

- Revenue;
- Finance costs;
- Share of the profit or loss of joint ventures;
- Tax expenses;
- A single amount comprising the total of:
  - » The post-tax profit or loss of discontinued operations; and
  - » The post-tax gain or loss recognized on the measurement to fair value less costs to sell, or on the disposal of the assets or disposal groups constituting a discontinued operation; and
- Net income.

G. CAPITAL

The word "capital" can mean many things in commercial and financial usage. For example:

- Share capital — contributed by the owners of the business;
- Loan capital — provided by creditors of a business;
- Retained earnings left in the business by the owners;
- Tangible capital, such as physical resources used in the business;
- Intangible capital, such as intellectual property in the form of patents, trade-marks, goodwill and trade names;

- Working capital — the difference between current assets and current liabilities.

In financial statements, however, capital refers to the consideration that shareholders pay for their stock. The share capital account is divided into classes according to their terms and conditions. In Canada, the term "preferred share" is a financial term and not a legal term. Duggan Inc has issued 1,496,000 Class A shares as at 30 September 20-2.

H. RETAINED EARNINGS STATEMENT

The equity portion of a corporate balance sheet comprises two principal components: share capital and retained earnings. A corporation's retained earnings is the accumulated income (deficit) net of dividends and other distributions to shareholders. If the balance is negative because of accumulated losses, the account is called "Accumulated Deficit," which shows under equity on the balance sheet.

There are very few transactions recorded directly in the retained earnings account. Typically, the most common entry is a transfer of the corporation's net income for the year from the income summary account to the retained earnings. For example, since Duggan Inc has net income of $6,807,000 after taxes, it will transfer the balance into the retained earnings account and close off the income summary for the year. The important point to observe is that retained earnings do not represent cash or any other specific assets. Retained earnings is simply a balancing account that derives from the fundamental balance sheet equation:

$$A = L + E$$

E (Equity) breaks down into two components:

$$E = \text{Capital} + \text{Retained Earnings.}$$

Thus, retained earnings is the difference between assets and liabilities and capital:

$$RE = A - L - C$$

In effect, the retained earnings account reflects the history of the corporation's earnings since its inception. The number does not reflect the market value of the entity.

1) Dividends

A corporation may pay dividends in cash, property, or its own shares (stock). There are three critical dates for dividends: the "declaration date," the date on which the corporation's board of directors authorizes the payment of the dividend and stipulates the amount payable; the "date of record," the date on which shareholder records are closed and the identity of shareholders entitled to receive the dividend is tabulated; finally, the "date of payment," the date on which the corporation actually pays the dividend to shareholders as of the date of record.

For example, a corporation may declare a dividend of $1 per share on 1 April payable to shareholders of record as of 15 April, with actual payment to be made on 30 April. Thus, the shareholder who owns the stock on the date of record (15 April) is entitled to the dividend of $1 per share. If the shareholder sells his stock after the date of record, the purchaser will receive her stock "ex-dividend" — that is, without the dividend.

a) Cash Dividends

Dividends are discretionary and there is no obligation on a corporation to pay a dividend. A cash dividend is the amount that the corporation pays in cash as of the declaration date. Once declared, the dividend becomes a legal obligation and a liability that is recorded as "Dividends Payable" on the balance sheet.

b) Dividends in Kind

Dividends in kind are the same as cash dividends, except that the distribution occurs in identified property rather than in cash. For example, a corporation may declare a dividend in the form of shares of another company that it owns. The same rules apply as with cash dividends. There will be a declaration date, date of record, and date of payment.

c) Stock Dividends

A stock dividend is a special dividend in kind, that involves a distribution of additional shares of the corporation's own shares to shareholders in proportion to their existing shareholdings. The accounting for stock dividends depends upon whether the distribution is considered "small" or "large."

With a small stock dividend — generally under 25 percent of the current outstanding shares — the company capitalizes retained earnings equal to the value of the dividend into share capital. For example, assume that a corporation declares a dividend of 200,000 shares that have a market value immediately before distribution of $10 per share. Prior to the distribution, the corporation has 2 million shares outstanding. The corporation will capitalize (transfer) $2 million from its retained earnings to its share capital account. After the distribution, the corporation will have 2,200,000 issued shares. Note, the corporation cannot ever do the reverse — that is, transfer share capital into retained earnings.

A large distribution of the corporation's shares is known as a "stock split." In the above example, the corporation might declare a stock split of 2 for 1, which would increase its issued shares to 4 million. A stock split does not require any capitalization of retained earnings into share capital. The shareholder simply receives (or is recorded on the share register) an additional certificate for each share that he owns. Hence, market value of the shares will usually drop by 50 percent to reflect the fact that there are twice the number of shares outstanding. Indeed, corporations often issue stock splits in order to bring down the market price of their shares to make them more attractive to retail investors. A stock split does not involve any change in the underlying financial structure of the corporation. It merely involves a proportional change in the number of shares outstanding and their per share price on the market.

A reverse stock split is similar in principle, except that the number of shares outstanding is reduced. In the above example, the corporation might decide to reduce the number of its outstanding shares by a ratio of 1:2, which would reduce the number of outstanding shares to 1 million. Typically, the market value of the shares should approximately double to reflect the fact that there are now 50 percent fewer shares outstanding. Once again, the transaction is entirely cosmetic and does not change the underlying financial structure of the corporation. Typically, a corporation will employ a reverse stock split to increase the market price of its shares to a "respectable" value that qualifies for investment by institutional investors.

I. STATEMENT OF CASH FLOWS

Cash management is an important aspect of a business. A successful business that reports growing net income may, nevertheless, run into financial difficulties if it cannot collect its revenues or there is undue delay between the time of sale and the time that it collects its cash. Similarly, businesses must be sensitive to their ability to pay their expenses as they become due. Even successful businesses can have difficulty in paying their accounts because of cash shortages.

The statement of cash flows essentially reconciles opening and closing cash (and cash equivalents) for the fiscal period. Unlike the income statement, which uses accrual accounting to record revenues and expenses, a cash flow statement classifies and reports transactions based upon actual cash receipts and disbursements. The statement of cash flows is important because it is easy to measure and report cash transactions, which do not involve judgment on accruals and allocations of expenses to particular periods. Thus, absent outright fraud, it is an extremely accurate statement.

As with the income statement, the statement of cash flows is a "period statement" that covers the same time horizon as the income statement. Thus, the statement supplements the income statement and the balance sheet and is the third dimension of financial statements.

There are three main segments of a cash flow statement: operations, investing, and financing.

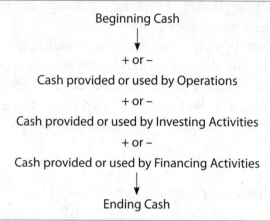

Beginning Cash

↓

+ or –

Cash provided or used by Operations

+ or –

Cash provided or used by Investing Activities

+ or –

Cash provided or used by Financing Activities

↓

Ending Cash

Duggan started the year with $1,263,000 in cash and cash equivalents and ended with $981,000. How did that happen? The cash flow statement tells the story.

1) Operations

The first segment shows the cash inflows and outflows from the business's primary income-producing and operating activities. This is the cash that the business receives from sales of its products or services and cash that it pays out for the ordinary operating expenses that it incurs in earning its sales revenues. Duggan Inc generated $8,122,000 from operations in the year ended 30 September 20-2.

We saw earlier that we calculate net income on an accrual basis — that is, recording revenues recognized from consummated sales and expenses incurred to match the revenues — regardless of when the entity actually collects or pays cash. The operations segment starts with the net income figure from the income statement. Then it adjusts income to reflect only actual cash receipts and disbursements.

Net income and cash are not the same thing. A business must calculate its income based upon accrual principles, recording revenues and expenses in the period that it makes its sales and not when it collects or pays out cash. The statement of cash flows is useful because it supplements the income statement by providing information about the sources of cash and where the business is expending cash.

The first adjustment of the cash flow statement is usually in respect of depreciation and amortization. Depreciation and amortization are non-cash expenses. The cash expenditure occurs when the company actually pays for its assets. Depreciation is merely the process of allocating the cost of the asset over its useful life. Thus, any depreciation that the company charges on its income statement is added back to net income because it does not involve any cash disbursement in the relevant period.

Example

ABC Ltd acquires a building on 31 December 20-1 for $10 million. The company pays 20 percent in cash and assumes a mortgage for the balance. Thus, in 20-1, ABC Ltd has a cash outflow of $2 million (assuming it does not pay anything on the mortgage). Assuming the building has a useful life of forty years and no residual value, ABC Ltd might depreciate it $250,000 annually. In 20-2, ABC Ltd will have depreciation expense of $250,000, which it will add back to net income to determine cash flow. Adding back depreciation converts the accrual net income to a cash figure.

The next set of adjustments to the operations component deals with current assets and liabilities. Accounts receivable, accounts payable, and inventories are the three most common adjustments.

When a business increases its accounts receivable, it means that the business has sold more on credit. In order to convert the sales income back to cash income, we deduct the increase in accounts receivable to reflect the actual amount of cash collected from sales. Similarly, we adjust inventories and accounts payable for increases and decreases from the prior year end.

2) Investing Activities

The second segment in the cash flow statement is investing activities. This segment discloses how much cash the business received or expended from investing — as opposed to operating — activities. For example, in 20-2, Duggan Inc expended $3,542,000 cash by purchasing capital and intangible assets. Hence, that number shows as a negative item in the cash flow statement. If the company had sold any capital assets during 20-2, it would have shown it as a source of cash from the sales.

3) Financing Activities

The third segment is financing activities. This segment shows how much cash the business derives or expends from selling financial instruments or financing operating activities. For example, we see that Duggan Inc obtained $2,120,000 from issuing long-term debt. The company also spent $6,102,000 in purchasing its shares and $3,052,000 in paying dividends.

In the result, Duggan Inc's cash and cash equivalent investments are $981,000 at 30 September 20-2. This is exactly the same number that appears on the balance sheet ended 30 September 20-2: cash of $268,000 and cash equivalents of $713,000, for a total of $981,000.

J. NOTES TO FINANCIAL STATEMENTS

The purpose of the notes to the financial statements is to enhance our understanding of the statements, and to provide context and some detail of accounting principles. The theory is that the notes should communicate relevant information in a readable form to assist the user in analyzing the statements. Unfortunately, management can also use the notes to obfuscate, minimize, or bury important information.

The notes to the financial statements are similar to footnotes in a document. They should provide supplemental information to the reader of the statements and disclose management choices in selecting between alternative accounting principles and methodologies. Since accounting involves choices between alternative methods of revealing financial information, management should select the method that is most appropriate to its particular business and operations. The notes describe the important accounting policies that management adopts and, where necessary, explain changes in such policies between successive financial statements.

The notes also contain information on aspects of business operations that cannot conveniently be disclosed in the body of the financial statements. For example, the notes may contain detailed discussions about an entity's legal obligations under long-term leases, retirement, and pension plans, and pending legal actions that may create liabilities in the future.

In addition, the notes can provide useful comparative data that is not in the body of the financial statements. For example, the notes may reveal comparative figures for the entity's sales and net income over a period of ten years. This type of detailed financial information is particularly useful for financial analysts and regulatory bodies.

Finally, the notes may contain a section on Management's Discussion and Analysis (MDA) of the entity and its financial operations. Regulatory bodies, such as the Ontario Securities Commission (OSC) and the Securities and Exchange Commission (SEC) require such disclosure in public filings.

To be sure, the notes to the financial statements are fairly boring, often tedious, and frequently ignored. They are, however, an integral part of the financial statements. As Pete Seeger said, "Education is when you read the fine print, experience is what you get when you don't." So it is with the notes.

Notes to financial statements will typically include the following:

- Significant accounting policies;
- Subsequent events;
- Contingencies;
- Related-party transactions;
- Principles and methods used in preparation;
- Explanations of significant items in the balance sheet, income statement and cash flow statement; and
- Buried skeletons.

K. CONTINGENCIES

Not everything about a business's financial results during a particular period of time is certain. There are many uncertainties about the future that may affect financial statements in the present. The simplest example is accounts receivable. A company sells goods and services on credit, and this creates accounts receivable that will be payable in the future. Some of the accounts receivable may never be collected. The company may not be certain as to which of its accounts it will not be able to collect, but past experience will teach it that it will not have a 100 percent collection record on its credit sales. Hence, the company might provide an "Allowance for Doubtful Accounts," and subtract the amount from its accounts receivable balance on the balance sheet. In effect, the company is providing for a future event (default) by taking a write-down of its receivables in the present set of financial statements.

There is, however, another type of uncertainty, which deals with the uncertainty of an event and not with the amount involved. We refer to these as "contingencies."

The *CICA Handbook* defines a contingency as:

> an existing condition or situation involving uncertainty as to possible gain or loss to an enterprise that will ultimately be resolved when one or more future events occur or fail to occur.[7]

Common examples include pending or threatened litigation, threat of expropriation of assets, guarantees of the indebtedness of others, and possible liabilities arising from discounted bills of exchange or promissory notes.

The treatment of future uncertain events varies depending upon the nature and degree of uncertainty. Under GAAP, the critical distinctions depend upon whether the event is probable, reasonably probable, or remote.

---

7   See Canadian Institute of Chartered Accountants, *CICA Handbook — Accounting*, loose-leaf (Toronto: Canadian Institute of Chartered Accountants, 2010), section 3290.02.

A company should accrue its contingent losses in the financial statements by a charge to current income if:

- The event is probable and likely to occur; and
- The amount of the loss can be reasonably estimated.[8]

The effect of the accrual is to reduce net income in the current period.

If, however, the occurrence of the future event is not determinable but is reasonably possible, the company should disclose the contingency in the notes to the financial statements and estimate the loss or range of losses that might occur.

The company should use notes disclosure if:

- The future event is likely to occur;
- The amount of the loss cannot be reasonably estimated; or
- The company is exposed to losses in excess of amounts already accrued in the income statement.[9]

The company should not disclose or accrue any amount if the future event is remote.

Non-disclosure of contingencies can have legal consequences. In *Endo v Albertine*,[10] for example, the company was liable for damages because it failed to disclose contingent tax deficiencies and environmental liabilities in its financial statements.

---

8   See *ibid*, section 3290.12.
9   See *ibid*, section 3290.15.
10   863 F Supp 708 (ND Ill 1994).

Chapter V: The Balance Sheet

In this chapter we look at the major and most common items on business balance sheets. Although balance sheets will vary between industries, they share common characteristics and principles. Business balance sheets have three components: assets, liabilities, and equity.

A. ASSETS

1) Current Assets

Assets are resources that a business uses in its operations to earn income. Current assets are a subset of assets that the business expects to use or consume within the next year or within the operating cycle of the business if the cycle is longer than one year. In a manufacturing business, for example, current assets would typically include cash, marketable securities, accounts receivable, inventories, and prepaid expenses. These are listed on the balance sheet in order of their liquidity.

a) Cash

Cash, the most liquid of all assets, includes all currency and bank accounts that can be withdrawn at any time without restrictions. Cash also includes "cash equivalents" — that is, short-term, liquid instruments such as money market funds and commercial paper that are readily available. Duggan Inc had a cash balance of $268,000 and cash equivalents of $713,000 at the end of 20-2.

Restricted funds are not included in cash. For example, a bank may loan money to a business, but require it to maintain a minimum cash balance. In effect, the minimum compensating balance increases the effective rate of interest that the bank charges on its loan. Assume, for example, that a bank loans a business $1 million at 5 percent, but requires the business to maintain a minimum of $100,000 in its account. Then, ignoring any time value of money considerations, the effective rate of interest on the loan is 5.56 percent. Restricted funds are reported as "Other Assets."

b) Marketable Securities

Marketable securities are liquid financial instruments — debt and equity — that the business holds as temporary investments. The securities should be available for sale at any time in order to meet cash requirements for the business. The rationale for holding marketable securities is that they generate a higher rate of return than cash sitting in a savings account. Marketable securities are reported on the balance sheet at their market values.

A business also may hold marketable securities that it does not intend to sell in the short term or that it is restricted from selling by virtue of contractual obligations with financial institutions. Such instruments are classified as "investments" in the non-current portion of the balance sheet.

c) Accounts Receivable

Accounts receivable, also called "trade receivables" arise from sales on credit and are legal rights to receive cash in the future. For example, assume that a business sells $150,000 of merchandise on terms of 1/10, net 30. This means that the business has extended credit and will give a discount of 1 percent if the customer pays $148,500 within ten days; otherwise the full amount is due in thirty days. Under accrual accounting principles the business would recognize the revenue from the sale and the accounts receivable as an asset. If the purchaser does not take the discount of $1,500, the business should record that as "cash discounts not taken," which is a form of interest revenue.

A business will record its receivables initially at their face value at the time that it sells the goods or services. Most businesses know, however, that they will not collect all of their receivables. At year-end, following the principle of conservatism, a business will estimate the uncollectable portion of its accounts receivable and set-up an "allowance for doubtful accounts" to recognize potential uncollectability. Thus, a business should report its accounts receivable at their "net realizable value" on the balance sheet date. Any estimated uncollectable receivables should be recognized as "bad debts" and charged to the income statement as an expense and set up as an allowance for doubtful accounts on the balance sheet. In Duggan Inc, for example, we see an accounts receivable balance as at 30 September 20-2 of $5,835,000, against which the company has created an allowance for doubtful accounts of $467,000.

The "allowance for doubtful accounts" is a "contra account" that is deducted from the accounts receivable balance on the balance sheet in the current assets section. This has the effect of showing the accounts receivable at their net realizable value. An account receivable that goes from being "doubtful" to "bad" is written off and the accounts receivable balance and the allowance for doubtful accounts are both reduced by the amount. There is no expense charge to the income statement at that time because, under accrual accounting principles, the charge was made at the time that the business estimated the allowance for doubtful accounts.

Example

Assume that X Ltd has sales revenues of $1 million in 20-0 and accounts receivable of $190,000 as at its year-end. The company estimates that it will not collect 5 percent of its accounts receivable. Then:

Income statement (partial) for year ended 20-0:

Sales revenue	$1,000,000
Bad debt expense	$ 9,500
Net income	$ 990,500

Balance sheet (partial) as at year ended 31 December 20-0:

Accounts receivable	$ 190,000
Allowance for doubtful accounts	$ 9,500
Net accounts receivable	$ 180,500

There are various methods for estimating the amount of accounts receivable that will not be collected. For example, based upon its past experience, a business may estimate a percentage of its total sales as potential uncollectable accounts. Alternatively, it may "age" its accounts receivable — that is, categorize them by the number of days outstanding — and then make an informed estimate of the uncollectable portion. The theory is that the older the account, the greater the risk of it becoming uncollectable. Regardless of the method used, a business should carefully review its estimate from time to time to see that it is appropriate. A business can create a hidden reserve and mislead investors if it overestimates its bad debt reserves.

Where a business assigns or pledges its accounts receivable as collateral for a loan, the amount assigned should be shown separately from the unassigned accounts receivable. For example, assume that a business with $1 million accounts receivable borrows $500,000 from a bank and assigns a similar amount to the bank as security for the loan. The business estimates that it will not collect 5 percent of its total receivables. The assigned receivables will remain as current assets, but will be segregated and shown as "Assigned Accounts Receivable" in the current assets section, as follows:

Balance sheet (partial) as at 31 December 20-0	
Accounts receivable	$ 500,000
Allowance for doubtful accounts	$ 50,000
Net accounts receivable	$ 450,000
Assigned accounts receivable (Note)	$ 500,000
Total accounts receivable	$ 950,000

d) Notes Receivable

Notes receivable are more formal accounts receivable where the customer signs a note showing the amount of the receivable and the terms and conditions attached. A note receivable may have some added interest, which the business will recognize as interest revenue. Where a business is doubtful about collecting the full value of its notes, it should provide for a reserve.

e) Inventories

Manufacturers, wholesalers, and retailers of goods and products almost always have unsold goods or products on hand at the end of their fiscal year. These unsold goods and products are "inventory" for resale and are considered "current assets" if the business intends to sell them within the next fiscal year or operating cycle. In a service firm, such as a law or accounting practice, unbilled services are work in progress (WIP) inventory.

Manufacturing companies have several categories of inventory depending upon where the product is in the manufacturing cycle. In a typical manufacturing operation, the enterprise purchases raw materials, which it uses to produce a finished product that it sells. At the end of any fiscal period, the business will typically have on hand raw materials, work-in-progress, and finished goods inventory (see stages 2, 3, and 4 of the Business Cycle). When inventories are sold their cost is recorded as costs of goods sold. The revenue from sales will show on the income statement. Hence, sales and the cost of goods sold will be matched in the same period.

Because of the inter-relationship between the balance sheet and income statement, any distortion of inventories and sales revenue affects both financial statements. For example, premature recognition of sales revenue overstates income and undervalues inventories on the balance sheet. The overstatement of income boosts the enterprise's "profit" and, ultimately, "retained earnings." Similarly, distortion of inventories because of valuation or timing flows through and affects the income statement, balance sheet, and statement of retained earnings.

i) Cost of Goods Sold

As its name implies, "Cost of Goods Sold" in the income statement is the cost of the merchandise that the enterprise sells during the fiscal period. A proper matching of sales revenue and cost of goods sold is essential in calculating gross margin and net income.

The following examples show the relationship between inventory on the balance sheet and cost of goods sold on the income statement.

Example

Opening inventory (asset)	$1,000
Add: Purchases in year	700
Inventory available for sale during year	$1,700
Less: Ending inventory (asset)	(800)
Cost of goods sold in year (expense)	$900

A misstatement of ending inventories will affect both the asset on the balance sheet and expenses on the income statement. For example, if we overstate ending inventory by $400, cost of goods sold falls by an equal amount and net income increases by $400.

Example

Assume that Chubb T-Shirts Inc sells $20,000 of merchandise inventory during January which it purchased for $4000. Then, its income statement for the month of January would show:

Sales	$20,000
Cost of Goods Sold	(4,000)
Gross Margin	$16,000

This is a very simple example because it assumes that Chubb T-Shirts Inc sold exactly the number of T-shirts that it purchased in January. A more likely scenario will be that Chubb will have some unsold T-shirts at the end of January, which it hopes it will sell in the following months.

Example

Assume that Chubb T-Shirts Inc purchased 4,000 T-shirts for $4,000 and sold 2,500 at $8 each. The income statement would show:

Sales	$20,000
Cost of Goods Sold	(2,500)
Gross Margin	$17,500

The remaining $1,500 invested in the T-shirts would show on the balance sheet as inventory.

In the following months, Chubb sells the remaining T-shirts at $6 each and earns sales revenue of $9,000. The Income Statement would show:

Sales	$9,000
Cost of Goods Sold	(1,500)
Gross Margin	$7,500

We see that accurately determining ending inventory is a key element in calculating gross margin, net profit, taxes payable, and asset values.

The cost of inventory includes not only the direct product costs, but also all other expenditures that the enterprise incurs in bringing the inventory to its existing condition and location. For example, if an enterprise purchases merchandise for $50,000 and then pays $3,000 for shipping it to its factory, and $2,000 as customs brokerage fees and delivery, its landed cost of inventory is $55,000 — the cost of bringing the inventory to the enterprise's place of business from which it will use or sell the product to earn revenues.

ii) Ending Inventory

There are two considerations that determine the value of inventory: 1) the cost of the inventory; and 2) the assumed flow of costs from time of purchase to recognition as a cost of goods sold. The purpose of inventory accounting is to allocate costs between the portion that the enterprise will utilize in a future fiscal year (assets) and the portion that it used in the current fiscal year (expenses).

There are two methods for determining the cost of ending inventory and the cost of goods sold: the perpetual inventory system and the periodic inventory method.

Under the perpetual inventory system, the enterprise keeps track of each item of merchandise that it purchases and sells. There are many sophisticated computer tracking programs that businesses use to keep count of their sales and inventories. If each product has a bar code, for example, the salesclerk will scan the code at point of sale. The computer will automatically log the transaction as a sale at the price that the salesclerk enters into the machine. At the same time, it will extract the cost of the product from inventory and enter it into a cost of goods account. Hence, the term "perpetual" is used to describe the system, which keeps a running balance of all transactions identified by their code numbers.

The perpetual system is useful for high value and unique products, each of which can be specifically identified and entered in the system. However, a perpetual system is expensive to maintain and not appropriate for businesses that sell large amounts of similar or identical products, which they acquire at different prices during the year.

An alternative method of determining inventory and the cost of goods is to physically count what is on hand at the end of the enterprise's fiscal period. The business can then deduce the cost of goods sold.

Example

Assuming that Chubb T-Shirts Inc started its fiscal year with an inventory of 1,500 T-shirts valued at cost (at the end of the prior year) at $1,500. During the current fiscal month, Chubb acquired 4,000 additional T-shirts at a cost of $1 each. Hence, its total cost of goods available for sale would be $5,500. If Chubb sold 4,800 of the T-shirts at $10 each, it would have sales revenue of $48,000. It would offset $4,800 as cost of goods sold against its revenues. The income statement would appear as follows:

We deduce the ending inventory of T-shirts as follows:

Opening Inventory	1,500
Add: purchases	4,000
Available for sale	5,500
Physical count	(700)
Amount sold	4,800
Sales	$48,000
Cost of Goods Sold	(4,800)
Gross Margin	$43,200

Since Chubb took a physical count and determined it had 700 T-shirts on hand at the end of the fiscal period, it deduces that it sold 4800 units during the fiscal period. Assuming that all of the T-shirts cost $1 per unit, the cost of goods sold would be $4,800 and the cost of the inventory on the balance sheet would show as $700. In fact, Chubb might have lost some inventory during the course of the fiscal period due to theft, obsolescence, and deterioration. We recognize these in cost of goods sold because theft, obsolescence, and deterioration are an intrinsic cost of business.

iii) Valuation

The valuation of inventory is more complicated if, as is likely, businesses buy identical products at different prices during the course of the fiscal year. The cost at which an enterprise values its ending inventory can be significant and has been the subject of many lawsuits and accounting frauds. Apart from blatant frauds, the issue often comes down to what should be included in the cost of inventory and which costs should be considered operating expenses. Overstated ending inventory may affect decisions on insurance claims and management of bonuses based on net profits. By including unrelated costs in inventory, an enterprise overstates its net income and asset values on the balance sheet.

Example	
Assume that the following applies to a business:	
Open Inventory	$10,000
Purchases	20,000
	$30,000
Ending Inventory	(8,000)
Costs of Goods Sold	$22,000
Sales	$100,000
Cost of Goods Sold	22,000
Gross Margin	$ 78,000

If the business incorrectly allocates $4,000 costs to ending inventory, the gross margin will increase by an equivalent amount because the cost of goods sold will fall by $4,000 to $18,000.

In *Berkowitz v Baron*,[1] for example, an action for securities fraud under Section 10(b) of the United States *Securities Exchange Act (1934)*, the vendor of a business included shipping costs as a component of manufacturing overhead instead of operating expenses. If the costs were an operating expense, the deduction would have been against gross profit. By including the costs in inventory, the effect was to increase net profit. Instead of showing a net income of $19,603

---

1   428 F Supp 1190 (US District Court, Southern District of New York 1977) [*Berkowitz*].

(as reported), the company would have had a loss of $24,960. The Court found the financial statements to be "materially misleading" and, therefore, in violation of Rule 10(b-5) of the *Securities Act*.

iv) Flow of Costs

In theory, one might suggest that the most accurate method of identifying the cost of goods sold and ending inventory would be to specifically identify each unit of material or product as it physically flowed through the business. In fact, specifically identifying each item of inventory through a production process is difficult, expensive, and, in many cases, impossible. Specific identification of products would also permit cherry-picking items for cost manipulation. One could pick low-cost items to increase profits or high-cost items to lower income.

To avoid income manipulation, accountants make assumptions about cost flows and then apply the assumptions consistently. One can make several different assumptions for valuing the flow of costs to determine cost of goods sold and ending inventory, each of which has its advantages and disadvantages. The important aspect is to understand the consequences of each method of valuation, apply the method consistently, and clearly disclose any changes in method (and financial consequences of the change) in the notes to the financial statements.

Example

In the first year of operations Young Stores Limited ("Young"), a retail store, orders 8,000 shirts for resale. The accounting records show the following:

Date	No. of units	Unit price	Total price
January 1	2,000	$20	$40,000
March 1	3,000	$22	$66,000
June 1	2,000	$23	$46,000
December 1	1,000	$21	$21,000
Total	8,000		$173,000

At the end of its first accounting year (31 December), Young counts 3,000 shirts in unsold stock in its warehouse and on its shelves in its store. Thus, Young must determine the cost of the 5,000 shirts that it sold (or lost through "shrinkage") during the year and value its ending inventory, which will also determine the cost of the merchandise that it sold during the year. To determine the value of ending inventory, Young must make assumptions about its flow of costs. For example, Young may assume that the cost of the shirts flowed through on a first-in, first-out (FIFO) basis. Alternatively, it may assume that the costs flowed through on a last-in, first-out (LIFO) basis. Alternatively, it may assume that the flow of costs was based on their weighted average during the year. Each assumption has financial consequences.

v) FIFO

Under FIFO, the 5,000 units sold have a cost of $106,000. If we assume a selling price of $40 per unit, the gross margin is $94,000 or 47 percent of sales.

$$\frac{\$ 94,000}{\$200,000} \times 100 = 47 \text{ percent}$$

FIFO presents a fair valuation on the balance sheet because the ending inventory (last-in, still-here) is priced at the most recent costs. The 3,000 units have a cost of $67,000. Thus the balance sheet reflects the most current value available to the enterprise. However, in a period of inflation, FIFO distorts the income statement by putting through the earliest (and cheapest) product costs as cost of goods sold. Thus, in inflationary periods, FIFO boosts profits by understating the cost of goods sold. Nevertheless, in many businesses, goods actually flow on a first-in, first-out basis to prevent inventory spoilage and obsolescence. Hence, the cost flow assumption often closely matches the actual physical flow of goods.

The increase in net income, however, is artificial because it does not properly reflect the operating results of the business and includes an element of "inventory profit" unrelated to operating efficiency. Thus, even an inefficient business can show an increase in profits simply by virtue of the impact of inflation on its inventory.

vi) LIFO

The LIFO method of inventory valuation emphasizes the impact of the most recent costs on the income statement. In times of rising prices (inflation), LIFO produces a lower net-income figure because the latest (most expensive) purchases go into determining the cost of goods sold during the year. Stated another way, LIFO means first-in, still-here. The earliest, and cheapest, inventory purchases show up on the balance sheet. Thus, LIFO can depress current net income and also understate the value of inventory on the balance sheet.

There are sound theoretical reasons for using LIFO in inflationary periods. When costs are rising, LIFO produces a conservative net income figure by showing the full impact of inflation on profits. The popularity of LIFO, however, depends upon more pragmatic considerations. LIFO became popular in the United States because, since 1939, American businesses can use LIFO for tax purposes under certain conditions. Since LIFO produces a lower net-income figure than FIFO, in inflationary times, it is entirely understandable that corporations may choose to use LIFO to reduce their current income taxes. IFRS does not permit the use of LIFO for financial reporting, which is different from US GAAP. Some US companies would pay higher income taxes if the United States adopted IFRS, which explains some of the resistance against IFRS.

Also for pragmatic reasons, LIFO is not a popular method of accounting for inventory in Canada. Since the somewhat unorthodox decision of the Privy Council in *Anaconda Brass*,[2] LIFO has not been accepted as a proper method for valuing inventory for Canadian income tax purposes. Hence, despite any theoretical arguments in its favour, Canadian businesses prefer to stay away from LIFO for financial statement purposes. This saves them from having to show two different net-income figures — one for financial statement purposes; the other for tax purposes.

---

2   *Minister of National Revenue v Anaconda American Brass Ltd*, [1956] 2 WLR 31 (PC).

Example

Using the same data for Young Stores Limited, the ending inventory using LIFO would be:

2,000 units @ $20 each	$40,000
1,000 units @ $22 each	22,000
Ending inventory	$62,000
The cost of goods sold is:	
Opening inventory	$0
Purchases during year	$173,000
Available for sale	$173,000
Ending inventory (LIFO)	(62,000)
Cost of goods sold	$111,000

At a selling price of $40 per unit, the gross margin is $89,000 or 45 percent of sales.

LIFO does, however, have some disadvantages. The inventory on the balance sheet is "understated," in that it reflects artificially low prices that do not prevail in the market. The lower net income reported under the method can distort certain ratios, particularly ratios that depend upon current assets, total assets or equity. For example, the lower balance sheet value of inventory under LIFO will affect the working capital ratio.[3]

LIFO also allows management to manipulate reported profits. Each addition to the inventory balance under LIFO is a "layer." Thus, the oldest layer can be the initial inventory balance from years past. Where a company increases the number of units in its inventory, each addition adds an additional layer. With the passage of time, the value of LIFO inventory on the balance sheet becomes dated. Thus, a business can significantly improve its net income by depleting its inventory and digging into its earlier lower costs as reflected in the inventory balance. For example, a business that wanted to increase its net profits for a period might simply deplete its inventory, thereby releasing "inventory profits" resulting from lower inventory costs into the cost of goods sold. In effect, previously unrealized

---

3   See Chapter 8.

gains and losses from inventory appreciation would suddenly appear in the accounting year in which management depleted inventory. A company that never depleted its inventory entirely would continue to show its earliest inventory costs on the balance sheet. Some of those inventory costs (first-in, still-here), would comprise costs from many years earlier.

vii) Weighted Average Cost

The average cost method is simply a compromise between FIFO and LIFO. Under this method, a business determines the weighted average cost of all of its inventory available for sale in the fiscal period and uses that cost in determining its ending inventory and costs of goods sold. In the previous example, the weighted average cost of ending inventory is $64,875.

viii) Lower of Cost or Market Value

GAAP (and the principle of conservatism) requires that inventory values on the balance sheet should be the lower of cost or market value. Thus, where market values fall below the costs of inventory, the business must write down its ending inventory and take the charge into its cost of goods sold. Following the principle of conservatism, increases in the value of inventory are not reflected on the balance sheet.

"Market value" can have several different meanings and the notes to the financial statement should disclose which meaning is applied in the particular circumstances. For example, market value can mean replacement value — the costs at which the business can replace its inventory. For example, where a business acquired 1,000 units of inventory at $10 per unit, the total cost of inventory available for sale would be $10,000. If the ending inventory of 300 units can now be replaced at $8 per unit, the inventory has a replacement value that is $2 less than its original cost. Thus, the business should write down its ending inventory by $600 to reflect the diminution in value of its ending inventory.

Market value can also mean "net realizable value" — that is, anticipated selling price minus costs of disposal. When net realizable value falls below replacement costs, the lower number should be used for purposes of the inventory write-down. In the above example, if the units can only be sold at $7 per unit less $1 in disposal costs, the net realizable value is $6 per unit. In these circumstances, the 300 units of ending inventory should be written down by $4 per unit, for a total write-down of $1,200.

There is a risk, particularly with publicly traded companies, that management will inflate ending inventory in order to boost net income and, therefore, share prices and stock option values. An outside reader of the financial statements will not be able to detect such overstatements and must rely on the company's management and auditors that the statements are fairly presented according to IFRS and GAAP.

For tax purposes, the behavioural incentive is exactly the opposite. Management is tempted to understate opening inventory, because understated inventory decreases net income and, therefore, current taxes payable. Similarly, for the purposes of profit-sharing arrangements with employees, management may shortchange employees by understating ending inventory to reduce profit-sharing payouts based upon net income.

The most common method of understating inventory is by charging as current expenses amounts that should otherwise properly be included in the cost of inventory. In this manner, expenses are increased, ending inventory is understated, and net income is reduced. In *Loveman & Son Export Corp v Commissioner*,[4] for example, the taxpayer deducted "freight-in" on purchase as current expenses when the charges should have been included in the cost of its inventory. The taxpayer was not allowed to deduct the freight charges as a current expense.

Lawyers should be careful in drafting warranties and covenants. For example, in *Berkowitz*,[5] the vendor warranted that the financial statement for the year ending 30 April 1970 "fully and accurately

---

4   34 TC 776 (1960), aff'd. 296 F 2d 732 (Sixth Circuit 1961), Cert denied, 369 US 860 (1962).
5   Above note 1.

present(s) as of its date financial condition in assets and liabilities of the Companies and fully and accurately present(s) the results of operations of the Companies for the period indicated."

Words such as "fully and accurately" are ambiguous in litigation. GAAP permits alternative treatment for many items that are all acceptable under accounting principles. In such circumstances, it is advisable for representations and warranties to track the language of the audit opinion currently in use. For example, the warranty might state: The financial statements present fairly, in all material respects, the financial position of the Companies as of . . . and the results of operations for the year ended . . . in conformity with generally accepted accounting principles (or alternatively, in accordance with IFRS).

f) Prepayments

Short-term prepaid expenses are amounts that the business has paid for goods or services in advance of their delivery or service. Prepaid expenses are also known as deferred charges and are not generally convertible into cash but are consumed over time. For example, a business with a calendar year-end may buy an insurance policy on 1 July and pay $20,000 premium for one year's coverage. At 31 December, the business would have utilized only six months of coverage and would recognize $10,000 on its balance sheet. Typical prepaid expenses include prepaid rent, prepaid insurance, prepaid subscription services, prepaid taxes, and prepaid interest.

2) Property, Plant, and Equipment

A fundamental principle underlying the measurement of income is the matching of revenues with expenses during a fiscal period. Where an enterprise purchases assets that will endure for several years, it must allocate their cost over their useful life in order to match the current portion of the cost against current revenues.

The starting point is to determine whether the expenditure is on account of long-lived (capital) assets or current expenses. If the former, the enterprise must estimate the useful or productive life of the capital asset, its residual value (if any) at the end of its useful life, and decide on the manner in which it will allocate the cost to various income statements over that life. These decisions require management estimates and choices.

In the historical cost model, the initial acquisition of capital assets is recorded at cost on the balance sheet. Hence, for example, where a business acquires (or constructs) a building for $60 million, it will record the asset at cost. The next question is: how long will the building last and what will be its residual (salvage) value at the end of its expected useful life? Let us assume that professional experts estimate the building's useful life to be fifty years with $10 million salvage value. Then, the next decision is the manner in which we allocate the net $50 million over the fifty years in each accounting period.

We refer to this allocation of cost of long-lived tangible assets as depreciation. Where the asset is an intangible asset (for example, intellectual property with a finite life), we refer to the allocation of cost as amortization. Where the asset is a natural resource (for example, an oil well or gold mine), the allocation process is called depletion.

IFRS allows an entity to record property, plant, and equipment at its fair value less any subsequent accumulated depreciation and accumulated impairment. Where an entity chooses to show its property, plant, and equipment at fair value, it must do so for all assets within the same class. Further, the entity must revalue the assets regularly to ensure that they are shown at current fair value.[6]

There are four principal factors to consider in determining the amount of depreciation that an enterprise should record as a charge against revenues in a fiscal period:

1) Cost of the asset;
2) Salvage value;
3) Useful life; and
4) Method of depreciation.

---

6   IAS 16 (Property, Plant, and Equipment).

Observe that the calculation for depreciation involves two estimates (salvage value and useful life) and a judgment call by management on the method of allocation. Thus, although the final depreciation number appears to be numerically precise, it is only as good as the estimates and judgment of management.

The annual depreciation charge based on the above factors does not involve any cash charge or transfer on the books of the enterprise. Depreciation is simply an allocation of the cost of capital assets over their useful life and does not involve any cash accumulation by the enterprise. We see this in the statement of cash flows where the annual depreciation charge is added back to operating income for the purposes of determining cash in-flows and out-flows.

a) Cost of Capital Assets

Capital assets are recorded initially at cost, which is the cash or cash equivalent price to bring the asset to its intended location and ready for use. Costs to set up the asset for its intended use are also included in the initial capital cost of the asset. Hence, the recorded cost will include the asset's purchase price, taxes, freight, installation, and set-up charges. In the case of buildings, we segregate the cost of the land from the cost of the building because land is not a depreciable asset.

b) Salvage Value

The salvage value of an asset is the amount that one estimates the asset will realize when the business ultimately disposes of it at the end of its useful life. The best that management can do is to estimate salvage value based upon its past experience, current market conditions, and professional expertise. The longer the expected life of the asset, the greater the difficulty in estimating its salvage value.

c) Useful Life

Management must also estimate useful life at the time that the enterprise acquires the capital asset based upon past experience and evolving technology. Useful life can be the actual physical life of the asset or useful life based upon technological developments and considerations of efficiency. Thus, useful life of an asset can be shorter than its physical life.

Example

On 1 January, a business acquires a machine for $72,000. The machine can last for ten years, but management estimates that it will have a useful productive life of only four years at the end of which it will be sold for $12,000. Hence, the net amount to be depreciated over the four years is $60,000.
The annual depreciation charge over the four years will depend upon the method of depreciation that management selects (see section that follows).

---

d) Depreciation Methods

The method of depreciation affects the annual expense charge to the income statement. There are various methods for allocating depreciation, but they all have the same objective: Allocate the net cost of the asset (initial cost minus salvage value) over its useful life to match revenues and expenses. Depreciation does not reflect the annual diminution in the market value of the asset. Similarly, the net book value of the asset on the balance sheet does not necessarily reflect the market value of the asset, unless management opts to disclose at fair value?

Here we will discuss three of the most common methods of calculating depreciation:

1) Straight line;
2) Declining balance; and
3) Units of production.

i) Straight Line

Straight line is the simplest of all the methods and results in the business charging an equal amount of depreciation expense to the income statement over the useful life of the asset. The formula for this method is as follows:

$$\text{Depreciation expense} = \frac{(\text{Original Cost} - \text{Salvage value})}{\text{Useful life in years}}$$

Example

Assuming the same facts for the machine as given in the preceding example, the annual depreciation charge for each of the four years of useful life would be $15,000 per year calculated as follows:

Year	Beginning Book Value	Depreciation at 25%	Ending Book Value
1	$72,000	$15,000	$57,000
2	$57,000	$15,000	$42,000
3	$42,000	$15,000	$27,000
4	$27,000	$15,000	$12,000*
		$60,000	

* Equals Salvage Value

Graphically, the annual depreciation charge is a straight line, from which it derives its label (see Figure 5-1).

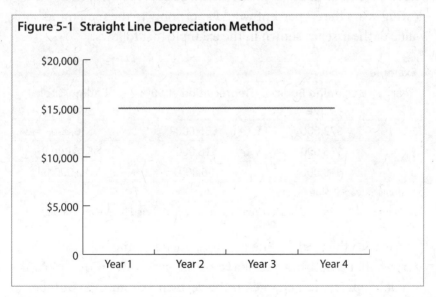

Figure 5-1 Straight Line Depreciation Method

The only adjustment that needs to be made to the straight line computation is if the asset is purchased and placed in use partway in the first year. In such a case the annual depreciation charge is proportionately allocated for the number of months in the year that it is actually in use.

ii) Declining Balance Method

The declining balance method applies a fixed percentage to the initial cost of the asset in the first year, and subsequently the same percentage to the remaining book value of the asset at the beginning of each year. The book value of the asset in the beginning of each year is the original cost of the asset less the amount of depreciation charged in prior years.

The most common percentage used in the declining balance method is double the percentage that one would use under the straight line method. There is no immediate adjustment made for the salvage value under this method. In the preceding example, the annual straight line percentage is equal to 25 percent (that is, 1 divided by the useful life of four years). Using the declining balance method we would charge 50 percent of the cost of the asset in the first year. Thus, the charge in the first year would be $36,000. In each of the following years the 50 percent would apply only to the remaining book value of the asset as shown in the example that follows.

Example

Year	Beginning Book Value	Depreciation at 50%	Ending Book Value
1	$72,000	$36,000	$36,000
2	$36,000	$18,000	$18,000
3	$18,000	$6,000	$12,000*

* Equals Salvage Value

No additional depreciation after Year 3 as asset has reached its Salvage Value.

As with the straight line method, the declining balance method derives its name from the shape of the graph when one plots the annual depreciation charge on the vertical axis and the number of years on the horizontal axis.

Now we can see the difference in the amount of depreciation expense between the straight line method and the declining balance method. Under the straight line method the annual charge was $15,000 per year, whereas under the declining balance method, the charge is $36,000 in the first year. Thus, the declining balance

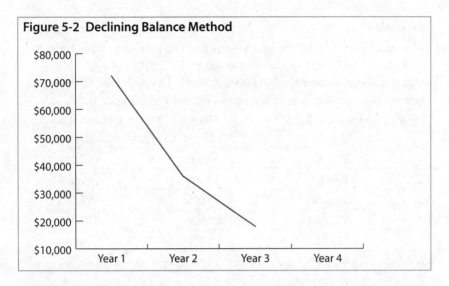

Figure 5-2 Declining Balance Method

method produces a higher write-off rate in the early years of an asset's useful life. In later years, however (for example, Year 3), the annual depreciation charge under the straight line method will exceed the amount charged under the declining balance method.

The difference between the two methods is important in considering the amount of income taxes payable during the life of the asset. The higher write-off under the declining balance method (referred to as capital cost allowance for Canadian income tax purposes) reduces net income and, therefore, income taxes payable in the early years. However, the higher write-off also creates a potential deferred income tax liability in the future when the write-off rate under the declining balance method drops below the amount charged under the straight line method.

iii) Units of Production Method

The units of production method is conceptually similar to the straight line method except that it is calculated on expected units of production from the asset rather than on its years of service. Thus, the first step is to determine the rate of depreciation per unit as follows:

$$\frac{\text{(Original cost − Estimated salvage value)}}{\text{Expected total units of production}} = \text{the depreciation per unit}$$

Example

Assuming the same data as given in the first example, the original cost of the asset is $72,000 with a salvage value of $12,000. It is estimated that the asset will produce 200,000 units during its useful life. Thus, the depreciation per unit (net of salvage value) will be $0.30 per unit.

Year	Beginning Book Value	Units	Depreciation at 0.30/unit
1	$72,000	40,000	$12,000
2	$60,000	50,000	$15,000
3	$45,000	30,000	$9,000
4	$36,000	60,000	$18,000
5	$18,000	20,000	$6,000
6	$12,000 (Salvage Value)		$60,000

e) Repairs and Improvements

Repairs and improvements to fixed assets pose a special problem in accounting. One must first determine whether an expenditure on account of repairs is a current expense or a capital expenditure. If it is a current expense, the cost goes to the income statement. If it is a capital expenditure, the cost is added to the capital asset and depreciated over time. The difficulty is in drawing the line between expenses and capital expenditures.

The distinction between routine repairs and capital improvements can be highly subjective and have a material effect on net income. For example, assume that a business spends $20,000 to repair a machine that has an estimated useful life of five years prior to the repairs. However, the repairs to the machine extend its life by another year. In these circumstances, one must determine whether the $20,000 should be charged as an expense in the current year or capitalized into the cost of the machinery. If it is expensed in the current year, net income will fall by an equivalent amount. This may affect a production manager's bonus payment based upon net income. What if the repairs extend useful life by four years? Here, the rationale for capitalizing the cost is more convincing.

3) Depletion

Depletion refers to the consumption of natural resources and is similar in concept to the depreciation of tangible assets, such as buildings, equipment, and fixtures. Depletion refers to the amount charged as expenses as natural resources are mined, extracted, or otherwise consumed.

The depletion rate is calculated in the same way as the units of production method for depreciation. The total cost of the natural resource is determined from the purchase documents. The salvage value (if any) is estimated. Finally, the total amount of the natural resource available is estimated. From these three figures we can determine the depletion rate per unit of the natural resource extracted.

For example, assume that a company purchases a mine for $500 million and expects to extract 400,000 ounces of ore from the mine. Then each ounce of ore extracted will deplete the mine by $1,250. If the company extracts 60,000 ounces in the first year, the depletion expense will be $75 million, which will reduce the net book value of the mine to $425 million. The depletion expense reduces income and an equivalent amount of accumulated depletion would show on the balance sheet at the end of the first year.

4) Intangible Assets

Intangible assets are identifiable non-monetary assets without physical substance. Intangible assets typically include legal rights — such as computer software, patents, trademarks, franchisees, and goodwill. The accounting for intangible assets depends upon the manner in which the business acquires or develops them. Internally generated goodwill is not recognized as an intangible because it cannot be measured reliably.

Intangibles are measured initially at cost and charged as expenses if the expenditure will produce future economic benefits.[7] The cost of the asset may be amortized over its useful life. If the fair value of the intangible can be measured by reference to an active market,

---

7   IAS 38.

the entity may revalue it at its fair value and show it net of accumulated amortization and any impairment.[8] Revaluation increases are recorded in the statement of comprehensive income and show on the balance sheet in the equity section as "Revaluation Surplus."

a) Patents

Patents are exclusive property rights granted by the federal government to protect inventions. In most cases, the legal life of a patent is twenty years from the date of filing, during which period the patentholder enjoys a monopoly for the use of the invention. Thus, in the simplest case, the cost of the patent may be written off or amortized over its protected life.

The concept of amortization is similar to that of depreciation in that both involve an allocation of cost of the asset over its life. However, because of technological developments, the useful life of a patent can be less than its legal life.

b) Copyright

Copyright refers to the legally protected right to publish, sell, or perform from books, music, films, and recordings. Copyrights are amortized over their useful life.

c) Trademarks

Trademarks are distinctive names, symbols, or designs that identify a particular product or service.

d) Amortization

The cost of acquiring identifiable intangible assets should be capitalized. Cost includes the purchase price of the property and all legal expenses incurred to perfect title to the property. The legal cost to defend intellectual property rights should also be capitalized.

An intangible asset with a finite life (for example, a patent) should be amortized over its useful life. The useful life of an intangible asset does not necessarily coincide with the period during

---

8   *Ibid* (the revaluation model).

which it is legally protected. For example, although a patent may have a legally protected life of seventeen years, the business may not enjoy its monopolistic protection of the patent for all those years because of changing technologies and competing products coming on the market. Thus, management must annually estimate the useful life of the property and make the appropriate expense charge.

Amortization of intangibles is generally straight-line based upon the full cost of the intangible. Unlike the charge for depreciation, which is accumulated in an account and shown as a deduction from capital assets on the balance sheet, amortization charges are usually written off directly against the cost of the intangible, with only the *net* remaining intangible cost showing on the balance sheet. For example, assume that a business purchases a patent for $1 million and that the patent has a remaining life of fifteen years. In the first year, the amortization charge would be $66,667 and the patent would show on the balance sheet as an intangible asset with a net capital cost of $933,333.

B. LIABILITIES

The characteristics of corporate liabilities are as follows:

- Debt does not represent ownership in a corporation, but merely creates a relationship of debtor and creditor between the lender and the corporation;
- Corporate creditors generally rank ahead of shareholders in claims against corporate assets;
- Debt may be secured by corporate assets or unsecured claims; and
- Interest on business debt is usually deductible for tax purposes.[9]

1) Accounts Payable

Accounts payable are debts that an enterprise incur when it purchases good or services on credit. Most accounts payable (such as credit

---

9   See *Income Tax Act* (ITA), para 20(1)(c).

card purchases) are due and payable within a short time — generally thirty or forty-five days, without interest charges.

Accounts payable are recorded at their face value and appear in the current liability section of the balance sheet. There is no imputed interest on the payable where the debt arises in the normal course of business and is due within one year from its creation.

2) Notes Payable

Notes payable are a more formal type of accounts payable that are recorded in a note and usually provide for interest and stipulate a due date. Most notes payable arise from cash loans to the business, such as bank loans and commercial paper. The note is recorded at its face value and shows in the current liability section of the balance sheet. Any interest payable on the note is interest expense.

3) Accrued Liabilities

Accrued liabilities are expenses that a business incurs but that have not been paid as at the fiscal year-end. The expense is recognized in the income statement and the accrued liability shows on the balance sheet. Accrued liabilities typically accumulate over time. For example, assume that a note payable of $100,000 has interest payable of 0.5 percent per month payable on the fifteenth day of each month. If the company's year-end is 31 December, there will be $250 accrued at that date for one-half month's interest, which the business will recognize as interest expense on the income statement for the year ended 31 December and show as an accrued liability on the balance sheet.

In some cases, however, estimating accrued liabilities can be an uncertain process involving difficult decisions by management and accountants. Adjustments to accrued liabilities can cause significant shifts in income and expenses.[10]

---

10   See, for example, *R v Dunn*, 2013 ONSC 137, which involved the criminal prosecution of three former executives of Nortel.

4) Deferred Revenues

Deferred revenues are unearned amounts received for goods and services to be delivered or rendered after the year-end of the business. Deferring the revenue recognizes that the business has not earned its income as at the year-end. In certain circumstances, the business may be liable to return the amount paid in advance if it does not ultimately deliver the goods or services.

Deferred revenues are the liability equivalent of prepayments on the asset side of the balance sheet. For example, assume that a business rents out a portion of its premises for $30,000 payable in semi-annual instalments of $15,000 on 1 October and 31 March. If the business has a calendar year-end, it would have deferred (unearned) revenues of $7,500 for the period of 1 January to 31 March. Hence, it would recognize the portion that it earned from 1 October to 31 December as revenues and defer recognizing the remaining $7,500 until the subsequent calendar year.

5) Estimated Liabilities

Estimated liabilities (or as IAS 37 calls them, "provisions") arise when a business knows that it will incur expenses in respect of its current sales, but cannot absolutely determine the amount of the expenditure that will arise in the future. For example, a car manufacturer may sell an automobile with a four-year warranty. The manufacturer knows that it will incur warranty expenses in the next four years but cannot be certain as to the exact amount of warranty work on each car sold. Hence, it will estimate its future warranty work as a reserve and recognize the expenditure as a current expense to match against the revenue from the sale of the car. The estimate should be the amount required to settle the liability.[11] The provision should be discounted to its present value using the appropriate pre-tax discount rate. The use of estimates is part of the accounting process.

---

11   IAS 37.

6) Contingent Liabilities

Unlike estimated liabilities, which involve uncertainty about the exact amount of cost that will be incurred in the future, contingent liabilities involve an additional uncertainty in that it is not known whether the liability will arise at all. The contingency depends upon events that have not been completed, but which create the distinct possibility that some amount may be created in the future if the event occurs.

Litigation and tax audits, for example, create difficult contingencies. As at the year-end, the business cannot be certain as to how litigation in which it is involved will eventually resolve and in what amount. Based on the principle of conservatism, the business may provide for an amount based upon the probability of future liability in the litigation and estimate to the best of its ability (based upon counsel's advice) the potential damages and costs payable. Thus, if it is probable that the business will incur a liability in the future and it is possible to reasonably estimate its amount, the contingent liability is accrued as an expense in the income statement and shows as a liability on the balance sheet.

For example, assume that a company is involved in a lawsuit in which the damages claimed are $5 million. Counsel advises that there is a likelihood that the company will be liable but, if it is, the damages will likely be no more than $500,000. The company would set up the $500,000 as a general liability expense and recognize $500,000 expense on the income statement. The contingent liability of $500,000 appears on the balance sheet. However, disclosure of the contingent liability creates difficulties for legal counsel defending the action.

If the likelihood of liability from the lawsuit is probable, but the amount cannot be reasonably estimated, the information about the contingent liability should be disclosed in the notes to the financial statements, but without recognizing any expense in the income statement.

Finally, where the likelihood of loss from the contingency is remote, there is no entry in the financial statements and there is no disclosure of the contingency in the notes to the financial statement.

7)   Audit Inquiry Letters

Disclosure of contingent liabilities in the financial statements is a diffi-cult issue for lawyers who are required to assess the likelihood of success in pending litigation and then estimate any potential liability or recov-eries from the action. There are also sensitive issues pertaining to legal privilege and the scope and extent of disclosure to non-clients.

The traditional approach was covered by a joint policy state-ment of the Canadian Bar Association and the Canadian Institute of Chartered Accountants (CBA/CICA). Clients were asked to evaluate whether potential losses from claims or possible claims were "likely, unlikely, or not determinable."

Under new rules adopted as part of the IFRS for public com-panies, the requirements for disclosure have been expanded to re-quire reporting of existing claims where it is "more likely than not" that resolution will require some outflow of resources. It is not at all clear how the new IFRS standard varies from the previous "likely" standard based upon an evaluation of probabilities.

Clients are to report contingent liabilities that include those claims that will not materialize until the occurrence of some future event be-yond their control, unless there is only a remote possibility that there will be an outflow of resources. Further, whereas the 1978 (CBA/CICA) standard only required clients to report the ultimate amount of losses from any claims or possible claims "if reasonably estimable," the new rules require clients to provide the "best estimate" of what they would "rationally pay" to settle a claim or transfer to a third party.

Finally, IFRS has a stricter threshold for non-disclosure of claims. Under the 1978 standard, entities could omit reportable information from their financial statements where disclosure would have a "signifi-cant adverse effect" on their businesses. Under IFRS, non-disclosure is confined to the "extremely rare" case in which reporting the informa-tion "can be expected to prejudice seriously the position of the [client] in a dispute with other parties on the subject matter" of the claim.

Lawyers should be extremely cautious about the scope of dis-closure to parties who are not able to claim legal privilege. Gen-erally, potential or contingent claims that are not identified in the audit inquiry letter should be raised directly with the client and not routed to the client's auditors.

8) Long-Term Liabilities

Long-term liabilities refer to debts with a maturity date that exceeds one year from the date of the balance sheet. Any portion of the debt that is payable in less than a year from the balance-sheet date is classified as a current liability.

Long-term liabilities take many forms, but they have certain common characteristics. First, and foremost, they are obligations that usually have a maturity date and stipulate an interest rate.[12] The obligations go by various names, depending upon their features. They may be in the form of a note payable, a bond, or mortgage. Obligations that are unsecured by assets of the corporation are called debentures. In contrast, bonds that are secured against the corporation's real property are referred to as mortgage bonds.

Where the debt is issued to multiple lenders, the terms and conditions of the loan are usually incorporated in a formal document, such as a bond indenture. The indenture contains the essential terms pertaining to the debt — such as maturity date, interest rate, dates for payment of interest, security (if any), designated trustee, and terms and conditions on default.

9) Issuance at Par

Where a corporation issues a bond at a rate of interest that is equal to the current market rate, it is said to be issued at par. For example, a corporation may issue $5 million of ten-year bonds at 6 percent when the market rate of interest is 6 percent. In these circumstances, the corporation will receive $5 million and will record the bonds on its books at their face value. If the bonds pay interest on 1 October and 31 March, bondholders will be entitled to 3 percent interest as of each date. If the corporation has a 31 December year-end, it will

---

12   In exceptional circumstances liabilities can be "perpetual" without a fixed maturity date.

record 1.5 percent interest as accrued interest for the amount that will become payable for October, November, and December.

10) Issuance of Bonds at Other than Par Value

A corporation may issue a bond at a rate of interest that is either below or above the prevailing rate of interest in the market. The purpose of bond discounts and premiums is to increase or decrease the effective rate of interest from the nominal rate. Where the bond is issued at less than the prevailing market rate, its face value will be discounted to account for the higher market rate. For example, a bond with a nominal interest rate of 6 percent when the market is yielding 7 percent must be discounted from its par (face) value so that the lender is compensated for the yield difference of 1 percent. In effect, by issuing the bonds at a discount from their face value, the corporation increases the effective yield to match prevailing market rates. The bonds will be recorded on the balance sheet at their face value. The discount on the bonds payable will be amortized over the life of the bond and charged to the interest expense account, so as to increase the effective interest rate on the bond and recognize it as an expense.

Where a corporation issues a bond at a rate of interest that is above the prevailing market rate, the issue price of the bond will be more than its face value to compensate for the differential in interest rates. For example, a corporation that issues a bond with a face value of $1,000 at a rate of 8 percent when the market rate is 6 percent will price the bond at a premium so as to lower the effective rate of interest payable. As with bond discounts, the premium is amortized over the life of the bond and charged against interest expense to lower the effective interest rate paid.

11) Amortization of Discounts and Premiums

Bonds issued at a discount or premium show on the balance sheet at their face value less or plus the discount or premium shown separately. There are two basic methods for calculating the amortization of bond discounts and premiums: the effective interest method and the straight line method.

The effective interest method results in the same effective yield reported on the bonds for each interest payment period. The amount amortized in each period is calculated by multiplying the carrying value of the bonds — that is, their face value less any discount or plus any premium — at the beginning of the period by the effective interest rate or yield to maturity implied by the initial purchase price of the bonds to determine the interest expense to be reported for the period.

Bond discount and premiums may also be amortized using the straight line method. Under this method, the bond discount or premium is amortized in equal amounts over the term of the bonds. The straight line method should only be used where the difference between the results that it yields is not substantially different from the effective interest rate method and the difference is not material.

12) Income Taxes

A business must calculate its income taxes payable according to the rules of tax law, which may differ from commercial principles, IFRS, or GAAP. These differences can affect the financial statements.

Timing differences between tax and financial accounting can create deferred tax liabilities and deferred tax assets.

13) Temporary Differences

Temporary differences arise when the *Income Tax Act* specifies the recognition of an income or expense item in a different period from that used under GAAP. For example, under GAAP we calculate "profit" from a business on the accrual basis of accounting. Generally accepted concepts of accrual accounting require a business to include in income only amounts that the business has earned in the period. Unearned revenue is a liability and is not income for accounting purposes.

For tax purposes, however, paragraph 12(1)(a) of the *Income Tax Act* (Canada) modifies the general accounting rule and requires all receipts, whether earned or unearned, to be included in income in the year that the business receives payment. Thus, a taxpayer must include in income an amount received on account of services to be rendered in the future ("unearned revenues"). The taxpayer may, however, claim a reserve against unearned income.[13] Hence, the profit reported for tax purposes will differ from the amount reported for financial statement purposes. The rule increases the tax payable in the current year when the corporation receives the unearned revenues and lowers it in the year when the corporation actually earns its revenues on which it has previously paid tax. Thus, the corporation has a deferred asset.

Similarly with interest income, there are several ways to account for interest income for tax purposes — cash basis, modified cash basis, receivable basis, accrual basis and modified accrual basis. For tax purposes, the term "receivable" means legally receivable and not "receivable" in the sense that one uses it in accounting.[14] For example, assume that a taxpayer buys a bond for $1,000 on 1 December. The bond pays interest at a rate of 12 percent per year, payable at the end of May and November of each year. By 31 December, the taxpayer will have earned one-twelfth of its annual interest income. In accrual accounting, the taxpayer is considered to have earned $10 in December even though he will not receive payment until 31 May. The $10 would be accrued as a receivable for general accounting purposes. For tax purposes, however, the $10 is not "receivable" because there is no legal obligation on the issuer of the bond to pay the interest as at 31 December. The legal obligation to pay the interest will arise on the date stipulated in the bond contract — 31 May of the following year.

We see this in the differences between depreciation accounting for financial reporting purposes and the rules for tax purposes. For financial reporting, a business may select to depreciate its assets on a straight line basis. For example, where a business acquires a machine that has an estimated life of five years for $100,000 (with zero salvage value), the straight line depreciation will be $20,000 per year for

---

13   ITA, para 20(1)(m).
14   *MNRJ v Colford Contracting Company*, [1962] SCR 8.

five years. For tax purposes, however, the business is allowed to depreciate (technically, called capital cost allowance or CCA) the asset at a declining balance rate of 30 percent. In the first year (assuming the business acquires the asset on 1 January), the business can claim $30,000 as a CCA expense in determining its net income for tax purposes. Thus, the business can claim $10,000 more as an expense in the first year than it does for accounting purposes. At a tax rate of 50 percent, the business saves $5,000 in taxes in the first year.

In the second year, the business once again claims $20,000 under the straight line method for financial statement purposes. However, for tax purposes, the business now claims 30 percent of the undepreciated amount of $70,000 — that is, $21,000. At a tax rate of 50 percent the business saves $500 in taxes.

By the third year the depreciation expense for financial statement purposes remains at $20,000 under the straight line method. For tax purposes, however, the business can claim only 30 percent of $49,000 (the undepreciated amount) — that is, $14,700. Hence, in Year 3 the business will pay $2,650 more tax than it would recognize for financial statement purposes.

Example

Year	CCA For Tax	Book Depreciation	Savings	Tax Saving
1	$30,000	$20,000	$10,000	$5,000
2	$21,000	$20,000	$1,000	$ 500
3	$14,700	$20,000	($5,300)	($2,650)

The preceding example shows that the tax savings in Years 1 and 2 are only temporary and that there is a crossover of expenses in Years 3, 4, and 5. This means that the tax savings in Years 1 and 2 created a deferred tax liability, which the business will face in Years 3, 4, and 5. The deferred tax liability appears on the balance sheet.

The converse situation arises when taxable income is greater than income for accounting purposes because of temporary timing differences. For example, a company that receives prepaid rental income will recognize it as income only in the year that it earns it and not when it receives payment. Assume that a company receives $30,000 of prepaid rent on 1 November, which covers six months of a lease. If the company has a calendar year-end, it will recognize one-third ($10,000) of the payment as income in the current year and show a liability for the $20,000 unearned income. For tax purposes, however, the company is required to include the entire $30,000 in income in the year that it receives the money. Thus, its tax bill will be higher than it would be under accounting rules. In the following year, the company would recognize the remaining $20,000 of its lease income for accounting purposes. It would not have to recognize the same amount for tax purposes because it would have paid tax on that amount in the preceding year. Hence, the company has a deferred tax asset.

14) Permanent Differences

Permanent differences arise when some items that are income for one purpose are not income for the other purpose. Similarly, some items that are deducted as expenses for one purpose may not be deducted as expenses for the other purpose. For example, gains on the sale of capital assets are considered income for accounting purposes. For tax purposes, however, only one-half of such gains are taxable (taxable capital gains). Conversely, while all losses from the sale of capital assets are deductible for accounting purposes, only one-half of such losses are deductible for tax purposes (allowable capital losses). The difference in recognition criteria is permanent. Thus, keeping "two sets of books" — one for tax and the other for accounting — is not always sinister.

15) Reserves

Accounting involves judgments on allocation of revenues and expenses to particular time periods. The underlying principle is simple: revenues and expenses should be allocated and matched in the time period to which they properly relate. There are, however, grey areas, which allow management to "manage" income in a particular period. The motivation can be to smooth income or enhance executive compensation.

For example, a corporation may have set aside or allocated amounts in prior years as reserves against future litigation costs. At the end of each fiscal year, management must determine whether the reserve is adequate in light of then-known circumstances concerning the litigation. If the reserve is considered too high, management can reduce it, which will have the effect of increasing earnings. In theory, the overestimated reserves should be allocated back to the years to which they relate. That may, however, be quite difficult because the circumstances may not have been fully understood in those earlier years but only became apparent as the litigation progressed. Conversely, management may estimate that the reserves are too low and choose to increase the reserve in the current year. The additional charge will depress current year earnings and increase the reserve account.

The temptation to manage reserve allocations increases depending upon management compensation schemes. In the Nortel fraud prosecution in the Ontario Superior Court in 2012, for example, the prosecution alleged that the company's former Chief Executive Officer, Frank Dunn (and others), manipulated the company's financial statements in 2002 and 2003 to trigger $5 million in bonus payments. The alleged motivation was to increase 2003 profits so that the executives could be paid a $73 million "return-to-profitability" bonus. The prosecution alleged that senior executives depressed 2002 profits through excessive accruals that properly belonged in 2003. By shifting the costs into 2002, the company was better able to increase its profits in 2003 because costs pertaining to the latter year had already been allocated to the preceding year.

In July 2010, First Horizon National Corp, a Memphis, Tennessee, bank that was exposed to housing problems surprised Wall Street when it announced its first quarterly profit in more than two years. How did it achieve such a result when still embroiled in a bad housing market? Its magic formula: it cut the cash reserves that it had set aside towards weak loans by 73 percent, which amount accounted for virtually the entire increase in its quarterly profit.

C. EQUITY

The capital structure of business corporations comprises two elements: equity and debt. Equity, in turn, comprises two categories: share capital and retained earnings. Thus, the characterization of capital as equity or debt is an important issue in corporate and tax law.

1) Share Capital

Equity or share capital represents an ownership interest in the corporation. The rights, restrictions, terms, and conditions attached to the shares determine the nature of the interest. In the absence of any special provisions, all shares of a corporation are presumed to be equal.[15] Shareholders rank behind creditors in claims on the corporation's assets. Thus, shareholders ultimately bear the financial risk of the corporation.

From an income tax perspective, share capital has two fundamental characteristics:

- A corporation can return share capital to its shareholders on a tax-free basis; and
- Dividends on shares are not deductible from income and are paid with after-tax dollars.

These two characteristics influence the corporate financial structure of most enterprises.

For purposes of corporate law, a corporation's share capital is its "stated capital," which has two distinct aspects:

1) Protection of creditors; and
2) Protection of shareholders.

A corporation's creditors look to its stated capital as a notional measure of the corporate ability to pay its debts. To be sure, the ability to pay ultimately depends upon available cash. However, creditors have an interest in the capital structure of the corpora-

---

15 CBCA, subs 24(3); OBCA, subs 22(3).

tion to which they loan money. They have a legitimate concern that the corporation does not dissipate its capital through unauthorized corporate distributions.[16]

Stated capital also serves as a measure of limiting shareholder liability for corporate debts. Corporate statutes generally limit a shareholder's exposure for corporate liabilities to the shareholder's contributions to stated capital. Thus, accounting for capital is an important stewardship function.

Neither the *Canada Business Corporations Act*[17] (CBCA) nor the *Business Corporations Act* of Ontario[18] (OBCA) define "capital." Generally, capital refers to proceeds from the sale of capital stock and represents money that the purchaser pays for an undivided interest in the assets of the corporation.[19] The owners' equity segment of the corporate balance sheet shows the nature and amount of stated capital.

The term "capital" also has other meanings depending upon the context and the adjective by which one modifies it. "Capital" sometimes describes all capital — whether from debt or the issuance of equity. In accounting, we use the term "working capital" to denote the excess of current assets over current liabilities and "liquid capital" to describe cash and marketable securities. In corporate law, however, one uses the term "capital" only to describe the share capital of a corporation. Thus, we must be aware of the context in which we use the term "capital."

2) Nature of Shares

A share represents the proportional financial interest of a shareholder in a corporation. It measures the liability of the shareholder to outside interests and the size of the financial interest in the corporate

---

16 *Re Inrig Shoe Co* (1924), 27 OWN 110 (SC); see *JMPM Ent Ltd v Danforth Fabrics (Humbertown) Ltd*, [1969] 1 OR 785 (HC) (issuance of additional shares to affect a change in control being "sale or other disposition" of control).

17 *Canada Business Corporations Act*, RSC 1985, c C-44.

18 *Business Corporations Act*, RSO 1990, c B.16.

19 *Toronto v Consumers' Gas Co*, [1927] 4 DLR 102 (PC [Ont]).

undertaking. Duggan Inc, for example, has issued $1,496,000 of share capital.

A share is not a sum of money: it is an interest measured by a sum of money. A share is a "chose in action" that forms a separate right of personal property.[20] It represents a fractional interest in the capital of the corporation. A share represents the bundle of rights contained in the share contract.[21] Thus, a share is that fraction of the capital of a corporation that confers on its owner a proportional proprietary interest in the corporation. Shareholders are not part owners of the assets of the undertaking.[22] Instead, they share certain rights, such as the right to participate in profits and capital.

3) Rights of Shares

Shares have three basic rights:

1) The right to vote;
2) The right to participate in profits through dividends; and
3) The right to share in the property of the corporation upon its dissolution.

Under the CBCA, where there is only one class of shares, the three rights attach to each share. Under the OBCA, however, only the right to vote and the right to receive property upon dissolution automatically attach to a single class of shares.[23] Unlike the CBCA,

---

20 OBCA, s 41; *Bradbury v English Sewing Cotton Co*, [1923] AC 744. The term "chose in action" only means that a share does not confer a right to possession of a physical thing; instead, it gives a personal right of property claimable by legal action.

21 *Borlands Trustee v Steel Bros & Co*, [1901] 1 Ch 279 at 288, Farwell J; see also *Re Paulin*, [1935] 1 KB 26 (CA); *IRC v Crossman*, [1937] AC 26 (HL).

22 *Short v Treasury Commrs*, [1948] 1 KB 116. The term "shareholder" merely describes a person who is a holder of shares; it does not mean that that person shares property in common with another.

23 CBCA, subs 24(3); OBCA, subs 22(3). Although there is no statutory right to dividends under the OBCA, all shareholders must be treated equally where there is only one class of shares.

the OBCA does not address the right of a shareholder to receive dividends.

A corporation may issue more than one class of shares. The rights, privileges, restrictions, and conditions that attach to each class of shares must be set out in its articles of incorporation.[24] If a corporation issues more than one class of shares, we must ensure that we attach each of the rights (the right to vote, the right to receive dividends and the right to share in property) to at least one of the classes of shares.[25] The equity section of the balance sheet should segregate each class of shares. The Notes should explain the rights of each class.

4) Issuance of Shares

i) No Par Value

Under the CBCA and most provincial corporate statutes, a corporation must issue its shares in registered form without nominal or par value.[26] Shares are considered to be issued when all the formalities in respect of their issuance are satisfied.[27] Shares with nominal or par value issued *prior to the enactment of* the CBCA and the OBCA *are deemed to be shares without nominal or par value.*[28]

A corporation issues a share in registered form if it satisfies one of two conditions: it names a person who is entitled to the share such that its transfer may be recorded on a securities register, or it bears a statement that it is in registered form.[29]

ii) Par Value

Some jurisdictions[30] are still using par value to denominate the nominal value of a corporation's shares. Par value shares can mis-

---

24 CBCA, subs 24(4); OBCA, subs 22(4).
25 CBCA, para 24(4)(b).
26 CBCA, subs 24(1); OBCA, subs 22(1).
27 See *Dale v Canada*, [1997] 2 CTC 286, 97 DTC 5252 (FCA); *National Westminster Bank v IRC*, [1994] STC 184 (CA).
28 CBCA, subs 24(2); OBCA, subs 22(2).
29 CBCA, subs 48(4); OBCA, subs 53(1) "registered form."
30 New York, for example, allows for par value shares.

lead investors. The par value generally denotes the nominal value of shares at the time that the corporation initially creates the shares. For example, a company may have been created in 1900 with a share capital of $100,000 divided into 100,000 shares, each having a par value of $1. This information would appear on the balance sheet.

Over time, however, the company may issue further capital as it requires financing. Later issuances of capital will be at the fair market value of the stock, which will generally be higher than the nominal or par value. For example, the company might issue an additional 100,000 shares in 2013 at an issue price of $100,000 per share. In a par value jurisdiction, the balance sheet would show additional share capital of only $100,000 at $1 par value and $99,900,000 as "Contributed Surplus."

iii) Unlimited Number

In the absence of a specific restriction in its articles of incorporation, a corporation can issue an unlimited number of shares of each class provided for in the articles. A corporation can set an upper limit, however, on the number of shares it will issue, even if the articles specify no such limit.[31] The financial statements should disclose any limits on the issuance of shares. Duggan Inc has no limits.

A corporation that restricts the number of shares it may issue may, at any time, by special resolution, amend its articles of incorporation to remove and or amend the restriction.[32] An amendment to a corporation's authorized capital entitles a shareholder of the corporation to dissent from the change and be paid the fair value of his or her shares.[33]

---

31   CBCA, para 6(1)(c).

32   CBCA, para 173(1)(d); OBCA, clause 168(1)(d). "Special resolution" is a defined term and, in effect, means a two-thirds majority; *Trans-Prairie Pipelines Ltd v MNR*, [1970] CTC 537, 70 DTC 6351 (Ex Ct) (interest on money borrowed used to redeem preferred shares deductible).

33   CBCA, s 190; OBCA, s 185.

5) Limited Liability

Shares issued by a corporation are non-assessable against its share-holders. Thus, they cannot be called upon to pay additional amounts either to the corporation or to its creditors.[34] Shareholders are not, *qua shareholders*, liable for the acts or default of the corporation.[35] Thus, the equity segment of financial statements shows the buffer that creditors have on the assets of the corporation.

6) Full Consideration

A corporation may not issue any shares until such time as it receives full consideration in the form of money, property, or past services, in return for the shares. If past services constitute the considera-tion for issued shares, the fair value of those services must not be less than the money the corporation would have received had the shares been issued for cash.[36]

A corporation may issue shares for non-cash property if the property is no less than equivalent in value to the fair cash con-sideration the corporation would have received had it issued its shares for money.[37]

The directors of a corporation determine the value of consider-ation received by the corporation in exchange for its shares (wheth-er in the form of property or past services). They must ensure that this amount is not less than the cash equivalent that it would have otherwise received.[38] In determining what constitutes a fair equiva-lent value for property or past services, directors may take into ac-count reasonable charges and any expenses of organization that are

---

34   CBCA, subs 25(2); OBCA, subs 23(2).
35   CBCA, subs 45(1); OBCA, subs 92(1).
36   CBCA, subs 25(3); OBCA, subs 23(3).
37   *Ibid.*
38   CBCA, subs 25(3); OBCA, subs 23(4). The CBCA does not specifically require directors to act on the determination of equivalent fair value. The power of determining share consideration is, however, an incident of the power and duty to manage the affairs of the corporation.

expected to benefit the corporation.[39] Directors may be personally liable for any shortfall of consideration.[40]

7) Stated Capital Account

Stated capital is the amount of money that a shareholder "commits" to the corporation and, in most cases, represents the shareholder's maximum liability to corporate creditors. Thus, in a sense, it is the financial measure of the limited liability of shareholders and represents to creditors the amount of funds or assets *initially* invested by shareholders. It is also the springboard for determining the "paid-up capital" of a corporation for tax purposes.

a) Separate Accounts for Each Class

A corporation must maintain a separate stated capital account for each class and series of shares that it issues.[41] Generally, the stated capital account is credited with the *full* amount of any consideration that the corporation receives in respect of the particular shares issued.[42] There are some exceptions (discussed below) to this rule in respect of non–arm's length transactions.

b) Shares Issued for Property

A corporation may not issue shares in exchange for any property (or past service) that is valued at less than the amount the corporation would have received had the shares been issued for money.[43] It can, however, issue shares for consideration of greater value than the cash equivalent of property or past services.

---

39 CBCA, subs 25(4); OBCA, subss 23(4) and 23(5).

40 See, for example, CBCA, subs 118(1) and OBCA, subs 130(1). Also, CBCA, subs 25(5) and OBCA, subs 23(6) generally do not allow a company to issue shares for debt.

41 CBCA, subs 26(1); OBCA, subs 24(1).

42 CBCA, subs 26(2); OBCA, subss 24(2), (8) (stated capital account may be maintained in foreign currency).

43 CBCA, subs 25(3); OBCA, subs 23(3).

c) Credit Full Consideration

Generally, a corporation must credit the *full* amount of the consideration received to its stated capital account. A corporation cannot credit to a stated capital account an amount that is greater than the amount of the consideration that it receives for its shares.[44] This rule also plays an important role in tax law because a corporation can generally pay back its "paid-up capital" (PUC) without any income tax cost to shareholders.[45]

The general rule is that PUC for income tax purposes is calculated by reference to the rules of corporate law. In the absence of technical adjustments, we determine the PUC of a class of shares of a corporation by dividing the stated capital account for that class of shares by the number of issued shares of that class.

8) Non–Arm's Length Transactions

There are several exceptions to the general rule that a corporation must credit the full amount of consideration that it receives to its stated capital account. A corporation may add, to its stated capital account, an amount that is *less* than the consideration that it receives for its shares if it issues the shares:[46]

1) In exchange for property of a person who, immediately before the exchange, does not deal with the corporation at arm's length;
2) In exchange for shares of a body corporate that immediately before the exchange, or because of the exchange, does not deal with the issuing corporation at arm's length;
3) Pursuant to an amalgamation with another corporation; or
4) Pursuant to an "arrangement" that is, in effect, an amalgamation of the issuing corporation with another corporation.

---

44   CBCA, subs 26(4); OBCA, subs 24(4).
45   "Paid-up capital" for tax purposes.
46   CBCA, subs 26(3); OBCA, subs 24(3). These exceptions all cater to income tax transactions and are intended to facilitate various rollovers under the *Income Tax Act*.

A corporation may also add an amount less than the fair market value of property to its stated capital account in respect of arm's length transactions if it, and all of the shareholders of the particular class, consent.[47]

In each of the above circumstances, the corporation may add either all or *some lesser part of* the consideration that it receives for its shares to the appropriate stated capital account. As already noted, it cannot add an amount that is greater than the amount it receives.[48] These exceptions facilitate corporate reorganizations under the *Income Tax Act*.

9) Stock Dividends

Where a corporation pays a stock dividend, it must add to the stated capital account of the class of shares on which it pays the dividend, the full financial equivalent of the declared amount of the dividend.[49] A stock dividend is a dividend paid by issuing additional fully paid shares of the corporation to existing shareholders. Thus, the corporation will capitalize a portion of its retained earnings to share capital for accounting purposes.

10) Continuances

A corporation continued under either the CBCA or the OBCA may add to its stated capital accounts any consideration that it receives for shares issued prior to its continuance. Also, it may, at any time, add to its stated capital account any amount credited to its retained earnings or other surplus accounts.[50]

---

47 See, for example, CBCA, subpara 26(3)(a)(iii).
48 CBCA, subs 26(4); OBCA, subs 24(4). Since 31 March 1977.
49 *See* CBCA, subs 43(2); OBCA, subs 38(2).
50 CBCA, subs 26(6); OBCA, subs 24(5).

11) Reduction of Stated Capital

Corporate statutes strictly control adjustments — particularly downward adjustments — in stated capital. The *Income Tax Act* also stringently controls adjustments to the paid-up capital of corporations.

The general rule is that a corporation may not reduce its stated capital.[51] There are exceptions to this rule, but the exceptions apply only in narrowly circumscribed circumstances.

A corporation may reduce its stated capital only if it satisfies two financial requirements: the reduction must not impair the solvency or liquidity of the corporation. Thus, a corporation may reduce its stated capital only if it is able to pay its obligations as they fall due and discharge its obligations to its shareholders and creditors.

The stringency of the financial tests varies with the reason for the reduction of capital and the potential for harm to investors. The less the risk of harm and the lower the potential for abuse, the less stringent the test that the corporation must satisfy to reduce its stated capital.

12) Acquisition of a Corporation's Own Shares

Under the common law, a corporation could not reduce its capital except with judicial approval. Thus, a corporation could not purchase its own shares, since the purchase would be tantamount to a reduction of capital.[52]

The common law rule has been incorporated into both the CBCA and the OBCA, but with substantial exceptions.[53] A corporation may reduce its capital if it protects the financial interests of its investors and creditors. We see, for example, that Duggan Inc has repurchased $18,456,000 of its shares, which show as treasury shares on its balance sheet as at 30 September 20-2.

---

51   CBCA, subs 26(10); OBCA, subs 24(9). This prohibition does not apply to mutual funds.
52   *Trevor v Whitworth* (1887), 12 App Cas 409 (HL).
53   CBCA, s 30; OBCA, s 28.

a) Financial Tests

Subject to restrictions in its articles of incorporation, a corporation may purchase its own shares if it does not have reasonable grounds for believing that the purchase will:[54]

- Render the corporation unable to pay its liabilities as they come due (the liquidity test); or
- Cause the realizable value of its assets to be less than the aggregate of its liabilities and the stated capital of all of its classes of shares (the solvency test).

Thus, the corporation must satisfy two financial tests: it must be liquid *and* solvent after it purchases its shares. We determine corporate liquidity from the financial statements stated in terms of current market values. Duggan Inc, for example, has cash and net accounts receivable of only $6,349,000 to pay substantially higher current liabilities. Long-term solvency is more difficult to measure because, unlike historical cost accounting, it relies on realizable value.

An Ontario corporation may also purchase its warrants. The financial tests are somewhat less stringent if the purchase of shares is to settle a claim against the corporation, eliminate fractional shares, or fulfil the terms of a non-assignable agreement under which the corporation is obliged to purchase the shares.

Directors of a corporation who authorize the purchase of its shares in contravention of the solvency and liquidity tests are jointly and severally liable to the corporation for the amount of the unauthorized disbursement of funds.[55] A director who dissents from the resolution authorizing the purchase of shares is not liable if the director records his or her dissent at the meeting. If the director is not present at the meeting, he or she must notify the secretary of the corporation and record the dissent in the minutes of the meeting.[56]

A director can rely upon reports presented by professionals who are qualified to comment on matters requiring technical expertise.

---

54 CBCA, s 34; OBCA, s 30.
55 CBCA, subs 118(2); OBCA, subs 130(2).
56 CBCA, s 123; OBCA, subs 135(3).

A director who relies upon the report of an auditor, accountant, appraiser, or other professional qualified to make valuation judgments is not liable if the purchase of shares subsequently proves to contravene the statutory financial tests.[57]

b) Dissenting Shareholders

A corporation that purchases its own shares to satisfy a dissenting shareholder's claim pursuant to the appraisal remedy faces a less stringent financial test.[58] For example, under a buy-out pursuant to the appraisal remedy, a corporation cannot purchase its own shares from a dissenting shareholder if the purchase would render the corporation unable to pay its obligations as they fall due (the liquidity test), or if the purchase reduces the realizable value of its assets to less than the value of its outstanding liabilities.[59] In these circumstances, the corporation's stated capital is not taken into account in the second prong of the two tests. Thus, a corporation may reduce its stated capital to purchase its own shares if it does not impair its liquidity and solvency towards creditors.

13) Alternative Acquisition of Corporation's Own Shares

There are three additional circumstances in which a corporation may acquire its own shares by satisfying a somewhat less stringent financial test than those generally applicable. Subject to its Articles, a corporation may purchase its own shares to:[60]

1) Settle or compromise debts asserted by or against the corporation;
2) Eliminate fractional shares; or
3) Fulfil the terms of a non-assignable agreement under which the corporation has an option or is obligated to purchase shares owned by a director, officer, or employee of the corporation.

---

57 CBCA, subs 123(4); OBCA, subs 135(4).
58 CBCA, para 35(2)(a); OBCA, cl 31(2)(a).
59 CBCA, subs 190(26); OBCA, subs 185(30).
60 CBCA, subs 35(1); OBCA, subs 31(1).

In any of these situations, the corporation may purchase its shares *unless:*[61]

- There are reasonable grounds for believing that the purchase will render the corporation unable to pay its obligations as they fall due; or
- The realizable value of the corporation's assets after the purchase will be less than the aggregate of its liabilities and the amount required to redeem all of its shares the holders of which have the right to be paid *prior* to the holders of the shares to be purchased.

The second prong of the financial tests ensures that a corporation that purchases its own shares does not prejudice the rights of "senior" shareholders who have a higher ranking claim to the assets of the corporation than the holders of the shares purchased. Thus, the corporation cannot prejudice the rights of preferred shareholders by purchasing shares that rank lower in corporate rights.

14) Redemption of Shares

A corporation can redeem its redeemable shares, but it cannot pay an amount that exceeds the redemption price stipulated in its articles of incorporation.[62] A "redeemable share" is a share that is redeemable at the option of either the corporation or the shareholder.[63]

A corporation can redeem its shares if it satisfies two financial tests:

1) It may redeem its shares only if there are reasonable grounds for believing that the redemption will not render the corpora-

---

61   CBCA, subs 35(3); OBCA, subs 31(3).
62   CBCA, subs 36(1); OBCA, subs 32(1).
63   CBCA, subs 2(1) "redeemable share"; OBCA, subs 1(1) "redeemable share." In financial jargon, a share that is redeemable at the option of the shareholder is referred to as a "retractable share."

tion unable to pay its obligations as they fall due.[64] Thus, the corporation must be liquid enough to pay its debts as they mature. Therefore, the working capital ratio is important, which we shall examine later.

2) The realizable value of the corporation's assets after the redemption must not be less than the aggregate of its liabilities and the amount required to pay other shareholders who rate equally with or have a higher claim than the holders of the redeemed shares.[65] The concern here is to protect only those who have a claim equal to or higher than the shares redeemed. The financial tests are less stringent because the shares would have been issued on the basis that they were redeemable and this information is available to the public. Here too, unlike historical cost accounting, the solvency test requires an assessment of the corporate assets based on market values.

15) Adjustments of Stated Capital Accounts

A corporation must maintain a separate stated capital account for each class and series of shares that it issues.[66] Generally, the corporation must credit the full amount of any consideration that it receives upon issuing shares to the appropriate stated capital account.[67]

A lesser amount may be credited to the stated capital account where the shares are issued in exchange for property in a non–arm's length transaction: CBCA, subsection 26(3); OBCA, subsection 24(3). The rationale of this exception is to accommodate income tax planning, particularly under section 84.1 of the *Income Tax Act*. CBCA, subparagraph 26(3)(a)(iii) also permits a corporation to add less than the FMV of property to its stated capital if the corporation and all the shareholders of the particular class consent.

---

64 CBCA, para 36(2)(a); OBCA, cl 32(2)(a).
65 CBCA, para 36(2)(b); OBCA, cl 32(2)(b).
66 CBCA, subs 26(1); OBCA, subs 24(1).
67 CBCA, subs 26(2); OBCA, subs 24(2).

16) Reduction

When a corporation reduces its share capital, it must adjust the amount shown in its stated capital account. The amount of the adjustment depends upon the manner in which the corporation acquires its own shares. Where the reduction in the share capital of a corporation is pursuant to:

- An acquisition of the corporation's own shares;[68]
- A settlement or compromise of a claim asserted against the corporation;[69]
- A plan to eliminate fractional shares;[70]
- The terms of a non-assignable agreement under which the corporation was obliged to purchase shares owned by its directors, officers, or employees;[71]
- A redemption of its shares;[72]
- The enforcement of a lien against its shares;[73]
- A transaction whereby a dissenting shareholder of the corporation exercised appraisal rights;[74] or
- A court order relieving a shareholder from oppression by the corporation.[75]

The amount to be deducted from the stated capital account is calculated according to a formula that reduces the stated capital account by the *average* issue price of all of the shares of the particular class or series.[76]

The formula reduces the stated capital account of the shares in proportion to the amount that was credited to the account when the shares were issued. The premium paid to a shareholder on the

---

68 CBCA, s 34; OBCA, s 30.
69 CBCA, para 35(1)(a); OBCA, cl 31(1)(a).
70 CBCA, para 35(1)(b); OBCA, cl 31(1)(b).
71 CBCA, para 35(1)(c); OBCA, cl 31(1)(c).
72 CBCA, s 36; OBCA, s 32.
73 CBCA, subs 45(3); OBCA, subs 40(3).
74 CBCA, s 190; OBCA, s 185.
75 CBCA, s 241; OBCA, s 248.
76 CBCA, subs 39(1); OBCA, subs 35(1).

redemption of shares in any of the above listed circumstances is not deducted from the stated capital account.[77]

In contrast, if a corporation is required to compensate a shareholder for the purchase price of the shares because of its oppressive conduct, the reduction in the stated capital account is the full amount paid to the shareholder.[78] This amount will not necessarily coincide with the amount credited to the corporation's stated capital account when the shares were initially issued as the shareholder may have purchased the shares from another shareholder at a later date.

Where a corporation reduces its stated capital account pursuant to a special resolution, the amount specified in the resolution is the amount deducted from the appropriate stated capital account.[79]

17) Conversion or Change of Shares

Where a corporation converts shares from one class into another, it must adjust the stated capital accounts of both of the classes to reflect the conversion. Similarly, when shares are changed from one class or series into shares of another class or series, the stated capital account of both classes or series must be adjusted.[80] A "conversion" of shares from one class into another occurs pursuant to the terms and conditions of the shares as described in the Articles of Incorporation. A "change" of shares from one class into another is usually pursuant to a subsequent amendment to the terms and conditions attached to the shares.

The stated capital account of the class from which the shares are converted is reduced by the amount derived from a formula. The stated capital account of the shares into which the shares are converted or changed is increased by an equivalent amount *plus* any additional consideration payable on the conversion or change of shares.[81]

---

77 *Ibid.*
78 CBCA, subs 39(2); OBCA, subs 35(2).
79 CBCA, subs 39(3); OBCA, subs 35(3).
80 CBCA, subs 39(4); OBCA, subs 35(4).
81 CBCA, para 39(4)(b); OBCA, cl 35(4)(b).

Where a corporation has two classes of shares with rights of conversion from one class into the other (that is, interconvertible shares), the adjustment to the stated capital account upon the conversion of a share from one class to the other is equal to the weighted average of the stated capital accounts of both classes of shares.[82]

When shares of one class or series are converted or changed into shares of another class or series, the old shares (that is, the converted or changed shares) are considered to be issued shares of the class or series into which the shares have been converted or changed.[83] Thus, to the extent of the number of shares converted, the issued capital of the old class or series *automatically* becomes issued shares of the new class or series. The automatic conversion of shares from one class into another applies only to the *issued* shares and does not apply to any *unissued* shares. The articles must be amended to convert the unissued shares of the old class into unissued shares of the new class.

18) Effect of Change of Shares on Authorized Capital

There are circumstances where a corporation may wish to restrict the amount of share capital that it issues.[84] Where a corporation limits the number of shares that it may issue by stipulating a maximum authorized capital, a conversion of shares from one class into another will have the effect of increasing the unissued but authorized shares of the old class by the number of shares converted or changed into shares of the new class. In other words, the authorized share capital of the old class is restored by the number of shares converted or changed into the new class.[85]

19) Cancellation of Shares

If its articles of incorporation do not limit the number of shares that a corporation may issue, any shares (or fractions of shares) that the

---

82   CBCA, subs 39(5); OBCA, subs 35(5).
83   CBCA, subs 39(9); OBCA, subs 35(8).
84   CBCA, para 6(1)(c).
85   CBCA, subs 39(10); OBCA, subs 35(8).

corporation issues and later acquires are automatically cancelled. Where, however, the authorized share capital of a corporation is limited, any of its shares acquired by the corporation are restored to the status of authorized but unissued shares of the particular class.[86] The rationale of these provisions is to prevent the corporation and its senior officials from manipulating the market in the corporation's shares or using corporate assets to acquire, or enhance, voting power.

20) Corporation Holding Its Own Shares

The common law rule against corporations "trafficking" in their own shares also prohibited a corporation from holding its shares: the retention of cancelled shares would be tantamount to a reduction of capital.[87]

The common law rule is entrenched in the CBCA and the OBCA.[88] The general rule is that a corporation may not hold shares in itself; nor may it hold shares in its parent corporation. A parent corporation is specifically prohibited from issuing its shares to any of its subsidiaries.[89] Although there are exceptions to these rules, each exception is circumscribed by financial tests that are intended to protect the interests of investors and creditors.

---

86   CBCA, subs 39(6); OBCA, subs 35(6).
87   *Trevor v Whitworth*, above note 52 at 423:

> Paid-up capital may be diminished or lost in the company's trading; that is a result which no legislation can prevent; but persons who deal with, and give credit to a limited company, naturally rely upon the fact that the company is trading with a certain amount of capital already paid, as well as upon the responsibility of its members for the capital remaining at call; and they are entitled to assume that no part of the capital which has been paid into the coffers of the company has been subsequently paid out, except in the legitimate course of its business.

88   CBCA, subs 30(1); OBCA, subs 28(1).
89   CBCA, subs 30(2); OBCA, subs 28(2) (a corporation acquiring a subsidiary that holds its shares must cause the subsidiary to dispose of those shares within five years of its becoming a subsidiary).

Chapter VI: Measurement of Income

A. GENERAL COMMENT

"Income" is a measure of gain over a period of time. Thus, measuring income requires that we identify the amount of the gain and relate it to the appropriate period when we should recognize it. Both of these aspects of measurement can be uncertain processes influenced by legal, economic, and accounting principles. As we shall see, the measurement of income is more art than science.

As with all languages, accounting has certain fundamental rules of structure and composition. We refer to these rules as the principles of accounting. Contrary to popular conceptions and, perhaps, most fortunately, accountants did not devise the fundamental structural rules of recording financial data. A Renaissance monk named Luca Pacioli devised the basic process of recording financial data. This process allows us to record information in a methodical manner for analysis and decision making. It is important to note, however, that the principles of accounting are neither rigid nor uniform. Variations in accounting principles can make comparisons of financial information difficult.

B. ACCOUNTING PRINCIPLES

Generally accepted accounting principles (GAAP) are the principles that underlie the preparation of financial statements for commercial use. We say "generally accepted" because they are accepted by various professional accounting bodies, regulatory agencies, securities commissions, and financial institutions as appropriate for financial statements. In Canada, the *CICA Handbook* is an authoritative source of GAAP. Thus, the *Canada Business Corporations Act* and regulatory statutes recognize it as the benchmark of accounting principles.[1]

GAAP, however, encompasses not only the specific recommendations and procedures set out in the *Handbook*, but also broad principles and conventions. These accounting principles develop over time and through usage. When the *Handbook* does not cover a matter, accountants refer to other sources of information. For example, the CICA's Emerging Issues Committee (EIC) Abstracts, International Accounting Standards, standards promulgated by the Financial Accounting Standards Board (FASB) in the United States, and accounting literature are useful sources. Unfortunately, these sources do not always agree on what constitutes GAAP. The *Handbook* addresses such potential differences by saying, "the relative importance of these various sources is a matter of professional judgment in the circumstances."

In practice, the order of importance of these sources is as follows:

- *CICA Handbook* and EIC Abstracts;
- CICA accounting guidelines;
- Established Canadian practices;
- Recommendations of the FASB in the United States;
- International Accounting standards; and
- Literature.

C. NET INCOME

Corporations registered with the Securities and Exchange Commission (SEC) in the United States may prepare their financials in accordance with US GAAP.[2]

---

1   CBCA, s 155, Reg 70, "Canadian GAAP" and "Canadian GAAS."
2   See CBCA, Reg 71.

Since GAAP represent authoritative guidelines for the preparation and presentation of financial statements for commercial purposes, we need to clearly understand their fundamental premises. These assumptions are the bedrock upon which we interpret financial information.

We saw earlier that net income essentially comprises two components, namely, revenue and expenses during a period of time. We calculate net profit or net income according to the formula:

NI = R – E

where:

NI = Net Income
R = Revenues
E = Expenses

All measurement of income for commercial purposes begins with this basic formula. The essence of the income statement formula is matching revenues and expenses over a period of time, usually one year for tax and regulatory purposes.

For tax purposes, the first step in the calculation of net profit is to look to accounting and commercial principles. In *Daley v MNR*, for example:[3]

> the first inquiry whether a particular disbursement or expense is deductible should not be whether it is excluded from deduction by [paragraph 18(1)(a) or (b)] but rather whether its deduction is permissible by the ordinary principles of commercial trading or accepted business and accounting practice.

"Net income" does not have a technical meaning. Whether or not the sum in question constitutes profit must be determined on ordinary commercial principles unless the provisions of the *Income Tax Act* specifically require a departure from such principles.

---

3   *Daley v MNR*, [1950] CTC 254 at 260, 4 DTC 877 at 880 (Ex Ct).

D. MEASUREMENT AND TIMING

Measurement and timing of income are actually two different concepts. There is, however, an inextricable relationship between the concepts. For example, suppose a business started up in 1900 and closed down in 2013. There might be a number of difficulties involved in measuring the aggregate income of the enterprise over the 113 years. If all we need to know is the net income figure for the 113 years, there is no issue of timing.

Serious problems of timing arise, however, if we need to measure income for 2013 only. Then, we need to match 2013 revenues and expenses. Thus, we need to know when we earn revenues, when we recognize the revenues in our financial statements, and the principles of matching of revenues and expenses.

We can illustrate these problems by examining the accounting concepts of "realization," "recognition," "accrual," "matching," and "conservatism."

E. REVENUE REALIZATION

A simple definition of "realization" would refer to the point of sale, the time at which X parts with property and receives a real gain in the form of cash. The following examples illustrate the inadequacy of this simple definition. If X sells Black Acre and takes back a mortgage, X realizes a gain. Similarly, we treat an exchange of Black Acre for White Acre, a property of equal value, or for stock in Black Acre Developments Ltd, as a realization. Even if X gives Black Acre away, he or she will realize a gain. In all these cases the rationale is the same: X has parted with his or her investment in Black Acre. We treat X as though he or she sold the property for cash.

There is a fundamental question, however, as to *when* we "realize" a gain or loss. Suppose, for example that X buys Black Acre for $50,000. By the end of the year the property is worth $60,000. Does X have a $10,000 gain? Certainly he or she has a potential gain, a "paper gain," an accrued economic gain in the Haig-Simons sense of economic income. Traditional accounting practice, however, ignores the gain as unrealized.

In the following year, X's property might decline in value to $45,000 or might rise to $70,000. Suppose, in either case, that X then sells the property. According to traditional practice, X is treated as "realizing" a $5,000 loss or a $20,000 gain in the year that he sells the property. In the first case, the $5,000 loss represents a $10,000 paper gain in Year 1 combined with a paper loss of $15,000 in Year 2. In the second case, X had a paper gain of $10,000 in each of Years 1 and 2.

F. REVENUE RECOGNITION

The second aspect of measurement is to identify the appropriate period in which we wish to recognize the gain. "Recognition" is the taking into account of an amount in computing income. Some accounting systems would recognize all the "paper" gains and losses in a year even though they are "unrealized."

There are good reasons for not recognizing paper gains. Accountants, true to the axiom of their conservatism in estimating income, normally disregard such gains because they may prove illusory if values decline in a subsequent period. On the other hand, the failure to recognize paper gains, and recognition of the entire gain at the point of realization, gives rise to problems of irregularity and "lumping" of income.

Accountants are not as reluctant to recognize unrealized losses as they are to recognize unrealized gains. Consistent with accounting conservatism in estimating income, and depending upon the nature of the asset concerned, it is sometimes considered good accounting practice to recognize a "paper" loss.

Proper revenue and expense recognition are crucial to an accurate measurement of net income. The consequences of improper revenue recognition, or delaying the recognition of expenses, hurts investors and damages the integrity of the capital markets. In addition, such practices can hurt employees who participate in profit sharing or bonus arrangements.

The fundamental principle of revenue recognition is that a business should recognize revenue only when:

1) It has a *bona fide* exchange transaction; and
2) The earnings process from the exchange has been substantially completed.

Thus, an enterprise should recognize revenue from sales transactions when the seller transfers to the buyer the significant risks and rewards of ownership and there is reasonable assurance of the price.[4]

Absent these conditions, a business should not recognize revenue in the current period and should defer recognition until the process is completed.

The matching principle requires that the enterprise offset expenses against related revenues in determining an enterprise's net income. Thus, if an enterprise defers its revenue, so also should it defer related expenses. This is a fundamental principle of all accrual accounting. The decision to recognize or defer revenue is based on the substance, rather than the form, of the transaction.

Some authorities, for example, the US Securities and Exchange Commission, enumerate a longer list of conditions that an enterprise must satisfy before it can recognize revenue.[5] A SEC staff study noted that an enterprise should recognize revenue only when:

1) There was evidence that persuasively demonstrated that an arrangement existed;
2) The enterprise had delivered the product or performed the services;
3) The arrangement provided for a fixed or determinable sale price; and
4) There was some reasonable assurance of collectability.

Thus, although an enterprise does not have to wait until it actually collects cash from the sale transaction, it must have reasonable assurance of ultimate collectability of the account.

---

4   Canadian Institute of Chartered Accountants, *CICA Handbook — Accounting*, loose-leaf (Toronto: Canadian Institute of Chartered Accountants, 2010), section 34005.05 [*CICA Handbook*].
5   See Staff Accounting Bulletin #101, "Revenue Recognition in Financial Statements."

Except for income tax purposes, most listed companies would prefer to increase their revenues in the current period and defer their expenses in order to enhance stock prices and bonuses. Hence, the usual problem in respect of revenue recognition is acceleration of sales revenue rather than delay.

"Channel stuffing" is a way of accelerating revenue recognition for financial reporting purposes. Channel stuffing refers to the practice of a business using its bargaining power or other financial incentives to pressure its customers to order more goods than they would want or need, so that the business can report additional revenues in the current period. The parties may agree that excess inventories may be returned after the year-end.

Bristol-Myers Squibb Co (BMS), a major drug company, used channel stuffing by providing financial incentives to its wholesalers to buy extra product to stockpile inventory that they did not need. BMS recorded the additional sales as current revenues and inflated its sales numbers by $2.5 billion between 1999 and 2001. This had the effect of inflating earnings by $900 million. The US Justice Department launched a criminal investigation. In 2005, BMS settled with the US Department of Justice and paid $300 million to a shareholders' restitution fund. The company also paid $150 million to settle the SEC's civil charges and $339 million to settle a class action lawsuit. Thus, the total bill to BMS was $800 million. Bearing in mind that these fines would probably be paid with after-tax dollars, the total cost to the company substantially exceeded the $900 million that went into its net income.

In addition, two of the company's executives were criminally indicted. The company itself agreed to a deferred prosecution arrangement, under which it escaped criminal charges if it complied with all the terms and conditions of the agreement. The deferred criminal prosecution arrangement purportedly penalized the corporation, without excessive loss to the employees and shareholders. Nevertheless, BMS's actions reflected in the company's stock price, thereby penalizing shareholders indirectly.

Given the importance of the capital markets in the United States, the response to the accounting misdeeds of the 1990s was brisk and hard. Congress enacted SOX, section 307, which directs the SEC to establish rules requiring lawyers who practise before the commission to report evidence of financial frauds that may violate the securities laws or breach fiduciary duties to the appropriate corporate officer or body, including the audit committee or board of directors.

Of course, lawyers often draft agreements that use "net income" in various provisions, for example, employment contracts, collective bargaining agreements, partnership, buy-sell agreements. In *Margonis v Rossi*,[6] the court found a lawyer had demonstrated an "ineptness of language" by confusing "net income" and "gross income" in drafting a partnership agreement.

G. CANADIAN GAAP

The *CICA Handbook* deals with revenue recognition in paragraph 3400.05, which states:

> In a transaction involving the sale of goods, performance should be regarded as having been achieved when the following conditions have been fulfilled:
> (a) the seller of the goods has transferred to the buyer the significant risks and rewards of ownership, in that all significant acts have been completed and the seller retains no continuing managerial involvement in, or effective control of, the goods transferred to a degree usually associated with ownership; and
> (b) reasonable assurance exists regarding the measurement of the consideration that will be derived from the sale of goods, and the extent to which goods may be returned.

In EIC-141 (17 December 2003), the *Handbook* accepted that the US Securities and Exchange Commission Staff Accounting Bulletin #101 (SAB 101) is consistent with the *Handbook* section 3400. The EIC also indicates that securities regulators in Canada would look to SAB 101 when determining whether Canadian reporting issuers have complied with Canadian GAAP.

---

6   253 NE 2d 577 (Illinois App Ct 1969).

The decision to recognize or defer revenue is ultimately a matter of professional accounting judgment based on an evaluation of all the underlying facts revealed in the course of an audit. To be sure, professional accountants may arrive at different conclusions. The important point is that they base their conclusions on the audited facts.

As the Supreme Court of the United States noted in its 1995 opinion in *Shalala v Guernsey Memorial Hospital*,[7] involving Medicare reimbursement regulations: "GAAP is not the lucid or encyclopaedic set of pre-existing rules it has been made out to be . . . . GAAP changes and, even at any one point, is often indeterminate."

The convictions of Bernie Madoff, Garth Drabinsky, and Myron Gottlieb for accounting and financial fraud are mere stepping-stones in the long history of financial debacles. If there is a lesson in the high-profile trials — Enron, WorldCom, Bre-X, Livent, and Tyco — of recent years, it is that determined and creative scoundrels can always find a way around the rules. Financial statement manipulation is not a novel phenomenon. History teaches us that bad financial statements and weak regulations are an intrinsic risk of publicly listed securities.

Accounting principles and auditing standards affect corporate behaviour. For example, WorldCom, recharacterized US $12 billion of its expenses as assets, thereby inflating its current profits to boost the value of its stock. Profits from stock manipulation are power incentives. The essential question is always the same: Are our standards ahead of the curve or merely responsive to events after the fact? New techniques of financial frauds are merely variations on old themes. They all have three ingredients: confidence, cooperative bookkeepers, and accounting respectability. Madoff set the record — $50 billion (US) for his Ponzi fraud! He will not be the last.

We have explored, in a very simple way, the concept of realization of gain. There remain a number of slightly more sophisticated problems concerning the time when gains should be recognized.

Suppose that X starts a business of manufacturing and selling widgets. The business cycle can be broken down into the following steps:

---

7   514 US 87 (1995).

1) Injection of capital in cash or assets;
2) Acquisition of inventory of raw metal;
3) Fabrication of metal into an inventory of widgets;
4) Sales activity that results in orders for widgets;
5) Delivery of widgets to customers;
6) Invoicing of customers; and
7) Collection of receivables and payment of invoices in cash.

We could make an argument for choosing several of the last five steps as the point at which X's gain should be recognized for the purposes of calculating income. Our earlier discussion would probably suggest that the gain should not be recognized at any point before Step 5. Standard accounting would lead to a choice of Step 6 as the point at which X should recognize a gain. In any event, as a matter of usual business practice, Steps 5 and 6 are merged. Commonly, the invoice accompanies the delivery of widgets. As we shall see later, if X's business adopts a cash basis of accounting, the gain will not be recognized until Step 7, when the business actually receives payment in cash.

One of the most important areas of income measurement is revenue recognition. Revenues derive from the sale of products, fees for services, and the use of intellectual property. Thus, the timing of revenues is the first decision in the measurement process. For accounting purposes, we generally recognize revenues at the point when the earning process is *substantially* complete.

The earning process is substantially complete when we pass title to the product to the purchaser, or when we complete the service. At this point, we have sufficient information to measure revenues objectively. The important point to observe here is that revenue does not necessarily relate in the earnings cycle to when we receive cash for the product or service. For example, if a company sells merchandise on credit (payable in thirty days), we recognize the full sales value when we ship the goods to the customer. The fact that the cash may not come in for thirty days or later does not matter. Indeed, in some cases, the customer might even pay in advance for the purchase of the goods. Nevertheless, we recognize revenues only when we ship the goods and title passes from the company to its customer. Until then, we consider the advance to be a debt owing to the customer. At the point of sale, we transform the debt into revenues.

To be sure, this principle of recognizing revenues at the time of sale and shipment does not make a great deal of difference in most cases, except at the end of the accounting cycle. For example, it matters little to a company with a 31 December year-end whether it takes its revenue for July sales into account in July, August, or September when it collects its cash from sales. Since all of the revenue falls in the same accounting period, it matters little for measurement purposes so long as the revenue falls in the current year.

The principle, however, is critical at the company's fiscal year-end. It makes a great deal of difference whether revenues from sales for merchandise shipped out in mid-December are taken into the current year's income or into the income of the year following. In this case, the timing of revenues affects the company's bottom-line profit for commercial purposes and the amount of tax payable in the current year. Thus, we need to match revenues and related expenses in the same period.

H. ACCRUAL

The principles of accrual accounting are central to the matching of revenues and expenses. Accrual accounting requires that we recognize revenues in the period to which they relate, rather than when we collect the cash. Similarly, we recognize expenses in the period when we incur the expense, rather than when we pay for it. For example, assume we purchase merchandise on 20 December of the current year and pay for it on 10 January of the following year. Accrual accounting requires us to recognize the purchase in the current year, even though we did not pay for it until the following year.

As we shall see, recognizing expenses in the appropriate period depends upon the nature of the expense. We recognize time-related expenses such as salaries and wages, utilities, interest, etc., at the end of the accounting period to which they relate. This is so even though we have not paid the expenses. Again, this may not make a great deal of difference to expenses we incur in the middle of an accounting period, but it can be important in terms of year-end accounting. Here also, accounting principles do not rely upon the outgoing of cash to determine when we take the expenditure into account in the financial books. The essential concept is matching the expense with revenues in the period in which we derive the benefit of the expense to earn the revenues.

I. MATCHING

So far we have been discussing the appropriate time to recognize gains and losses. In an accounting sense, gains and losses are measured by reflecting expenditures and receipts. "Gains" or "losses" in themselves are net concepts, as is the "income" of a business, since it reflects all expenditures and all receipts.

Accrual and matching are closely related. The matching principle requires us to deduct expenses (E) in the same period as they contribute to the earning of revenues (R). Hence, if we incur expenses in one time period but the expenses will benefit several periods, we allocate the expense in some reasonable manner between the various periods. This principle lies at the core of the income equation. In other words, the "R" and "E" in the formula must match each other. The "E" must track the "R" so that both match for accounting purposes.

For example, assume that a company orders and receives merchandise on 15 December 2012. We allocate the cost of the merchandise to 2012 or beyond depending upon when we sell the goods and pass title. Hence, if we sell the merchandise and recognize revenues in 2012, we also recognize the expenses (cost of goods sold) of the sale in the same year. If, however, the merchandise remains on hand as inventory, we recognize the cost as an asset in the current year. We then recognize the expense when we sell the merchandise in the following year. Thus, expenses are merely resources and assets consumed in the current year.

Matching is essentially an allocation process between time periods. We recognize expenses that benefit the current time period in that period. Expenses that will benefit future time periods are "held" in asset accounts. We recognize them in subsequent time periods when we flow them out of "assets" and match them against revenues.

Mismatching of revenues and expenses distorts the net income figure and can seriously mislead users of financial statements. For example, for tax purposes, mismatching leads to tax deferral if we delay recognizing revenues or accelerate recognizing expenses. From a tax perspective, the most extreme scenario is one where the taxpayer delays recognizing revenues and concurrently accelerates the time when he or she charges off the expenses. This might occur, for example, if the taxpayer receives a lump sum for two years' rental that he or she does not recognize until the second year, but recognizes the rental expenses in the first year. Such mismatching would be wrong both for accounting and tax purposes.

The following example illustrates the resolution of the problem of matching.

Assume that City Dairy Ltd delivers milk door to door and for this purpose requires 100 trucks costing $6,000 each. The trucks will have a useful life of approximately five years and will be disposed of for $1,000 each at the end of that time. Thus, over the course of five years, each truck represents a $5,000 expense of City Dairy's business. If, however, City Dairy bought and expensed 100 trucks in its first business year, it would dramatically distort its income for the year by recognizing the entire cost of $600,000 as an expenditure for that year. We resolve this particular problem by applying the notion of "depreciation" to spread the cost that arises from exhausting such assets over an appropriate number of years.

Although "matching" is a well-accepted business principle, it is simply an interpretive aid that assists, but is not determinative, in arriving at an accurate picture of the taxpayer's income.[8] We do not

---

8   See, for example, *Canderel Ltd v Canada*, [1998] 1 SCR 147, [1998] 2 CTC 35, 98 DTC 6100 (tenant inducement payment paid to secure 10-year lease

need to match if an expenditure does not directly relate to future revenues, or if it relates to future revenues but also refers to benefits realized in the year of expenditure.

J. CONSERVATISM

Conservatism is all about attitude. Conservatism refers to the accounting profession's approach to measuring profits. Measuring income means allocating costs and values to time periods and then matching revenues and expenses in the periods. Since we do not always know how much to allocate with absolute certainty, measuring profits requires professional judgment. Conservatism requires a cautious approach in allocating values and recognizing revenues and losses.

In effect, conservatism means that an enterprise should not recognize revenues before earning them, but should recognize all anticipated losses even before they actually occur. Some call this a pessimistic approach; others say it is merely being prudent. Regardless of the label, conservatism implies caution and prudence. Recognize no gains in advance of realizing them but recognize all losses at the earliest signal of trouble.

Conservatism and matching can conflict. For example, should we write-off research and development costs over time to match revenues through increased sales? The matching principle requires that we recognize research and development as capital costs that we allocate over time as the new products generate revenues. The concept of conservatism, however, dictates prudence. Should we recognize the

---

from key tenant deductible entirely in year paid rather than over the period of the lease since sufficient benefit [preserved reputation, ensured future income stream, satisfied interim financing requirements] realized in first year to match expense); *Ikea Ltd v Canada*, [1998] 1 SCR 196, [1998] 2 CTC 61, 98 DTC 6092 (tenant inducement payment received for signing a 10-year lease taxable as income entirely in year received); *Toronto College Park Ltd v Canada*, [1998] 1 SCR 183, [1998] 2 CTC 78, 98 DTC 6088 (tenant inducement payment paid to secure lease deductible entirely in year made since amortization over period of lease would not present a more accurate picture of income).

research expenditures as early as possible without waiting for future revenues that might never materialize? Thus, measuring profit according to accounting principles is fraught with judgment calls that can materially affect an enterprise's bottom line. Indeed, it is entirely possible for two accountants to look at the same set of numbers and arrive at entirely different conclusions on net income. Nor should we underestimate the powerful incentives for executives — think stock options and bonuses — to overstate current net income.

Policy makers responsible for the development of tax law are fully aware of the variances that occur from discretionary judgments. Thus, we see many provisions in the *Income Tax Act* that provide for a particular and specific method of measuring profit, regardless of accounting principles. In almost all cases, the Act prescribes a method of measuring profit that is more onerous than that allowed under accounting principles. This is understandable. Given a choice, why would the tax collector prescribe a method of accounting that produces a better result for the taxpayer?

K. ACCOUNTING STATEMENTS

Financial statements provide information about an economic entity's financial performance, economic resources and legal obligations to investors, creditors, management, tax authorities, and other regulators. Thus, we can use financial statements to assess management's performance, predict the entity's ability to generate future cash flows to meet obligations, assess the return to shareholders, and measure tax liabilities.

Two statements, the Balance Sheet and the Income Statement, are closely inter-related and must be read together in order to present a complete and meaningful picture of the profitability and solvency of a business. The Statement of Comprehensive Income provides additional information that IFRS requires.

As an illustration, assume that A and B opened a retail business on 1 January, Year 1 with each person contributing $2,500, and a bank loan of $10,000. The opening balance sheet *as at* 1 January, Year 1, would appear as follows:

Balance Sheet

As at 1 January, Year 1

Assets		Liabilities and Equity	
Cash	$15,000	Bank loan	$10,000
		Owner's equity:	
		Capital A	2,500
		Capital B	2,500
	$15,000		$15,000

We observe that the Balance Sheet balances: the left side of the statement that lists all the property owned by the business is *exactly equal* to the right side of the statement that lists its sources of financing. In other words, the statement informs the reader as to *what* the business owns (assets), and discloses *how* it financed the assets (liabilities and equity). Hence, the above Balance Sheet informs any reader without further explanation that the business entity (the retail business) owned $15,000 of property (assets) as at 1 January, Year 1, and that it held it in the form of cash. Further, it informs the reader that two individuals and an outsider financed the firm from two sources — one external (bank loan $10,000) and the other internal (owner's equity $5,000).

L. DOUBLE-ENTRY BOOKKEEPING

The mention of double-entry bookkeeping strikes terror in the hearts of most people. The whole idea of debits and credits is a chilling experience, even for grown adults who can be reduced to tears after a five-minute discourse on the subject. Practically speaking, however, double-entry bookkeeping simply means that every transaction is recorded for accounting purposes from two perspectives: the use of funds and the source of financing. Thus, by definition, since every transaction is recorded from the same two perspectives, the result must be that the sum of all assets will exactly equal the sum of all financing. This is a metaphysical truth.

That is enough of bookkeeping for a lifetime. The only point that we should note is that even balanced books can be completely wrong. Balancing is simply a mathematical by-product of the system. Wrong and fraudulent books will still balance. Indeed, it would be a foolish corporate fraudster who would not first balance the books. A balance sheet out of balance is a red flag. But a balanced balance sheet should not be a sedative.

The following transactions illustrate the operation of the fundamental Balance Sheet accounting equation $A = L + E$:

On 2 January, Year 1, the business leased office space at an annual rent of $6,000 and pays two months' rent on that date.

Balance Sheet
As at 2 January, Year 1

Assets		Liabilities and Equity	
Cash	$14,000	Bank loan	$10,000
Prepaid rent	$1,000	Owner's equity:	
		Capital A	2,500
		Capital B	2,500
	$15,000		$15,000

Here, the business exchanged one type of asset — cash — for another asset — prepaid rent. The prepaid rent is an asset because it is an unexpired cost as at 2 January. It will become an expense with the passage of time.

On 4 January, Year 1, the business acquired office furniture at a cost of $3,000, paying $1,500 in cash with a promise to pay the balance in 90 days.

Balance Sheet
As at 4 January, Year 1

Assets		Liabilities and Equity	
Cash	$12,500	Accounts payable	$1,500
Prepaid rent	1,000	Bank loan	10,000
Office furniture	3,000	Owner's equity:	
		Capital A	2,500
		Capital B	2,500
	$16,500		$16,500

Here, the business acquires an asset — furniture — and finances it by paying with another asset (cash) and by credit (accounts payable).

On 15 January, Year 1, the business hired two employees at a monthly salary of $1,000 each, and paid their salaries on 31 January, Year 1.

Balance Sheet
As at 31 January, Year 1

Assets		Liabilities and Equity	
Cash	$11,500	Accounts payable	$1,500
Prepaid rent	500	Bank loan	10,000
Office furniture	3,000	Owner's equity:	
		Capital A	1,750
		Capital B	1,750
	$15,000		$15,000

The points to note in the 15 January Balance Sheet are: First, the prepaid rent is now only $500 because one month has passed and the rent for January is now an expired cost or an expense. Second, cash is $1,000 lower than before because the business paid $500 to each of two employees for half a month's salary. Third, retained earnings has dropped by $1,500 because the business has incurred expenses:

Rent	$500
Salaries	1,000
Total	$1,500

without any corresponding sales income.

Cash has gone up by $4,000 because the business had cash sales of $6,000 and salary expense of $2,000. Note that by the end of February, all of the prepaid rent has now expired and become an expense.

During the month of February, Year 1, the business sold merchandise and collected $6,000 cash, again paying its staff $2,000 in salary.

Balance Sheet
As at 28 February, Year 1

Assets		Liabilities and Equity	
Cash	$15,500	Accounts payable	$1,500
Office furniture	3,000	Bank loan	10,000
		Owner's equity:	
		Capital A	3,500
		Capital B	3,500
	$18,500		$18,500

Each of the transactions described has been recorded using the fundamental equation: A = L + E. The reader sees that the business owns property (assets) that cost $18,500, now held in two forms, cash and office furniture, and that the firm is financed, as at 28 February, Year 1, by outsiders to the extent of $11,500, with insiders (owner's equity) providing the balance of $7,000. The balance sheet does not, however, disclose any information as to *how* and *why* the owners' interest in the business increased from $5,000 (2 January) to $7,000 (28 February) during the two months of operations.

The balance sheet tells only one-half of the story. Based on the balance sheet alone it would be difficult, if not impossible, for any user to assess the profitability of the business. Should the owners, A and B, for example, be required to pay income tax on the increase in their equity of $2,000, or on some other amount? We find the answer in the income statement.

The purpose of the income statement is to disclose *how* a business has performed between two successive points in time. In this sense, it is a connecting link between successive balance sheets. Whereas a balance sheet informs a reader *where* a business stands as at a given time, an income statement reveals *how* the business moved from its opening position to the closing balance sheet.

Continuing with the previous illustration, the income statement reveals the following information:

Income Statement

For the *Two Months* ended 28 February, Year 1

Sales Revenue		$6,000
Expenses		
Wages	$3,000	
Rent	1,000	
Net Income:		($4,000)
		$2,000

Allocation of Net Income
To A at 50% of $2,000 = $1,000
To B at 50% of $2,000 = $1,000

This statement now informs the reader *how* the owner's equity increased by $2,000 from 2 January to 28 February. Specifically, the business generated revenues of $6,000 and expended $4,000 in the process of generating those revenues, leaving an excess of revenues over expenses (net income) of $2,000. Thus, the purpose of the income statement is to match revenues earned with expenses incurred to generate the revenue. The statement usually explains the change in the owners' equity between successive points in time.

M. ACCOUNTING METHODS

Accounting principles and conventions deal with the methodology behind the task of matching revenues and expenses.

To this point, we have used the term "income" to denote the excess of revenues earned over expenses incurred to generate those revenues. Hence, in one sense income is an increase in net wealth; conversely, a loss is a decrease in net wealth. This definition is terse and obvious but mathematically demonstrable. The essence of the concept is thereby reduced to "gain during an interval of time." "Gain" is the *sine qua non* of income. While this definition satisfies the purpose of conceptual explanation, it is necessary to adapt it to use it in the preparation of financial statements.

N. TIME INTERVALS

As a preliminary matter, it is essential to select the appropriate "interval of time" between successive financial statements. For no other reason than that of administrative convenience, we conventionally prepare financial statements at least annually. Thus, annual financial statements for external reporting and tax purposes are now, with limited exceptions, the general rule. It is the statutory requirement of annual reporting that gives rise to several income measurement problems.

O. CASH VS. ACCRUAL ACCOUNTING

The first of the measurement problems is to determine whether we should prepare financial statements on a "cash basis" or on an "accrual basis." The principal distinction between the two methods of accounting arises in connection with the treatment of accounts receivable and payable. Accounts receivable from customers and employers are not included in income under the cash method until the entity actually receives the cash. In contrast, under the accrual method, we must report income when services are completed and billed, regardless of when the customer actually pays the account. Thus, the distinction between the two is one of timing.

In cash basis accounting, we record business transactions at the time, and in the accounting period, when the business receives the cash or disburses the amount. Assuming an accounting period of 1 January to 31 December and the sale of merchandise on 15 December, Year 1 for $3,000 with payment received on 15 January, Year 2, a cash basis business would record and report the $3,000 revenue in Year 2. Further assume that the cost of the merchandise to the business was $1,000, paid in cash at time of purchase on 1 December, Year 1. A cash basis business would record and report the cost of merchandise sold in Year 1. The effect of the purchase and sale of merchandise would be reflected in the income statements of the business as follows:

(Cash Basis)			
	Year 1	Year 2	Combined
Sales Revenue	$0	$3,000	$3,000
Cost of Merchandise Sold	(1,000)	0	(1,000)
Net Income (Loss)	$(1,000)	$3,000	$2,000

Regardless of the accounting method, the *combined* net income of the business in the forgoing circumstances would always amount to $2,000.

The disadvantage of the cash basis method lies, however, in the mismatching in a particular accounting (fiscal) period of revenues earned and expenses incurred to earn those revenues. Thus, Year 1 shows a net loss of $1,000 due to the combined effect of early expense recognition and delayed revenue recognition. A year later the statement shows net income of $3,000 by ignoring the earlier expense write-off. Each of Years 1 and 2 viewed in isolation present a distorted result of the underlying business transaction: an economic increase of $2,000 in net wealth.

We said earlier that we can determine net income with absolute accuracy when the reporting period for financial statements covers the entire life of a business. The selection of a time period shorter than the life of the business, changes the task from income determination to estimation of net income. The sacrifice in mathematical accuracy, however, is well justified by the regulatory and business convenience that results from timely financial statements.

In most situations, cash basis accounting distorts the financial statements of an entity and conceals the true impact of business transactions. A notable exception is in the reporting of employment income, for tax purposes. Individuals must report employment income on a cash basis. This requirement results from a balancing of the enhanced administrative convenience to the employee, the employer, and the Canada Revenue Agency, and the minimal distortion that occurs in measuring employment income on a cash basis.

In contrast with the cash basis of accounting, accrual accounting recognizes revenue when it is realized, and expenses are reported in the same time period as the revenues for which they were incurred.

The accrual basis is premised on the rationale that reporting revenues earned and expenses incurred in the same accounting period provides a better "matching," and that such matching more accurately depicts the underlying business transaction. Using the same figures as in the previous example, an income statement prepared on an accrual basis would disclose the following:

(Accrual Basis)

	Year 1	Year 2	Combined
Sales Revenue	$3000	$0	3000
Cost of Merchandise Sold	(1000)	0	(1000)
Net Income (Loss)	$(2000)	$0	$2000

Although the combined net incomes of the two years is the same in both the cash basis and accrual basis methods of reporting, the latter method more accurately reflects the increase in net wealth in each period. (The outstanding accounts receivable of $3,000 as at 31 December, Year 1, represent debt that increased net wealth.)

Regardless of when the accounting entity actually receives cash, accrual accounting requires the reporting of revenue in the fiscal period in which the entity realizes it. The rationale that debt, as much as cash, represents an increase in wealth is one that is particularly appropriate to any modern economy. At the same time, the accrual method requires that expenses incurred to earn revenue be matched with corresponding revenues earned in the same fiscal period.

The accrual method generally also prevents tax deferral. For example, if a person pays five years' worth of lease payments in advance, the lump sum is capitalized and written off over a five-year period. Similarly, the lessor will treat the prepaid rents as an asset and recognize only one-fifth of the lump sum in each of the five succeeding years.

Unfortunately, tax and commercial accounting do not always arrive at the same solution. Tax accounting puts the lessor on the cash method and compels him or her to recognize the full five-year lump sum payment in the year that he or she receives it. The lessee, however, is not entitled to deduct the lump sum in the year that he or she pays it, but must spread it out over five years. This asymmetric policy works to the advantage of the government and against the taxpayer.

P. TESTS FOR REVENUE RECOGNITION

The important task remains to determine the criteria for selection of a given time when we may consider revenue to be realized, and thus recognized as earned, in a particular fiscal period.

Two tests determine the appropriate time period for revenue recognition. First, the accounting entity must have substantially completed the economic activity concerned with the earning process. Second, there should be some objective measurement available. Thus, we should only recognize revenue when major uncertainties in respect of its measurement are substantially resolved.

When one examines these criteria it is easy to see the rationale for selection of point of sale as the most usual time of revenue recognition. In most merchandising and service businesses, the point of sale represents completion of the major portion of economic activity. In these situations the point of sale is assumed to be the primary economic event and it provides an objective measurement yardstick, namely, sale price.

At the same time, a sale generates a flow of assets that converts inventory into accounts receivable. Concurrently with the objective measurement of revenue, related expenses are determinable with reasonable certainty, and any remaining uncertainty is reduced, for pragmatic purposes, to an acceptable level. Finally, the point of sale is clear and determinable. For all these reasons, time of sale is considered to be the point of revenue recognition in most business transactions. Note, however, that point of sale for recognizing revenue and passage of legal title do not necessarily coincide.

Q. ACCOUNTING ADJUSTMENTS

Let us assume that X Widgets is preparing its accounting statements for its fiscal year ending 31 October, Year 1. In order to comply with the matching principle, we must make some special accounting entries to implement the system of accruing expenses and revenue earned. In the preceding section we saw the entries we make when an invoice is received or rendered, even though no cash changes hands. At the year-end, we make some special entries to reflect expense or income that has accrued but as to which no transaction is currently taking place. These entries are designed to adjust the "timing" and recognition of expenses and revenue. A further group of entries may also be made to adjust the "measurement" of revenues or expenses.

1) The "Timing" Adjustments

Some transactions that give rise to normal accounting entries represent expense or revenue for a period that straddles the year-end. Assume the following about X Widgets:

1) On 1 July, Year 1 it paid a $900 premium for insurance for one year to 30 June, Year 2.
2) Its employees are paid monthly on the 15th of the month and the monthly salary expense is $8,000.
3) It owns a bond that pays $1,200 interest each 30 November.
4) It rents an unused part of the land adjacent to its building to a company that parks its trucks there. The annual rent is $1,200, paid each 31 January and 31 July in advance.

To avoid a misstatement of the expenses and revenues for the year ending 31 October, Year 1, four adjustments are necessary:

1) A reduction in insurance expense to reflect the fact that two-thirds of the insurance benefit paid for in July still remains.
2) An increase in salary expense to reflect the one-half month's labour already enjoyed by the business, but which will not be paid for until 15 November.
3) An increase in investment income to reflect the eleven-twelfths of the bond interest accrued to 31 October.
4) A decrease in rental income to reflect the receipt of three months' rent not yet earned.

The following four entries reflect the adjustments:

1) Insurance expense will be reduced by $600 and a balance sheet asset, "prepaid expense," will be set up.
2) Salary expense will be increased by $4,000 and a balance sheet liability, "salary expense payable," will be set up.
3) Investment income will be increased by $1,100 and a balance sheet asset, "accrued bond interest," will be set up.
4) Rental income will be reduced by $300 and a balance sheet liability, "rent received in advance," will be set up.

2) The "Measurement" Adjustments

It is consistent with accounting conservatism to recognize, at the year-end, that the value of some of the business assets may be over-stated and therefore, that business profitability may be exaggerated.

One of the most obvious adjustments to correct for this danger is an allowance for doubtful debts. If X Widgets shows $20,000 in accounts receivable at the year-end, it may well be realistic to pre-dict that some of the debts will never be collected. On that assump-tion, we reduce the balance sheet asset, "Accounts Receivable," by an amount (referred to as an allowance for doubtful accounts) that would also reduce the current year's income.

A business may also face contingencies and hazards, which a careful accountant and a prudent business manager would like to provide for by making similar "allowances." All of them will have the effect of reducing the statement of current profitability.

One adjustment that must be mentioned is the allowance for depreciation. In our earlier hypothetical situation, City Dairy will experience, over five years, a cost of $500,000 in respect of its fleet of trucks. To allocate this cost appropriately in order to match expense and revenue, it may reflect a depreciation expense of $100,000 at the end of each year. This is essentially a "timing" adjustment de-signed to spread a large cost over the appropriate accounting per-iods. There is, however, an element of uncertainty involved: both the assumed useful life of the trucks and their assumed salvage value are based on estimates.

R. OTHER ACCOUNTING METHODS

Some businesses involve such unusual features that the standard accrual basis of accounting fails to achieve an appropriate matching of expenses and revenues. For example, some businesses involve a high volume of sales on terms that call for instalment payments over an extended period of time. Such a business may have significant costs associated with the selling activity but, notionally, a large "profit margin" as judged by the difference between selling price and cost of sales. The incidence of uncollectable accounts in such a business, however, is usually higher than for most other businesses. At best, the accounts are not "receivable" on a current basis, but are going to be received over a much longer period than is usual for businesses generally. This kind of business might adopt the instalment method of accounting which does not recognize the accounts receivable in revenue. In effect, the business uses a hybrid accounting system, which recognizes all expenses except the cost of goods sold on an accrual basis, but recognizes revenue on a cash basis by ignoring its accounts receivable.

Other businesses carry on long-term projects that may involve several years' work to complete. Payment for work completed may be by way of advances or there may be significant delays in receiving payment; and there may be a holdback to satisfy liens or to give the payer a guaranteed opportunity to judge whether the work is satisfactory. Again, because of the difficulty of appropriately matching expenses and revenues, such a business may use a "completed contract" method of accounting.

S. THE BALANCE SHEET

The balance sheet of an entity tells us what it owns and how it is financed. The financing side of the balance sheet — liabilities and owners' equity — shows the interests of creditors and shareholders in the entity. This relationship is particularly important in corporate law as creditors rank ahead of shareholders in their claims against corporate assets. Corporate law determines the accounting for capital accounts and their presentation on the balance sheet.

Hence, lawyers must understand both the legal and accounting aspects of equity capital. Transactions in corporate capital also have significant tax implications.

As between creditors, there can be a hierarchy of claims and priorities. For example, a secured creditor will stand ahead of unsecured creditors. Within the subclass of secured creditors, there may be further refinements in the priority of each group. Some, for example, may hold first mortgages as security; others second mortgages; and others third mortgages. The balance sheet will show the general hierarchy of claims on corporate assets.

Shareholders are the residual owners of a company. Shareholders, however, may also have their own hierarchy and priorities within their group. Some, for example, may have priority to assets upon liquidation; others may have priority in claims on dividends; others may have "super voting" rights. The balance sheet and notes will generally reveal the relevant ranking of shareholders according to their priority on corporate assets. Thus, lawyers are interested in the financial and legal structure of claims on corporate assets

The financial structure of a corporation ultimately depends upon two principal factors:

- Access to funds; and
- The cost of available funds.

We can fund a corporation in several ways. The conventional sources of corporate funding are:

- Share (equity) capital;
- Debt capital;
- Retained earnings;
- Off-balance-sheet financial instruments (warrants, options, leases, etc.); and
- Government grants and subsidies.

The method that one uses to finance a corporation depends upon the type of corporation, its size, access to capital markets, and qualification for government programs.

Small businesses generally access debt, share capital, retained earnings, and government grants. Large, publicly listed corporations with access to capital markets can also issue derivatives such as rights and warrants.

Market and tax considerations influence the cost of funds. Thus, where a corporation has a choice between alternative sources of funding, its decision to opt for one source over another, or to balance between different sources of funds, may depend upon income tax considerations. For example, a corporation may determine the ratio of its debt to equity capital (debt/equity ratio) by tax considerations — such as the residence of shareholders, which determines the withholding tax rate, or the thin capitalization rules,[9] which determine the deductibility of interest expense for tax purposes.

---

9   *Income Tax Act*, subs 18(4).

Chapter VII: Reports on Financial Statements

A. GENERAL COMMENT

Reports on financial statements are an integral part of the verification and accountability of financial statements. Even if not legally required to produce formal reports and financial statements, many companies will prepare such statements for accounting to their proprietors and creditors. Thus, such reports are referred to as "assurance reports."

Financial statements may be audited or unaudited. In either case, the auditor may express an opinion — unrestricted or restricted — on the statements. The degree to which readers of the statements can assure themselves of the integrity of the financial statements depends, in part, upon the nature of the report prepared. Audits are intended to enhance the degree of confidence of users of the financial statements.[1] The auditors' report is a key communication item that, although brief, contains valuable information. The report is the foundation on which many legal actions proceed.

An auditor is an independent person called upon to review the enterprise, its processes, and internal controls, and express an opinion on the financial statements. Corporate and securities statutes require publicly held corporations to appoint auditors, and file

---

1   See, generally, Canadian Institute of Chartered Accountants, *CICA Handbook — Assurance*, loose-leaf (Toronto: Canadian Institute of Chartered Accountants, 2010), section 200 [*CICA Handbook — Assurance*].

audited financial statements with the appropriate regulatory authorities. Section 162 of the *Canada Business Corporations Act*, for example, requires the shareholders of every distributing corporation to appoint an auditor at their first annual meeting of shareholders and at each successive annual meeting thereafter. Section 163 allows non-distributing corporations not to appoint an auditor. Section 167 of the CBCA allows a court to appoint and fix the remuneration of an auditor if the corporation does not have one and a shareholder applies to have one appointed.

Similarly, section 78 of the *Securities Act* (Ontario) requires every reporting issuer to file annually audited comparative financial statements within 140 days of the end of its financial year.

The auditor has considerable statutory rights and powers. For example, he or she is entitled under section 168 CBCA to receive notice of every meeting of shareholders and to attend, at the expense of the corporation, at such meetings and be heard on matters relating to his or her duties. Any shareholder can give notice to the corporation and have the auditor attend at a shareholder meeting at the expense of the corporation.

There are three types of reports on financial statements:

1) Auditors' reports;
2) Review engagement reports; and
3) Notice to reader reports.

In this chapter we describe briefly the nature of these reports and the degree of prudent reliance that one can place on them in analyzing financial statements.

B. AUDITORS' REPORTS

The overall objective of the auditor is to obtain reasonable assurance that the financial statements as a whole are free from material misstatement.

The first point to observe is that the financial statements belong to management. The auditor reports on management's financial statements. The auditors' report belongs to the author/auditor. This is made quite clear in the general representation letter that management signs for the auditors and in the body of the report itself.

C. GENERAL REPRESENTATION LETTER

The following is an example of a general representation letter that an auditor would expect from an audit client.

> Duggan Inc
> Licensed Public Accountants, LLP
> Toronto, ON
> Canada
>
> Dear ...
>
> In connection with your audit of the financial statements of Duggan Inc as of 30 September 20-2 and for the year then ended, for the purpose of expressing an opinion as to whether the financial statements present fairly, in all material respects, the financial position, results of operations and changes in financial position of Duggan Inc in conformity with IFRS and Canadian generally accepted accounting principles, we confirm, to the best of our knowledge and belief, the following representations made to you during your audit:
>
> 1. We are responsible for the fair presentation in the financial statements of financial position, results of operations and changes in financial position in conformity with generally accepted accounting principles.
> 2. We have made available to you all financial records and related data.
> 3. There have been no:
>   a. Irregularities involving management or employees who have significant roles in the internal control structure.
>   b. Irregularities involving other employees that could have a material effect on the financial statements.
>   c. Communications from regulatory agencies concerning non-compliance with, or deficiencies in, financial re-

porting practices that could have a material effect on the financial statements.

4. We have no plans or intentions that may materially affect the carrying value or classification of assets and liabilities.

5. The following have been disclosed to you and properly recorded or disclosed in the financial statements:

   a. Related-party transactions and related amounts receivable or payable, including sales, purchases, loans, transfers, leasing arrangements, and guarantees.

   b. Arrangements with financial institutions involving restrictions on cash balances and line-of-credit or similar arrangements.

   c. Agreements to repurchase assets previously sold.

   d. All financial instruments, including those with off-balance-sheet risk (such as swaps, forwards, and futures), as required under generally accepted accounting principles.

   e. The nature of our operations, that the preparation of financial statements requires the use of estimates, and when applicable, specific information regarding significant estimates embodied in the financial statements.

6. There are no:

   a. Violations or possible violations of laws or regulations (other than those previously disclosed) whose effects should be considered for disclosure in the financial statements or as a basis for recording a loss contingency.

   b. Other material liabilities or gain or loss contingencies that are required to be accrued or disclosed.

7. There are no unasserted claims or assessments that our lawyers have advised us are probable of assertion and must be disclosed.

8. The accounting records underlying the financial statements accurately and fairly reflect, in reasonable detail, the transactions of the Company.

9. Duggan Inc has satisfactory title to all owned assets, and there are no liens or encumbrances on such assets nor has any asset been pledged.

10. Provision has been made for any material loss to be sustained in the fulfilment of, or from inability to fulfil, any commitments.

11. We have complied with all aspects of contractual agreements that would have a material effect on the financial statements in the event of noncompliance.

12. No events have occurred subsequent to the balance sheet date that would require adjustment to, or disclosure in, the financial statements.

Per: ....

Chief Executive Officer
Chief Financial Officer
Duggan Inc
November 10, 20-2

D. STRUCTURE OF AUDIT REPORT

There is a clear distinction between ownership of the financial statements and the report thereon. The financial statements belong to the company and its management.

Based on representations by management to the auditor, the auditor will conduct his or her audit and report on the financial statements. The audit report belongs to the auditor and he or she is responsible for its contents.

The auditors' report comprises five segments, all of which appear on one page. The five components are as follows:[2]

1) Addressee;
2) Scope of opinion;
3) Generally accepted auditing standards;
4) Opinion; and
5) Date of report.

---

2   See, generally, *CICA Handbook — Assurance*, section 700.

The one-page report contains a lot of information. The opinion paragraph is the most important in the report. All of the paragraphs preceding it are essentially exoneration clauses crafted to protect the audit firm.

E. EXAMPLE OF AUDITORS' REPORT

To the Shareholder of Duggan Inc

We have audited the accompanying financial statements of Duggan Inc, which comprise the statements of financial position as at 30 September 20-2 and 20-1, and the statements of income, comprehensive income, changes in equity, and cash flows for the years ended 30 September 20-2 and 20-1 and a summary of significant accounting policies and other explanatory information.

Management's Responsibility for the Financial Statements
Management is responsible for the preparation and fair presentation of these financial statements in accordance with International Financial Reporting Standards, and for such internal control as management determines is necessary to enable the preparation of financial statements that are free from material misstatement, whether due to fraud or error.

Auditor's Responsibility
Our responsibility is to express an opinion on these financial statements based on our audits. We conducted our audits in accordance with Canadian generally accepted auditing standards and IFRS. Those standards require that we comply with ethical requirements and plan and perform the audit to obtain reasonable assurance about whether the financial statements are free from material misstatement.

An audit involves performing procedures to obtain audit evidence about the amounts and disclosures in the financial statements. The procedures selected depend on the auditor's judgment, including the assessment of the risks of material misstatement of the financial statements, whether due to fraud or error. In making those risk assessments, the auditor considers internal control relevant to the entity's preparation and fair presentation of the financial statements in order to design audit procedures that are appropriate in the circumstances, but not for the purpose of expressing an opinion on the effectiveness of the entity's internal control. An audit also includes evaluating the appropriateness of accounting policies used and the reasonableness of accounting estimates made by management, as well as evaluating the overall presentation of the financial statements.

We believe that the audit evidence we have obtained in our audits is sufficient and appropriate to provide a basis for our audit opinion.

Opinion

In our opinion, the financial statements present fairly, in all material respects, the financial position of Duggan Inc as at 30 September 20-2 and 20-1, and its financial performance and its cash flows for the years ended 30 September 20-2 and 20-1 in accordance with Canadian generally accepted accounting principles and International Financial Reporting Standards.

Chartered Accountants
Licensed Public Accountants
10 November 20-2

The point to observe is the boilerplate language of the opinion, which is devoid of commentary. The auditor is not an insurer and his or her report does not constitute a guarantee of absolute accuracy.[3] Hence, it is important to understand the limitations of the auditors' report and the degree to which one may rely upon it.

The management representation letter that Duggan Inc signed illustrates the types of representations that companies make to their auditors. The representation letter covers various aspects of the corporation's financial and business operations. It is a comprehensive document of exonerations that audit firms insist upon before signing off on any opinion. An audit firm will rely upon the general represen-

---

3   *CICA Handbook*, section 5135.15.

tation letter as its first line of defence in any litigation that shareholders or management may file against the firm. Note, particularly, the responsibility for the fair presentation of the financial statements in compliance with GAAP and IFRS is squarely on the shoulders of the company. Management will certify that the financial statements include amounts based on its best estimates and judgment. Thus, we repeat: accounting is as much art as it is a science.

Management will also certify that it maintains a system of internal accounting controls to provide reasonable assurance that assets are safeguarded and that transactions are authorized, recorded and reported properly. Further, that the internal audit department reviews these accounting controls on an ongoing basis and reports its findings and recommendations to management and the Audit, Finance, and Risk Management Committee of the Board of Directors.

1) Addressee

The report starts out by identifying the party to whom it is addressed. In the case of Duggan Inc, it clearly states that it is addressed to the shareholders of the company. In theory, identification of the addressee determines the scope of liability of the audit firm. It is clear that the auditor is the auditor for the shareholders.

Unfortunately, the Court decision in *Hercules* severely limited the liability of auditors to shareholders on policy grounds.[4] The decision protects auditors at the expense of investors. As the events of 1990 through 2013 show, however, it is the investors, employees, and creditors who bear the brunt of auditor protection policies developed by the courts.

2) Scope

The next component identifies the scope of the auditors' opinion. The scope paragraph states:

---

4   See the decision of the Supreme Court of Canada in *Hercules Managements Ltd v Ernst & Young*, [1997] 2 SCR 165 [*Hercules*].

We have audited the balance sheets of Duggan Inc ("Company") as at 30 September 20-2 and 20-1, and the statements of income, retained earnings (deficit) and cash flows then ended. These financial statements are the responsibility of the Company's management. Our responsibility is to express an opinion on these financial statements based on our audit.

Note again, the clear and unequivocal statement that the auditor makes in placing the responsibility for the financial statements on the shoulders of corporate management.

3) Generally Accepted Auditing Standards (GAAS)

GAAS defines the scope of the report, which states:

We conducted our audits in accordance with Canadian generally accepted auditing standards. Those statements require that we plan and perform an audit to obtain reasonable assurance whether the financial statements are free of material misstatement. An audit includes examining, on a test basis, evidence supporting the amounts and disclosures in the financial statements. An audit also includes assessment of the accounting principles used and significant estimates made by management, as well as, evaluating the overall financial statement presentation.

The quality and integrity of the auditors' opinion depends upon the scope of the work that he or she performs in order to arrive at the opinion.

4) Opinions

The objective of an audit is to obtain *reasonable* assurance whether the financial statements are free of *material* misstatement. Having identified the party to whom the opinion is addressed and the scope of the work performed, the auditor's report will state an opinion.

Typically, audit opinions are terse boilerplate statements. Where the auditor gives a qualified (modified) opinion, he or she should articulate any scope limitations and disclaimers on particular aspects of the financial statements. The auditor may also address concerns with the "going concern" assumption. There are four types of audit opinions:

1) Unqualified (Unmodified);
2) Qualified (Modified);
3) Adverse; and
4) Disclaimed.

The following is a clean, unqualified (unmodified) opinion:

> In our opinion, these financial statements present fairly, in all material respects, the financial position of the Company as at 30 September 20-2 and 20-1, and the results of its operations and its cash flows for the year then ended in accordance with Canadian GAAP and International Financial Reporting Standards.

Note the key terms: "present fairly" and "in all material respects." The audit report is not a guarantee. It merely assures fair presentation.[5]

5) Date of Report

The date of the report serves several purposes. First, it tells us how relevant the report is by identifying the time that has lapsed since the auditor issued it. The more stale-dated the report, the less relevant it is for analysis. Second, the date tells us the effective date for disclosure of contingent liabilities — that is, liabilities that potentially exist between the year-end of the financial statements and the disclosure date of the audit report.[6] In the case of Duggan Inc, for example, the auditors' report is dated 10 November 20-2. This

---

5   In an earlier era, the opinion paragraph used to use the words that the financial statements presented a "true and correct" view of the financials. The words "true and correct" leave the impression of a much more accurate compilation of financial data than is intended.

6   See *CICA Handbook — Assurance*, sections 580 and 200.

means that all contingent liabilities between 30 September and 10 November must be disclosed in the Notes to the financial statements. Third, the date effectively frames the time limits of liability for the report.

F. QUALIFIED REPORTS

As its name implies, a qualified (modified) report limits some aspects of the audit opinion and is less than an unqualified (clean) opinion. The auditor will express a qualified opinion when, having obtained sufficient appropriate audit evidence, concludes that there are material misstatements, but that they are not pervasive.[7] A qualified report will start with the same introductory and scope paragraphs, as in any audit opinion. It will, however, disclose the nature of the qualification by saying: "In our opinion, except for the effects of (reason for the reservation) discussed in the preceding paragraph, these financial statements present fairly, etc."

One must review carefully the reservation and qualification. It may pertain to a relatively small issue or a substantial and significant aspect of the corporation's operations. If there are several qualifications and reservations, their cumulative effect may render the entire report meaningless and unreliable.

G. REVIEW ENGAGEMENTS

Going down the hierarchy of auditors' reports, the next rung on the ladder is the review engagement. A review engagement limits the scope and work of the auditor. The auditor will describe the limits of the engagement as follows:

> We have reviewed the balance sheet of "X" Company as at December 20-2 and the statements of income, retained earnings, and changes in financial position for the year then ended. Our review was made in accordance with generally accepted standards

---

7   See *ibid*, section 705.6.

for review engagements and accordingly consisted primarily of enquiry, analytical procedures and discussion related to information supplied to us by the Company.

Review engagements typically do not require testing of the corporation's financial records but rely on enquiry, analysis of procedures, and discussions with management.

The auditor will disclaim any audit opinion by stating:

A review does not constitute an audit and consequently we do not express an audit opinion on these financial statements.

Despite the reservations, review engagements do have some value in that they provide a form of negative assurance to the reader, such as:

Based upon our review, nothing has come to our attention that causes us to believe that these financial statements are not, in all material respects, in accordance with generally accepted accounting principles.

Thus, unlike the qualified opinion, which provides positive assurance that the statements are prepared in accordance with GAAP and IFRS and present fairly the financial state of affairs, a review engagement tells us that the auditor did not see anything unfavourable in the limited work that he or she performed on the corporation's books and records.

H. NOTICE TO READER REPORTS

Compilations are at the bottom of the hierarchy of opinions. A compilation does not require any audit and does not meet even with the limited aspects of review engagements. Compilations are simply a simulation of data with a notice to the reader, such as:

We have compiled the balance sheet of "X" Company as at 31 December 20-2 and the statements of income, retained earnings and changes in financial position for the period then ended from information provided by management. We have not audited, reviewed or otherwise attempt to verify the accuracy or completeness of such information. Readers are cautioned that these statements may be not be appropriate for their purpose.

Notice to reader statements following a compilation engagement are of minimal value to any person who is an outsider of the corporation. Thus, notice to reader statements for external users are sometimes characterized as "burn before you read" statements. They may, however, have some value to the owners of a business who are actively involved in, and have substantial knowledge of, the business and its financial position.

I.   RECENT DEVELOPMENTS

Traditional audit reports are brief boilerplate documents that cast minimal light on issues of interest to most users. The IASB has published "Invitation to Comment: Improving the Audit Report" (June 2012) that suggests various improvements and enhancements.

The first is that the opinion should be the first paragraph of the auditors' report. This is hardly a radical proposal, since it is the most important part of the report.

Another proposal to highlight "auditor commentary" and highlight outstanding litigation, valuation of financial instruments and internal control, and management's assessment of the going concern assumption faces opposition from the large audit firms. A less than complete endorsement, for example, of the going concern assumption may well be the catalyst that drives a company under and exposes the audit firm to litigation. Audit firms do not want to take on the added risk of lawsuits.

J.   SOME PROBLEM AREAS

1)   Write-Downs

Write-downs occur when costs and values diverge and current values fall below cost. Thus, we write down assets in order to preserve the tenet of conservatism. For example, the traditional view in accounting is that long-lived assets, such as property, plant, and equipment, should be recorded at cost less accumulated depreciation, unless they are permanently impaired and their value has declined below their net book value. In such circumstances, a company may reduce its long-lived assets to their fair market value by taking a charge against earnings so as to reflect the lower and more conservative value. The difficulty with write-downs is in determining when the company should do so and the effect that it will have on earnings, stock prices, and stock options.

Nortel was a classic example of delusion and despair in recognizing its financial picture. Nortel's operating profit for fiscal year 2000 was US $1.73 billion. The CEO of the company, John Roth, said on 25 June 2000 that Nortel is "firing on all cylinders."

On 8 September 2000, the *National Post* reported that Mr Roth said: "It isn't that Nortel is overvalued, its maybe that everything else is undervalued." By 17 November 2000, Nortel's shares plunged by 8.9 percent on rumours that it was losing business to rivals. Nortel called the claim "nonsense." In a speech to the Canadian Club on 19 February 2001, Mr Roth said: "We don't have any control over the stock prices. We are just running a terrific business here."

On 21 April 2001, Mr Roth went on to say: "I'm not going to pretend we grew efficiently. You don't grow that fast in elegant fashion." By 15 June 2001, Nortel's tone had deteriorated from exuberance to despair. Mr Roth said: "We have had better times. Is this the end? God, we sure hope so, this is a brutal experience."

Nortel's financial profile had changed remarkably from a year earlier. The company had an operating loss of US $1.5 billion and total losses of US $19.2 billion. It took restructuring charges of $12.3 billion, $2 billion in amortization charges, and $959 million on receivables, inventory, and investments. It spent $830 million on 20,000 job cuts and announced 10,000 more job cuts to come in the future.

In 2012, three of its senior executives, charged with fraud and accounting manipulation ("earnings management") to perk up their bonuses, went on trial in the Superior Court of Ontario.

2) Restructuring Charges

"Restructuring" is one of those fluid accounting terms that can cover a multitude of events and changes in business operations — some voluntary; some imposed. Restructuring charges are write-downs that clean up the balance sheet and can improve future earnings. They also remove redundant assets from the balance sheet.

Restructuring charges or write-downs generally arise when corporations write off excessive goodwill resulting from extravagant acquisitions at inflated prices. For example, in 2013, Barrick Gold Corp, the world's biggest gold miner, wrote down US $4.2 billion, most of which related to its copper mine in Zambia.

Restructuring charges can also accumulate and have dramatic effects on the financial statements. For example, restructuring charges for American Telephone & Telegraph from 1986 to 1996 amounted to US $14.2 billion, which exceeded its total net income of $10.3 billion during the those years.[8]

3) Goodwill

Goodwill is the premium that a company pays over the fair value of assets that it purchases from another company. The premium that the purchaser pays is supposed to reflect the anticipated "superior earnings" from the assets acquired. For example, if a purchaser company buys another company that has assets with a fair value of $10 million, but is willing to pay $13 million for the assets, the premium is presumably attributable to the perceived superior earnings that the purchaser anticipates it will generate from the assets. For accounting purposes, the premium of $3 million is reported as purchased "goodwill" — a loose term that describes factors that will generate superior earnings attributable to customer relationships, good labour union relationships and contracts, supplier reliability, or lucrative government licences.

During boom times, companies can use their inflated stock to buy other companies, often at substantial premiums. When lean times follow the boom, companies may be stuck with over-inflated

---

8   *Wall Street Journal* (1996).

assets on their books — typically buried in their goodwill account. Where goodwill is substantially impaired, companies will write-down the account to reflect the reduced values. We saw this in 2002 following the technology bust. JDS Uniphase, for example, wrote down US $56.1 billion on assets that it had previously acquired at inflated prices. AOL Time Warner took write-downs in 2002 of US $99.7 billion, which was an all-time record at that time. The company acknowledged substantial and permanent impairment of its assets. The total impact on profits from technology companies' write-downs in 2002 was estimated to be US $235 billion.

The net effect of corporate write-downs is to leave a cleaner and more conservative balance sheet going forward. Of course, from the investor's perspective write-downs can be either good news or bad news. They are good news if the investor purchases after the write-down; they are bad news if the investor went in before the write-downs when asset values were inflated.

4) Stock Options

Stock options are contracts that give the holder the option to purchase shares at predetermined prices. The holder will exercise his option only if the stock is above the price at which he can buy. Option values rise as the price of the underlying stock increases.

One of the main propellants behind stock prices is earnings. As earnings increase, stock prices will generally react favourably and increase. Stock prices are the principal impetus behind stock option prices, which management typically reserves for employees and senior officers. Hence, there is a direct relationship between earnings and stock option prices, which is a powerful incentive for corporate management to "improve" earnings, either by increasing revenues or decreasing expenses.

During the Internet boom in 2000, investors focused more on revenues that technology companies earned and not as much on bottom-line earnings. As stock prices increased, so did the value of stock options. In fact, a very large number of Internet companies never had any earnings at all. Nevertheless, they hyped up their stock options.

There are various methods for determining the fair value of stock options, but none of them are entirely appropriate for stock market and accounting purposes. The Black-Scholes formula, for example, is not ideally suited for accounting purposes. It is designed essentially for determining values in short-term trading. Thus, the formula makes options on highly volatile stocks unduly valuable.

The discretion to use "fair value" opens up the potential for manipulation of values. Some companies simply ignore the cost of stock options and consider them to be "free compensation" notwithstanding their dilutive effect on future share values. Others backdated their options retroactively to take advantage of hindsight — a practice akin to placing a bet on a horse after the race is over. The 2002 technology bust and scandals associated with fictional stock option prices produced some reforms. The accounting rules were changed to account for stock options as expenses.

5) Pensions

The stock market boom of the 2000s enabled companies to look at their pension surpluses and take some surpluses into income to bolster their net income. With the market bust, pension shortfalls became the norm and there were (and are) continuing deficiencies in many defined benefit plans. Air Canada, for example, had a major pension shortfall that caused the company to seek bankruptcy protection.

6) Special Accounting Jargon

Accounting is the language that we use to communicate financial information. Thus, terms such as "revenues," "expenses," "capital assets," "capital expenditures," and "accrual and cash basis" have a special meaning in the context of accounting and financial statements. If accounting is the language of communication, it can also be an instrument of obfuscation. Here are some jargon phrases that one should view with caution.

Accelerating the booking of contracts	Loosely translated, this means that the company is recognizing revenue early by signing and recognizing contracts that may not generate the revenues until sometime in the future.
Premature revenue recognition	This is another phrase that simply says that the company did not adhere to "GAAP" and recognized and accrued its revenues before it should have.
Aggressive accounting	This phrase can cover a multitude of circumstances when management prepares its financial statements and stretches accounting principles to their limits. Management may do this to inflate revenues or decrease expenses.
Income smoothing	The objective here is to smooth income between successive financial periods to show a steady increase and to conceal volatility in earnings. Stock markets react favourably to consistently increasing earnings, rather than erratic fluctuations. By adjusting accounting entries, a company can level out the troughs and pare down the peaks in earnings to produce a nice steady earnings per share graph.
Options selected with some hindsight	This innocuous phrase refers to the practice of backdating options to a favourable price after the trigger date of option execution has passed. It is a form of contractual retroactivity with the benefit of hindsight. In horse racing, it would be comparable to betting on the winner of the Kentucky Derby after the race was over. Bookmakers do not pay on such bets. Corporate management may, however, do so with the shareholders' money! Securities regulators frown on such activities.
Earnings management	This term refers to manipulation of revenues and expenses to achieve desired goods – generally to enhance executive compensation.

7) Audit Inquiry Letters

Audit inquiry letters pose particular difficulties for companies because they create a conflict between the auditor's desire to disclose relevant contingencies and litigation risks and the lawyer's desire to protect confidential information on behalf of his or her clients.

A lawyer cannot disclose confidential information without the consent of his or her client. If the lawyer discloses with the client's consent, the information may lose its solicitor-client privilege. There is no comparable accountant-client privilege.

Note 6 to Duggan's financial statements shows how some companies handle disclosure. The note reads:

> The Company is vigorously defending the lawsuit. The Company is not able to predict the probable outcome of this matter or its potential impact on the Company's business or operations.

Law firms regularly receive inquiry letters from accountants asking whether the lawyer (or law firm) is aware of any outstanding claims against a particular client. Such letters should be carefully managed to ensure that confidentiality and privilege are not compromised in any reply, which should be addressed to the client and not the audit firm.

Chapter VIII: Interpretation of Financial Statements

A. GENERAL COMMENT

We prepare corporate financial statements for various purposes and audiences. They report on the financial stewardship of an enterprise based upon historical and, under IFRS, some fair value information about the entity. Stewardship stops when the report is delivered to the person to whom the enterprise is accountable — for example, the trustees of a trust, directors and shareholders of a corporation, officials of a regulatory agency, or the tax authorities. However, there are additional users of financial statements.

Financial analysts are an important constituency interested in corporate statements. They pore over the statements to detect future trends and report their findings to investors, private clients, and investment media. Indeed, some specialized television channels — such as, CNBC — do little else other than analyze financial information, economic trends, and the general business environment for their investor-oriented audiences.

Lawyers who are responsible for their clients' corporate transactions and agreements that contain financial covenants and restrictions are also interested in financial statements. Lawyers, acting for creditors, partners, joint venturers, trustee stakeholders or labour unions, look at the financial statements and ensure that they comply with the terms of agreements.

Management is interested in all aspects and perspectives of financial statements — past, present, and future. They must ensure that the statements properly report information as part of their custodial and fiduciary responsibilities to the corporation and that the enterprise complies with all of its legal covenants and contractual arrangements with creditors and regulators. Management must also make decisions about the direction in which they should steer the corporation in order to maximize its return on equity to create wealth for their shareholders.

B. MEASURING FINANCIAL SUCCESS

From a shareholder's or owner's perspective, the primary objective of a business is to maximize its return on equity (ROE) and control risk, which, requires reliable tools of measurement and analysis. Absolute numbers are not very helpful in financial analysis. Ratios are a better tool to analyze businesses of varying size. For example, absolute numbers mean little if we are comparing IBM with a small startup technology company.

Ratios allow us to use a common denominator to measure status or performance. For example, if one company earns $100 million in sales and another has $10 million in sales, but both earn $5 million in net income, we must adjust for relative size of the businesses. One has a rate of return of 5 percent on sales; the other a return of 50 percent. By reducing the numbers to a common ratio — net income as a percentage of sales — we obtain a more meaningful snapshot of the two companies than we would by looking at their absolute numbers.

We must be careful with numbers analysis. There is a psychological tendency to draw comfort from numbers. There is also a danger in interpreting numbers as absolutes. There is no predetermined "good" ratio for financial analysis. Each situation requires analysis in the context of the particular business, its environment, stage of development and the economic climate. Thus, properly used, a ratio is an analytical tool for financial interpretation and not an end in itself.

Ratio analysis plays different roles depending upon the purpose for which one engages in it. In a legal document — such as, a bond indenture or loan contract — a covenant on a particular ratio — for example, working capital — is an absolute requirement that the borrower must comply with to avoid legal sanctions. Thus, the question that we ask is whether the borrower has complied with the covenant in the lending document. We do not enquire into whether the ratio, *per se*, is good, bad, or indifferent. In contract law, ratios play a rigid role to measure compliance. In financial analysis, however, ratios are a predictive tool.

C. RETURN ON EQUITY

Return on Equity (ROE) is the granddaddy of all ratios in "for profit" companies. A business corporation exists to make a profit for its shareholders. Thus, for a shareholder, ROE is the critical performance indicator of the corporation's success. The formula is simple. A company's return on equity is:

ROE = Net Income/Equity

Although ROE appears as a single number, it is actually the product of three separate components:

1) Profit margin (Net income/Sales)
2) Asset turnover (Sales/Assets)
3) Leverage (Assets/Equity)

If we multiply the three components, we obtain the net after-tax return on equity. This is the classic Dupont formula.

$$\frac{\text{Net Income}}{\text{Sales}} \times \frac{\text{Sales}}{\text{Assets}} \times \frac{\text{Assets}}{\text{Equity}}$$

When expressed as a percentage, it gives us the overall return on the shareholders' investment. In Duggan Inc, for example, we see that after-tax ROE is equal to:

$6,807 \div \$17,134 = 40\%$

In order to determine whether Duggan's ROE is good or poor, we must compare the percentage return with comparable returns with its competitors in the same industry. We should also look at ROE in the context of past performance and general trends. Finally, we need to satisfy ourselves that the return is indicative of normal returns and is not distorted by a unique event. Hence, we must be satisfied that the net income figure properly reflects the income of the enterprise and that it has not been boosted by accounting manipulation — so-called earnings management.

D. PROFITABILITY RATIOS

1) Earnings per Share

Corporate financial statements do not actually show financial ratios. One must compute these ratios from the data in the statements. The exception is the "earnings per share" (EPS) ratio, or earnings yield, which is disclosed in the body of the financial statements, usually at the bottom of the Income Statement. The basic EPS is earnings attributable to the common stock divided by the weighted average number of shares of such stock outstanding for the year.

EPS is probably the most used financial tool in analyzing and predicting corporate performance. The number tells us how much money each share is earning: The higher, the better. There are, however, various forms of EPS.

The earnings attributable to common stock are net income for the year less any dividends and accumulations of dividends on preferred shares. The ratio measures the amount of earnings left for the residual owners of the corporation who invested in its common stock. Thus, it is the amount of earnings for a particular year that is allocable to each share of the corporation's residual security interest — the common shares of the corporation.

Since EPS can be affected by changes in the number of common shares outstanding — for example, through stock splits and stock consolidations (reverse splits) — it requires further analysis.

a) Dilution of Shares

Even more significant than the basic EPS is the diluted EPS of a business corporation. Diluted EPS takes into account the dilutive effect of issuing additional shares through stock options, warrants, or other agreements that require the company to issue additional shares in the future. The denominator is the fully diluted number of shares.

Basic EPS may also be adjusted for extraordinary items, changes in accounting principles, or gains or losses on the disposal of a business. In such cases, there may be several EPS calculations and amounts disclosed on the income statement.

b) Convertible Securities

In considering EPS, one must also take into account the effect of convertible securities and their potential dilutive effect on earnings. Thus, we can report EPS on a "if converted" basis — that is, assuming that the convertibles are actually converted into common stock.

There are two effects to the "if converted" calculation of EPS. First, the number of common shares outstanding is deemed to increase. Thus, the denominator increases. Second, we must adjust the earnings in the numerator by assuming that there will be no priority payment of interest or preferred cumulative dividends if the convertibles are converted into common stock. Thus, the numerator will also increase.

If the combined effect of these two adjustments is to increase the EPS, the convertible securities are anti-dilutive and they are not deemed to be converted in calculating EPS. If the conversion is dilutive, the diluted EPS should be disclosed.

c) Preferred Dividends

We must also adjust EPS for dividends on senior stock. For example, if a corporation has a net income of $2 million and 200,000 of only one class of shares outstanding all year, the EPS is $10 per share. If the corporation also has cumulative preferred shares outstanding, we deduct the amount attributable to the preferred shares before calculating the EPS per common share. For example, if the corporation has 30,000 preferred shares with a dividend of $8 per share, we would subtract the $240,000 in preferred dividends (whether paid or accumulated) from the $2 million net income. The remaining $1,760,000 of net income available to the common shares would provide an EPS of only $8.80 for common stockholders.

d) Weighted Average

The denominator in the EPS calculation is the weighted average of common charges outstanding during the year. For example, if a corporation has 80,000 shares outstanding on 1 January, the beginning of its fiscal year, and issues 20,000 additional common shares on 1 October of the year, the weighted average of shares outstanding for the calendar year is 85,000.

Example

Assume that a corporation with a calendar fiscal year has net income of $12,500,000. The company has a capital structure as follows:

- 100,000 Preferred shares with a cumulative dividend of $7 per share.
- 100,000 Common shares outstanding at its year-end (20,000 shares of which it issued on 1 October.)

We calculate EPS by first deducting the $700,000 preferred stock dividend from net income. That leaves us with net income of $11,800,000, which becomes the numerator in the EPS calculation.

Since the company issued 20,000 shares on 1 October, the weighted average of the outstanding common shares is determined by taking 100 percent of the 80,000 shares outstanding during the entire calendar year and 25 percent of the 20,000 shares outstanding for one-quarter of the year. This gives us a weighted average of 85,000 common shares, which is the denominator in the EPS calculation.

Thus, the EPS is $138.82 per share.

---

2) Price/Earnings Multiple

The price to earnings ratio (P/E) is probably the most single important measure of stock price valuation and the one that most analysts and investors follow.

What does the P/E ratio really tell us? When one buys corporate stock, one is, in effect, buying the corporation's future earnings, a surrogate for ROE. The P/E ratio is a measure of the amount that one is willing to pay for those earnings into the future.

For example, assume that ABC Ltd's EPS is $10 a share, and one is willing to purchase the share for $150. Then its P/E ratio is 15. This means that one is willing to pay fifteen times the company's current earnings for the shares. Stated another way, if earnings and stock prices remained constant, it would take us fifteen years to recover the share price of ABC Ltd through corporate earnings. This implies an annual rate of return of 6.7 percent if earnings remain constant.

The P/E ratio is important because it allows us to compare companies, industries, countries, and indices using a common yardstick. For example, we know that investors are willing to pay a higher multiple for technology companies than they are for utilities. This is entirely reasonable because technology is a growth industry, whereas utilities are stable. Thus, a growth investor might be willing to pay more (and risk more) for a growing company than for a stable company. In contrast, an income investor might prefer a stable and boring (but less risky) utility company with a steady cash flow and dividends.

As valuable as the P/E ratio is, it has its limitations and we should interpret it with care. The classic P/E is a measure of *past* earnings compared to current stock prices. It tells us about the relationship between last year's earnings and today's stock price. This information is useful, but can be misleading. If the company has taken a substantial write-off or recorded an unusual one-time gain in the preceding year, the earnings may not reflect a typical pattern that is useful for predicting future values. In 2008 and 2009, for example, many companies — especially financial institutions — took large write-offs and provided substantial reserves against future losses. All of this had the effect of reducing current earnings and enlarging P/E ratios. The backward-looking P/E ratio is not useful in these circumstances for predicting future earnings.

The forward P/E ratio is a more useful number for financial analysis. The earnings in the ratio are the expected future earnings of the company. Since a stock investor purchases future earnings, this is a more meaningful number. It tells us how much an investor is willing to pay for stock ownership in the future. For example, if the EPS of ABC Ltd in the previous example is expected to be $15 next year, the P/E ratio drops to 10 and the yield on the investment increases to 10 percent. This presents a different picture from the backward-looking P/E.

To be sure, the prospective P/E ratio is more difficult to estimate because, by definition, it involves looking into the future and predicting earnings. Hence, we do not have the benefit of hindsight as we have in the case of the backward-looking P/E ratio. However, for analytical purposes, we trade off historical precision for relevance of information in predicting the future.

The PE multiple for a stock is less susceptible to manipulation than EPS. For example, assume that a company with 100,000 shares outstanding has an EPS of $2 that trade at $10. The PE is 5. If it increases the number of shares outstanding through a 2:1 stock split, it will have 200,000 shares outstanding after the split, which will reduce its EPS to $1 per share. In these circumstances, the price of the stock should fall to $5 per share after the split. The PE multiple will remain 5.

EPS is reduced by one-half because there are double the number of outstanding shares. The drop in the EPS from $2 to $1 is not meaningful in and of itself. All that has happened is that the number of outstanding shares has increased from 100,000 to 200,000 and, therefore, net income is being divided by a larger figure. Each shareholder now owns two shares for every one share that he or she owned previously. The stockholder's *pro rata* share of corporate earnings is exactly the same. A stockholder who owned one share trading at $10, now owns two shares trading at $5 per share.

Example

Assume that a corporation has net income as follows:

	Year 1	Year 2
Net Income	$15,000,000	$15,000,000
Weighted average common shares	2,000,000	
EPS	$7.50	
The corporation splits its stock 3:1		
Weighted average common shares		6,000,000
EPS		$2.50

If Jane Doe owns 5,000 shares, her proportionate interest in corporate earnings is $37,500 in each of Years 1 and 2.

Conversely, a company can increase its EPS by doing a reverse stock split — a stock consolidation. For example, a company with 90,000 outstanding shares can consolidate its outstanding shares on a 3:1 basis and reduce the number of shares outstanding to 30,000. The number of outstanding shares is now that much lower, so the EPS of the company will increase proportionately if net income remains at the same level.

3) Financial Yields

In the private, for-profit sector "yield" is an important measure for evaluating business enterprises. There are, however, many different aspects of yield and each of them looks at financial results from a different perspective. In combination, they are valuable tools of analysis.

a) Dividend Yield

Dividend yield is the easiest of financial yields to understand. It is simply a company's annual dividend payout divided by its stock price. For example, if Company A pays an annual dividend of $2 per share and its stock is trading at $40, the dividend yield is 5 percent. Dividend yield tells us how much income an investor can expect to earn annually from his or her stock if the dividend remains constant.

A company's yield varies inversely to its stock price. As the price of stock goes up, the yield of its dividend will fall. In the above example, if Company A's stock price goes up to $50 and it maintains its payout at $2 per share, the yield falls to 4 percent. Conversely, as stock prices fall, yields go up.

Yields vary between industries and over time. We evaluate the dividend yield of stock by comparing it with the comparable yield on government bonds. However, not everyone is enamoured by dividend yields. Warren Buffett, for example, has never paid out a dividend on his Berkshire Hathaway stock since it went public in 1985. Nevertheless, the stock has done very well, giving its owners large capital gains.

Taxes are also a significant factor in evaluating dividend yields and capital gains. Not all dollars are equal. The Canadian income tax system, for example, taxes dividends, capital gains, and interest income at different rates. At the top marginal rate of tax, for example, dividends are taxed at approximately 31 percent, capital gains at 23 percent, and interest at 46 percent (in Ontario). Thus, in comparing the yield on investments, it is important to take into account the net after-tax yield, which is the amount that the investor actually keeps after paying the government its share in taxes.

b) Earnings Yield

We can also look at a company's performance by measuring its earnings yield as opposed to the payout yield of its dividends. Earnings yield is the company's annual earnings divided by its share price — also known as earning per share (EPS). For example, if Company B has EPS of $5 per share and its stock is trading at $60, the earnings yield is 8.3 percent.

Earnings yield tells us how well the company is doing, regardless of its payout ratio. Berkshire Hathaway, for example, has a high earnings yield, but pays out no dividends. In these circumstances, investors must make their decisions based upon their particular requirements and other economic considerations. For example, an income investor may prefer stock with a high dividend yield because of his or her cash requirements. A younger and more aggressive investor may prefer zero dividend yield and invest for longer-term capital gains. In Canada, the income investor would be taxed at 31 percent. The growth investor would eventually be taxed at 23 percent, but only when he or she disposes, or is deemed to dispose, of the stock. Thus, in addition to the differential tax rates that apply, there is also the time value of money.

4) Cash Flow Yield

A company's financial statements are prepared using accrual accounting principles. Accrual accounting requires a company to recognize its revenues and expenses when it earns them or incurs its costs, regardless of when it actually collects or pays out cash. For example, if a company sells $100 of merchandise on ninety days credit, it will recognize its sales revenue of $100 immediately even though it may not collect its accounts receivable for ninety days.

Cash flow measures the actual amount of cash that a company receives or pays out in the course of its operations. Cash measurement is, of course, much more certain than income measured on accrual principles. Hence, cash flow is considered a reliable indicator of corporate operations. At the end of the day, a company pays dividends from its cash. Hence, cash flow is an important measure of the safety of future dividends.

A company's free cash flow yield is its free cash flow per share divided by its share price. Free cash flow is the amount of cash that the company has after it pays out all of its expenses and expenditures on capital assets.

5) Bond Yields

Bond yields are more complicated calculations. Bond yield refers to the amount that an investor can expect to earn on his or her investment in a bond over its term. An investor's bond yield to maturity is made up of two components: periodic interest payments and the capital gain or loss when he or she redeems the bond.

In the simplest case, where an investor buys a bond at par, the yield to maturity is equal to the coupon rate on the bond. For example, if an investor buys a $1,000 bond at its face value when it is initially issued and the bond pays 6 percent interest annually, the yield to maturity is 6 percent. Thus, the yield is equal to the coupon interest rate on the bond without any capital gain or loss on maturity.

Where an investor purchases a bond at a price above or below its par value, the yield to maturity will be made up of the interest components and the capital gain or loss. In the preceding example, if the investor purchased the bond at $950, the yield to maturity would be made up of the 6 percent ($60) annual coupon rate and the capital gain of $50, upon maturity. The capital gain is the difference between the investor's cost of $950 and the redemption price of $1,000 at par.

As with the earnings yield on stock, the maturity yield on bonds fluctuates. As interest rates rise, the capital value of the bond will fall in order to maintain parity between the coupon rate on the bond and market rates of interest. Similarly, when interest rates fall, the capital value of bonds will increase in order to equalize the effective yield on the bond coupon with current market interest rates. As bond yields fluctuate, stock investors also make decisions to rationalize stock earnings yields with bond yields.

6) Price to Book Value

The price to book value ratio is a conservative number that measures the relationship between the price of shares and the book value — assets minus liabilities — of a company. Stated another way, the price to book value looks at the relationship between stock prices and the company's equity, which is assets minus liabilities, mostly valued on an historical cost basis.

E. LIQUIDITY RATIOS

The balance sheet provides a lot of useful information concerning an enterprise's financial liquidity, solvency, leverage, and debt to equity relationships. Each ratio provides us with a different snapshot of the enterprise's financial standing.

Liquidity ratios measure the ability of a company to meet its financial obligations in a timely manner. Thus, these ratios measure liquidity, as opposed to long-term solvency. Liquidity ratios supplement information that the cash flow statement provides.

There are several liquidity ratios, but the two most commonly used ones are:

1) Current (working capital) ratio; and
2) Quick ratio.

1) Current Ratio

The current ratio is calculated as follows:

Current Assets/Current Liabilities

Current assets include cash (and cash equivalents), accounts receivable, marketable securities, inventory, and short-term prepayments. Depending upon a company's industry, there is a time lag between the manufacture of its product into inventory, which, when sold, become accounts receivable, and then, ultimately, are collected in cash. The time lag from inventory to cash may be 120 days or longer.

Current liabilities include accounts payable, accrued liabilities, and other short-term liabilities that will come due during the year.

Duggan's current ratio is:

$12,451/$12,146 = 1:1

Thus, Duggan has just about enough current assets to be able to pay for its current obligations as they become due. The margin of safety is minimal. Any downturn in Duggan's cash collection from its business operations may cause financial stress. For example, Duggan may have to resort to short-term borrowing or credit facilities to cover its current liabilities.

The conventional view is that a working capital ratio of 2:1 is "good" because there is ample safety margin. In fact, there is no such thing as "good" in evaluating ratios. Much depends upon the nature of the business, its industry, access to credit lines, predict-ability, and stability of cash flows. Safety margin comes at a price: current assets reduce risk but produce minimal (if any) income.

2) The Quick Ratio

The quick ratio is a more stringent measure of liquidity than the current ratio. The quick ratio is:

Monetary Assets/Current Liabilities

Monetary assets include cash, cash equivalents, marketable securities, and net accounts receivable. These assets are the most easily and quickly convertible into cash. Receivables can usually be turned into cash within thirty to sixty days. Hence, we some-times refer to the quick ratio as an "acid test," because it tells us how quickly a company can meet its obligations without having to sell its inventory and, then, collect its receivables.

Monetary assets exclude inventory and prepaid expenses. (*Note:* prepaid expenses do not convert into cash, but are amounts that the company pays in advance and represent an outflow of cash.)

Duggan's quick ratio is:

$6,349/$12,146 = 0:5

The ratio is on the low side. A ratio of 1:1 would be more con-servative in most cases.

F. SOLVENCY RATIOS

Solvency ratios measure financial leverage — that is, the manner in which a corporation uses debt to finance its capital structure. Thus, solvency ratios focus on a longer term than liquidity ratios.

A company can improve its ROE by using debt capital if it earns more from the debt than its cost. For example, if a company can borrow at 6 percent interest and use the money to earn 10 percent, it will enhance its net income by the amount of the spread between its borrowing cost and the earnings rate. The reverse is also true. A company with interest costs that are higher than its earnings rate will diminish its ROE. Debt also increases risk. Thus, a firm must balance the benefits of leverage against risk.

1) Debt/Equity Ratio

The debt/equity ratio is the standard measure of leverage. The ratio measures the relative use of debt and equity in a company's capital structure. The formula for the debt/equity ratio is:

Debt (long-term)/Equity

Duggan's debt/equity ratio is:

$13,091/$17,134 = 0.8:1

Thus, debt represents 43 percent of the company's overall financial structure.

Too much debt can be risky, particularly if earnings are not stable and predictable. There is no absolute measure of the right amount of debt for an enterprise. Too little debt can lead to lost financial opportunities.

2) Return on Capital

A company's return on capital is:

Net Income/Total Capital

A company with strong earnings can have a low return on capital if it carries a high level of debt.

Both short- and long-term debt can be used to leverage earnings if the cost of capital is less than the rate of earnings. There are variations of the debt/equity ratio depending upon how one measures "debt." Some analysts include all debt; others include only long-term debt. Since the working-capital ratio measures the ability of a company to pay its short-term debt, it is usually more meaningful to measure only long-term debt when measuring leverage.

G. FINANCIAL LEVERAGE

Another measure of leverage is to see how much of the total assets of a company are financed through equity. The financial leverage ratio is:

$$\frac{\text{Total Assets}}{\text{Equity}}$$

In the case of Duggan Inc, for example, the financial leverage is:

$$\frac{\text{Total Assets} = \$42,371}{\text{Equity} = \$17,134}$$

Leverage = 2.47

Thus, the company has two and one-half times as much in assets as its owner's equity; the remainder is financed by debt.

1) Times Interest Earned

Times interest earned — or interest coverage — is a measure of solvency that is of particular interest to the company's long-term creditors. The ratio measures the degree of safety that the creditors have from the earnings of the company.

Times interest earned is:

$$\frac{\text{Net Income before Interest \& Taxes}}{\text{Interest Expense}}$$

In the case of Duggan, its interest coverage is:

$$\frac{\$10,674}{\$333}$$

Interest coverage equals 32.

Duggan's creditors are very well secured by its earnings — the company is earning thirty-two times what it needs to pay its creditors.

Stated another way, interest coverage tells us how much a company's income can deteriorate without prejudicing the creditors or putting them at risk. (*Note:* we add back taxes to the net income because interest is a deductible expense for tax purposes. Thus, taxes do not affect the company's ability to pay interest.)

2) Preferred Dividends

There are other variations on interest coverage and solvency measures. Some analysts, for example, will add dividends on preferred shares to the interest expense in the denominator. Although, preferred share dividends are not fixed legal obligations, they represent, in a business sense, obligations that a company will not want to default on. Hence, from a business perspective, interest expense and preferred share dividends are both "fixed" obligations.

H. ACTIVITY RATIOS

Activity ratios measure a firm's efficiency in utilizing its assets. We measure activity by comparing the relationship between two connected and relevant numbers to see how effectively or efficiently the business is operating. As a group, we refer to these as "turnover" ratios.

1) Asset Turnover

The broadest turnover ratio is that of the company's total assets — usually at the average of the opening and the closing balance of assets. This ratio measures how efficiently the company uses its total assets. The formula for asset turnover is:

$$\frac{\text{Sales Revenue}}{\text{Average Assets}}$$

In Duggan's financial statements, the asset turnover is:

$$\frac{\text{Sales Revenue} = \$62,954}{\text{Total Assets} = \$41,261}$$

Asset Turnover = 1.53

The higher the asset turnover, the more efficiently the business is using its assets to generate sales. If a company can use a small base of assets to generate large volume of profitable sales, it will be operating efficiently.

2) Accounts Receivable Turnover

Accounts receivable turnover measures the amount of receivables that a company carries in relation to its sales. The formula for receivables turnover is:

$$\frac{\text{Sales Revenue}}{\text{Average Receivables}}$$

Duggan's accounts receivable turnover is:

$$\frac{\$62,954}{\$5,280} = 11.9$$

The higher the receivables turnover, the better the company is in terms of converting its sales into cash. Clearly, a short period for outstanding accounts receivable is in the company's interest as it does not have to tie up its capital, but can use it in its business. For example, a receivables turnover of 10 implies that the accounts receivable are outstanding for 10 percent of the year — that is, thirty-six days.

As an absolute number, the number of days outstanding is not particularly helpful. We must compare the number with the actual terms of sale to see whether the company is performing efficiently. For example, if the terms of sale are thirty days for net payment, thirty-six days of actual outstanding receivables reflects well on the company's sales and credit operations. If the terms of sale are net ten days, the thirty-six days of outstanding receivables indicates a cash collection problem.

3) Inventory Turnover

Another measure that tests the efficiency of asset usage is inventory turnover, which measures the amount of inventory to the volume of goods produced and sold. The formula for inventory turnover is:

$$\frac{\text{Cost of Goods Sold}}{\text{Average Inventory}}$$

Duggan's inventory turnover is:

$$\frac{29{,}890}{4{,}098} = 7.3$$

This ratio tells us how quickly an enterprise is consuming its inventory. The higher the ratio, the faster the utilization of inventory. A high turnover ratio implies that the company does not have its capital tied up in inventory for a long time. For example, an inventory turnover of 15 implies that the business holds its inventory for approximately twenty-four days of sales.

I. PROFITABILITY RATIOS

We measure the profitability of a business by comparing profits to sales, investment, and market price of its shares.

The most important profitability measure is profit margin — that is, the portion of each sales dollar that the company realizes as a profit from the business:

$$\frac{\text{Net Income}}{\text{Sales}}$$

There are actually three measures of profitability: gross profit, net profit, and net return on common equity. The most commonly used is net profit margin, which is net income as a percentage of sales. In Duggan, for example:

$$\frac{\$10{,}341}{\$62{,}954} = 16\%$$

The profitability of a business depends, in part, upon its profit margin. The business may have a high or low profit margin depending upon the industry within which it operates and the segment of that industry that it occupies.

It is not possible to generalize about profit margins. A business may have a high profit margin but a low turnover of assets (for example, a high-end restaurant). Another business may be equally profitable by maintaining a low profit margin with a high turnover of assets (for example, a fast-food restaurant, such as McDonald's). Thus, although profit margin is a very useful figure, it is only the starting point in analyzing an enterprise's profitability. Clearly, a negative margin over a long-term spells trouble for the business. On the positive side, the profit margin tells us how much of its sales dollars the enterprise keeps.

There are many competitive and industry reasons that will determine a company's profit margin. Businesses in highly competitive industries must maintain a profit margin commensurate with their competitors. Excessively high margins will drive away customers to competitors.

In monopolies and oligopolies, companies can maintain higher profit margins than in competitive industries. For example, a liquor licensing board that has a monopoly over all liquor, beer, and wine sales can set a high profit margin and not be concerned about its competitors going elsewhere to purchase their supplies. Hence, governments like liquor monopolies because they provide a steady and predictable source of revenue from a captive market.

Profit margin is determined by numerous factors, all the way from the top of the income statement (the top line) down to the bottom (the bottom line). An increase or decrease in any of the items in the income statement will ultimately affect the profit margin. There are differences, however, between top-line versus bottom-line effects on profit margin that depend upon the particular industry. For example, Table 8-1 shows the effect of a 1 percent price cut on the operating profits of industries (in 2009 figures).

Table 8-1 Effect of a One Percent Price Cut on Major Industries, 2009	
Industry	Percentage Effect on Operating Profit
Food & Drugs	−23.7
Airlines	−12.9
Computers	−11.0
Average	**−8.0**
Tobacco	−4.9
Semiconductors	−3.9
Diversified Financials	−2.4

As we see, on average, a top-line price cut of 1 percent reduces bottom-line earnings by 8 percent. The food industry, however, is much more sensitive than diversified financials.

Profit margins, are only one indicator of overall profitability. One is tempted to think that the higher the profit margin, the better off the company. In fact, low profit margins can also be very good if the company's turnover is high. For example, a company with $100 per unit profit margin that turns over its assets only once has a profitability of $100. In contrast, another company with a lower profit margin of $50 that can turn over its assets three times will earn $150. Apple Inc, for example, is a classic case of high gross margins in a highly competitive industry.

We see this also in the restaurant business. Some restaurants are high-end establishments with large profit margins on food and liquor. Patrons who go to such establishments usually stay for quite a while. Dinner guests, for example, may stay for a couple of hours or more. The restaurant's nightly turnover of tables may be only 1.5 or 2 sittings. In contrast, a lower-end, fast-food service will have lower profit margins, but high turnover. The classic case is McDonald's, which may have 10 or more sittings during the evening dinner hour. It can afford to earn less on each sale, but makes more sales to increase net earnings.

Table 8-2 is a list of Canadian banks showing what analysts look at in evaluating businesses.

Table 8-2 How the Big Five Banks Stacked Up, September 2012

Company	Symbol	Market Cap ($MIL)	1-Yr Total Return (%)	Expected Dividend Yield (%)	P/B Ratio (x)	Price to Reported Earnings (x)	Trailing ROE (%)
Royal Bank of Canada	RY-T	79,375	14.1	4.4	2.1	11.3	19.0
Toronto-Dominion Bank	TD-T	73,429	7.7	3.8	1.7	10.9	15.9
Bank of Nova Scotia	BNS-T	59,713	-0.2	4.4	1.9	11.4	17.2
Bank of Montreal	BMO-T	37,128	-2.0	5.0	1.5	10.1	14.6
CIBC	CM-T	30,534	3.3	5.0	2.1	9.6	22.0

Source: Morningstar Canada, as published in the *Globe and Mail* (7 September 2012).

J. SUMMARY OF FINANCIAL STATEMENT RATIOS

#	Ratio	Formula	Description
1	Return on equity (ROE)	$\dfrac{\text{Net Income}}{\text{Equity}}$	This is the granddaddy of all ratios and can be disaggregated.
2	Return on assets (ROA)	$\dfrac{\text{Net income}}{\text{Total assets}}$	Measures net income in relation to assets. It is a function of the company's asset turnover and its net profit margin.
3	Profit margin (PM)	$\dfrac{\text{Net income}}{\text{Sales}}$	Measures the amount of *after-tax* income as a percentage of sales.
4	Asset turnover (AT)	$\dfrac{\text{Sales}}{\text{Assets}}$	Measures the volume of sales produced by the assets of the company.
5	Financial leverage (FL)	$\dfrac{\text{Assets}}{\text{Equity}}$	The larger this ratio, the more the company has been financed with debt.
6	ROE = PM × AT × FL		This is known as Dupont analysis.
7	Gross profit margin (GPM)	$\dfrac{\text{Gross profit}}{\text{Sales}}$	Gives an indication of the relationship between sales prices and cost of goods sold.
8	Inventory turnover (ITO)	$\dfrac{\text{Cost of goods}}{\text{Inventory}}$	Low value indicates slow-moving inventory while a very high ratio indicates the possibility of inventory shortages.
9	Average collection period (ACP)	$\dfrac{\text{Accounts receivable}}{\text{Average daily sales}}$	Average daily sales is equal to total sales divided by 365 days.
10	Current ratio (CR)	$\dfrac{\text{Current assets}}{\text{Current liabilities}}$	Measures the ability of a company to pay off current liabilities.

#	Ratio	Formula	Description
11	Debt to equity (DE)	$\dfrac{\text{Total debt}}{\text{Total equity}}$	Total debt is equal to total liabilities. When this ratio rises, the FL ratio also rises.
12	Times interest earned (TIE)	$\dfrac{\text{EBIT}}{\text{Interest expense}}$	EBIT is earnings before interest and taxes. Measures the ability to generate sufficient earnings to pay interest on debt.
13	Income tax rate	$\dfrac{\text{Income tax expense}}{\text{EBT}}$	EBT is earnings before income taxes.
14	Earnings per share (EPS)	$\dfrac{\text{Net Income} - \text{Pref \$/share}}{\text{\# of Common shares}}$	Measures earnings on a per share basis.
15	Price earnings	$\dfrac{\text{Common share price}}{\text{Earnings per share}}$	Measures the relationship of stock price to earnings.
16	Dividend payout	$\dfrac{\text{Dividends per share}}{\text{EPS}}$	Indicates the percentage of earnings distributed as dividends.
17	Dividend yield (YLD)	$\dfrac{\text{Dividends per share}}{\text{Common share price}}$	Measures return via dividends relative to share price.

K. SUMMARY OF DUGGAN INC'S RATIOS

Liquidity & Solvency			
Current Ratio	$\dfrac{\text{Current assets}}{\text{Current liabilities}}$	$\dfrac{\$12,451}{\$12,146}$	$= 1.0$
Acid test Ratio	$\dfrac{\text{Monetary current assets}}{\text{Current liabilities}}$	$\dfrac{\$6,349}{\$12,146}$	$= 0.5$
Financial Leverage Ratio	$\dfrac{\text{Total assets}}{\text{Shareholders' equity}}$	$\dfrac{\$42,371}{\$17,134}$	$= 2.473$
Debt/equity Ratio	$\dfrac{\text{Long-term liabilities}}{\text{Shareholders' equity}}$	$\dfrac{\$13,091}{\$17,134}$	$= 76\%$
Times interest earned	$\dfrac{\text{Pre-tax operating profit + Interest}}{\text{Interest}}$	$\dfrac{\$10,674}{\$333}$	$= 32$ times
Investment Utilization			
Asset turnover ratio	$\dfrac{\text{Sales revenue}}{\text{Total assets}}$	$\dfrac{\$62,954}{\$42,371}$	$= 1.486$
Profitability			
Profit margin percentage	$\dfrac{\text{Net income before taxes}}{\text{Net sales revenue}}$	$\dfrac{\$10,341}{\$62,954}$	$= 16.40\%$
Tax retention rate			
1 – tax rate			65.80%
Effective tax rate		$\dfrac{\$3,534}{\$10,341}$	$= 34.20\%$
Overall performance			
Return on shareholders' equity	$\dfrac{\text{Net income}}{\text{Shareholders' equity}}$	$\dfrac{\$6,807}{\$17,134}$	$= 40\%$
Same as:	Profit margin percentage* (NPM)	16.40%	
	Asset turnover* (AT)	1.486	
	Financial leverage* (FL)	2.473	
	Tax retention rate (TRR)	65.80%	
	NRM $\times$ AT $\times$ FL $\times$ TRR		$= 39.70\%$

Chapter IX: Accounting and Law

A. GENERAL COMMENT

Accountants and auditors can be liable under contract, tort, securities, or tax law to users of financial statements. The scope and extent of their liability depends upon the particular branch of law, the user of the financial statements, the nature of the claims, statutory structures, and public policy considerations.

Although public accountants perform a wide variety of services for their clients, their primary function, and the one that most frequently generates lawsuits against them, is financial auditing. Accountants are the traditional target in business lawsuits. This is because most business failures, whether of public or private companies, involve some aspect of corporate financials. The plaintiff might complain that the statements were prepared without adequate care in the audit process or that the auditors misapplied GAAP or IFRS. For example, the plaintiff may allege that the statements are misleading, whether innocently or fraudulently, and caused the plaintiff (or class of plaintiffs) financial harm.

There is another reason, however, why accountants are often in the crosshairs of plaintiffs' lawyers. Accounting firms do not like to be dragged into court, where litigation can extend for years and attract attention in the business press. In many cases, it is the insurance coverage that attracts plaintiffs' lawyers, like bees to honey. Thus, accountants and accounting firms are amenable to settlement, if the settlement is within their professional insurance limits, and their legal fees are covered. In the final analysis, it is the insurance company that loses. However, it makes up its losses through increased premiums and tax write-offs. Ultimately, the taxpayer pays.

For example, in the 1990s, the "Big Five" (now reduced to the Big Four) faced more than US $30 billion in legal actions against them. Laventhol & Horwarth — the seventh largest accounting firm at the time — declared bankruptcy in 1990 because it could not meet its liability claims. A 1995 study of accounting firm payouts in the United States found that the "Big Six" (as they then were) paid out US $1.7 billion since 1991 in securities fraud cases.[1]

B. GENERAL PRINCIPLES

There are various types of reports on financial statements, each of which specifies the nature and extent of work done by the auditors, the standards applied and the assurance given. Liability for each of these types of reports also varies. The less intense the involvement of the auditor in preparing the report, the higher the threshold for legal liability.

Audit reports alert the reader to the degree of confidence or reliance that he or she can place on the financial statements. They are the centrepiece of the communication process. Although they are short, they contain valuable information. The auditors' report is the basis of liability for public accountants.

The first consideration in determining liability in contract is the scope of the task for which the business retains the auditor. The auditors' potential liability in contract is highest when the auditor is retained for a complete audit. Potential exposure diminishes as the scope of the work that the auditor is asked to perform is reduced. For example, a "review engagement" requires less detailed examination and no testing of financial transactions. It is basically enquiry, analysis of procedures, and discussions with management. Hence, the accountant's exposure to liability is less than for a complete audit with an unqualified (unmodified) assurance opinion.

---

1   "Big Six Have Paid $1.7 Billion since 1991 in Securities Fraud Cases, Study Finds" (1995) 27 Sec Reg & L Rep 1723.

To establish liability and collect damages from an accountant, the plaintiff must prove that the auditor's negligence or intentional misconduct caused the financial damage. But the issue of liability does not stop there. The plaintiff must also establish that he or she is within the class of persons who warrant protection from the auditor's negligence that results from audit, review, or compilation engagements, as well as from other services that accounting firms provide — such as tax, consulting, and litigation support.

There are two preliminary issues to decide in accounting malpractice litigation: 1) Did the accountant owe the plaintiff or class of plaintiffs a duty of care in the preparation of an independent audit of the client's financial statements? and 2) Did the accountant breach the appropriate standard of care in conducting the independent audit? These are fundamental and basic questions of tort liability that first-year law students study in principle, but which have a slightly different hue in cases involving accounting malpractice.

Clients may commission audits for a variety of purposes. Some must be audited; for example, public companies must be audited under statutory and regulatory requirements of the *Canada Business Corporations Act* and the *Ontario Securities Act*. Others request audits to establish their financial credibility with lenders and government agencies, such as the tax authorities and regulatory rate setting commissions. Indeed, a so-called clean opinion from one of the Big Four accounting firms is often the *sine qua non* for admission into the capital markets. Fraudsters also understand and use the stamp of approval of one of the Big Four firms to perpetrate securities frauds in the public markets. See, for example, McKesson & Robbins.[2]

1) Privity of Relationship

The first issue to consider is the scope of the duty of care and to whom the auditor owes the duty.

---

2   McKesson & Robbins is the company involved in one of the most notorious accounting scandals of the 20th century, a watershed event that led to major changes in American auditing standards for physical inventory counts and securities regulations after being exposed in 1938.

In *Ultra Mares*,[3] for example, the plaintiff made three unsecured loans totalling $165,000 to a company that went bankrupt. The company obtained a "clean opinion" from its auditors that its balance sheet "presented a true and correct view of the financial condition of the company." The balance sheet showed a net worth of $1 million. In fact, the company was insolvent. The auditors had failed to follow paper trails to "off-the-books" transactions that, if properly analyzed, would have revealed the company's impecunious situation. The auditors supplied thirty-two copies of the financial statements and opinion, all with serial numbers as counterpart originals. In what is considered to be the seminal opinion on auditor malpractice, Chief Judge Cardozo reversed the jury verdict.

> The auditor in Ultra Mares knew the company was in need of capital and that its audit opinion would be displayed to third parties "as the basis of financial dealings."
>
> The Plaintiff's name, however, was not mentioned to the auditor, nor was the auditor told about any actual or proposed credit or investment transactions in which its audit opinion would be presented to a third party.

The Court found that the auditor owed no duty to the third-party creditor for an "erroneous opinion." Chief Judge Cardozo narrowed the scope of the duty of care on public policy grounds.

> If liability for negligence exists, a thoughtless slip or blunder, the failure to detect a theft or forgery beneath the cover of deceptive entries, may expose accountants to a liability in an indeterminate amount for an indeterminate time to an indeterminate class. The hazards of a business conducted on these terms are so extreme as to enkindle doubt whether a flaw may not exist in the implication of a duty that exposes to these consequences payment.
>
> Thus, the class of persons to whom accountants owe a duty of care is narrower than one might otherwise imagine because of public policy considerations.

---

3   *Ultra Mares Corp v Touche*, 255 NY 170, 174 NE 441 (New York Court of Appeals 1931) [*Ultra Mares*].

Chief Judge Cardozo did not exonerate auditors from liability to third parties for fraud, but merely for "honest blunder."

The essential issue is whether the auditor has sufficient nexus with the third party to constitute a relationship approaching privity. This is essentially a question of fact. The auditor's liability to his client with whom he has a contract is clear if the auditor breaches the standard of care in providing services. The client and the auditor are in a relationship of privity.

The more difficult question is determining the standard of auditor liability to third parties. As one moves away from privity of contract to privity of relationship, the line for liability becomes obscure. In *Credit Alliance v Arthur Andersen & Co*,[4] for example, the New York Court of Appeals restated the American law of liability as follows:

> Before accountants may be held liable in negligence to non-contractual parties who rely to their detriment on inaccurate financial reports, certain prerequisites must be satisfied: (1) the accountant must have been aware that the financial reports were to be used for a particular purpose or purposes; (2) in the furtherance of which a known party or parties was intended to rely; and (3) there must have been some conduct on the part of the accountants linking them to that party or parties, which evinces the accountants' understanding of what that party or parties' reliance.

Thus, the essential question is whether accountants should be subject to liability to third persons (persons not in contractual relationships with the auditor) on the same basis as all other tortfeasors or whether they should enjoy special protection from the doctrine of foreseeability on public policy ground.

2) Foreseeability and Duty of Care

Ultra Mares is an "anachronistic protection" of accountants. In a 1983 law review article, Justice Howard Weiner wrote that "accountant

---

4   65 NY 2d 536, 493 NYS 2d 435, 483 NE 2d 110 (New York Court of Appeals 1985).

liability based on foreseeable injury would serve the dual functions of compensation for injury and deterrence of negligent conduct."[5] Other judges have said that it is a just and rational judicial policy that the same criteria govern the imposition of negligence liability, regardless of the context in which it arises. As Chief Justice Lucas said in *Billy v Arthur Young & Company*,[6] "the accountant, the investor, and the general public will in the long run benefit when the liability of the certified public accountant for negligent misrepresentation is measured by the foreseeability standard."

There is really no reason to distinguish accountants from other professionals and suppliers of services and goods to the public. To be sure, the public policy limitation protects accountants. However, the rule impairs the potential deterrent effect of liability based on negligent conduct. As Weiner said:

> The imposition of a duty to foreseeable users may cause accounting firms to engage in more thorough reviews. This might be setting up stricter standards and applying closer supervision, which should tend to reduce the number of instances in which liability would ensue. Much of the additional cost incurred because of more thorough auditing review or increased insurance premiums would be borne by the business entity and its stockholders or its customers.

In *Hercules*,[7] the Supreme Court of Canada followed Cardozo's reasoning and limited the scope of auditors' liability to shareholders, investors, and other potential users of financial statements. The plaintiffs were two shareholders of two companies that carried on business of lending and investing money on the security of real property mortgages. The defendants (Ernst & Young), a firm of public accountants, performed the annual audits of the financial statements of the two companies and provided their reports to the

---

5   Weiner, "Common Law Liability of the Certified Public Accountant for Negligent Misrepresentation" (1983) 20 San Diego L Rev 233.

6   3 Cal 4th 370, 11 Cal Rptr 2d 51, 834 P 2d 745 (Supreme Court of California 1992).

7   *Hercules Managements Ltd v Ernst & Young*, [1997] 2 SCR 165 [*Hercules*].

companies' shareholders. The two companies went into receivership. The plaintiffs, who had relied on the auditors' reports, suffered damages on account of their investments in the companies. They alleged that the audit reports were negligently prepared.

The principal issue was the scope of the duty of care in cases involving negligent misrepresentation. The Court reiterated the two-part test that the House of Lords used in *Anns*:[8]

> First one has to ask whether, as between the alleged wrongdoer and the person who has suffered damage there is a sufficient relationship of proximity or neighbourhood such that, in the reasonable contemplation of the former, carelessness on his part may be likely to cause damage to the latter — in which case a prima facie duty of care arises. Secondly, if the first question is answered affirmatively, it is necessary to consider whether there are any considerations which ought to negative, or to reduce or limit the scope of the duty or the class of person to whom it is owed, or the damages to which a breach of it may give rise.

"Proximity" is simply an alternative articulation of the "duty of care" test that Lord Atkin first developed in *Donoghue v Stevenson*.[9] Professor Fleming called proximity a "vacuous test."[10]

Negligent misrepresentation actions differ from physical damage cases. In physical damage cases, the reasonableness of the plaintiff's expectations is not really an issue. Where there is a duty of care, injury is sufficient to support an action. In negligent misrepresentation actions, however, the plaintiff relies on detrimental reliance on the negligent statement. Thus, the reliance must be reasonable and is not taken for granted. It is in respect of the reasonableness of the reliance that public policy considerations may override the simple "duty of care."

---

8   *Anns v Merton London Borough Council*, [1978] AC 728 at 751–52 (HL), Lord Wilberforce [*Anns*].
9   [1932] AC 562 at 580–81.
10   John G Fleming, "The Negligent Auditor and Shareholders" (1990) 106 Law Q Rev 349 at 351.

3) Policy Considerations

Policy considerations are an additional burden on a plaintiff in negligent misrepresentation actions. As Justice LaForest said in *Hercules*:

> Plainly stated, adding further requirements to the duty of care test provides a means by which policy concerns that are extrinsic to simple justice — but that are, nevertheless, fundamentally important — may be taken into account in assessing whether the defendant should be compelled to compensate the plaintiff for losses suffered. In other words, these further requirements serve a policy-based limiting function with respect to the ambit of the duty of care in negligent misrepresentation actions.[11]

Ultimately, all policy making is a compromise between competing values. The Supreme Court of Canada considered the competing values in *Hercules*, balancing the interests of the auditors against the interests of individual shareholders. The Court went with the auditors, whose interests prevail in their role as auditors of corporations under statutory requirements.

There are many people who rely upon audit reports in making decisions. Shareholders, creditors, potential investors, financial analysts, and financial planners all use audit reports in various decisions that rely on financial statements to be fairly presented and in accordance with sound accounting principles. It is entirely reasonable for such users to expect, at the very least, that the auditors' opinion that the financial statements present fairly the results of operations is a stamp of approval. Indeed, in the case of the Big Four accounting firms, users of financial statements treat their signature at the bottom of the audit opinion as the hallmark of financial probity. Should auditors who benefit from such reverence from the business and investment community be accountable in law for their audit opinions? If so, to whom?

There are conflicting and competing interests in determining the scope of auditor liability. Since all rules are behavioural, broad-based liability for negligent misrepresentation to users who rely

---

11   Above note 7 at para 28.

on financial statements would deter negligent conduct. As liability costs go up, the auditor would become more self-conscious that his or her professional liability insurance costs would also go up. As insurance premiums escalate for liability insurance, the cost of audit services would increase and, eventually, get passed on to the ultimate consumer.

In *Hercules*, however, the Supreme Court considered that the deterrence of negligent conduct was outweighed by "socially undesirable consequences" that would flow from imposing indeterminate liability on auditors: the spectre of "liability in an indeterminate amount for an indeterminate time to an indeterminate class."[12]

Thus, despite the interest that the plaintiffs had as individual shareholders in the defendant company, the Supreme Court restricted the scope of auditors' liability to their statutory mandate, which was to report to the corporation and the collectivity of shareholders, but not to any individual shareholders who made personal investment decisions based on the audit report. Relying on the corporate doctrine that the duty that auditors owe is to the corporation — a separate fictional legal entity — and not to the shareholders personally, the Supreme Court restricted the scope of the potential liability of auditors. As Lord Oliver said in *Caparo*[13] (quoted with approval by the Supreme Court of Canada):

> My Lords, the primary purpose of the statutory requirement that a company's accounts shall be audited annually is almost self-evident . . . . The management is confided to a board of directors which operates in a fiduciary capacity and is answerable to and removable by the shareholders who can act, if they act at all, only collectively and only through the medium of a general meeting. Hence the legislative provisions requiring the board annually to give an account of its stewardship to a general meeting of the shareholders . . . . It is the auditors' function to ensure, so far as

---

12 Per Justice LaForest: "In the general run of auditors' cases, concerns over indeterminate liability will serve to negate a *prima facie* duty of care."

13 *Caparo Industries PLC v Dickman*, [1990] 1 All ER 568 at 583 (HL) [*Caparo*].

possible, that the financial information as to the company's affairs prepared by the directors accurately reflects the company's position in order first, to protect the company itself from the consequences of undetected errors, or, possibly wrong doing . . . . And, second, to provide shareholders with reliable intelligence for the purpose of enabling them to scrutinize the conduct of the company's affairs and to exercise their collective powers to reward or control or remove those to whom that conduct has been confided.

Similarly in *Roman Corp Ltd*,[14] Farley J stated:

As a matter of law, the only purpose for which the shareholders receive an auditor's report is to provide the shareholders with information for the purpose of overseeing the management and affairs of the corporation and not for the purpose of guiding personal investment decisions or personal speculation with a view to profit.

Thus, we emphasize the responsibility of the auditor to the corporation and the "collectivity" of shareholders, but not to individual shareholders who may use the audit information in making personal investment decisions. This despite the fact that it is the shareholders who finance the corporation with risk capital! Financial statements, preferably audited, are the first step in financial analysis by investors and analysts.

Most shareholders' meetings are in fact perfunctory, superficial and pithy, programmed to a script. Retail investors are not usually well informed and have limited understanding of financial statements.

The real financial analysis is done by professionals who scour the financial statements, the audit report, the notes to the financial statements (which under IFRS are voluminous), and the more detailed information usually provided to securities regulators in quarterly and annual filings. How effective is their analysis? In 2008, the Congressional Budget Office of the United States reported that Americans lost over $2 trillion in accumulated retirement assets in their

---

14   *Roman Corp Ltd v Peat Marwick Thorne* (1992), 11 OR (3d) 248 (Gen Div).

401(k) accounts, pensions, and other traditional retirement savings during the preceding fifteen months. Absent accountability of auditors to investors, we can expect more of the same in the future.

4) American *Restatement*: Intent to Benefit Third Persons

Section 552 of the *Restatement Second of Torts*[15] covers "Information Negligently Supplied for the Guidance of Others." It states that a supplier of information should be liable for negligence to a third party only if he or she intends to supply the information for the benefit of one or more third parties in a specific transaction identified to the supplier. Thus, it states the general principle that a person who negligently supplies false information "for the guidance of others in their business transactions" is liable for economic loss suffered by the recipients in justifiable reliance on the information.

However, the restatement limits the scope of liability for loss suffered. To be liable to a third party, the loss must be suffered:

1) by the person or one of a limited group of persons for whose benefit and guidance he intends to supply the information or knows that the recipient intends to supply it; and
2) through reliance upon it in a transaction that he intends the information to influence or knows that the recipient so intends or in a substantially similar transition.

For example, an auditor who is engaged to perform an audit and render a report to a third person whom the auditor knows is making a substantial investment in the client's business is on notice of specific potential liability. The third person is clearly within the scope of foreseeability. The auditor can act to encounter, limit, or avoid the risk. In contrast, an auditor who is simply asked for a generic audit report to the client has no comparable notice and, according to the restatement, should not be held liable to third parties.

---

15 *Restatement of the Law Second: Torts* (Philadelphia, PA: American Law Institute, 1957–) s 552.

Chapter X: Tax Aspects of Equity

A. GENERAL COMMENT

A corporation's share capital represents its permanent capital base and is a key component of equity, the denominator in calculating return on equity (ROE). A corporation is generally not obliged to re-purchase its shares and return capital to shareholders. Since, in most cases, the payment of dividends is within the discretion of the board of directors, a corporation need not pay dividends when it is not financially secure. Indeed, as we have seen, a corporation is prohibited from paying dividends if the payment would impair its financial ability to repay its debts as they become due.

One measures a shareholder's ownership of a corporation by the number of shares that he or she owns. For tax purposes, the paid-up capital (PUC) of a share represents the owner's capital interest in the corporation for tax purposes.

Two fundamental tax aspects of corporate share capital influence a corporation's tax structure:

1) Dividends are paid from after-tax dollars and are not deductible from income; and
2) The paid-up capital of shares can be returned to shareholders on a tax-free basis.

Thus, these two features play an important role in determining the overall debt/equity ratio and corporate leverage.

B. PAID-UP CAPITAL

The *Income Tax Act* (Act) levies a tax on income, not on capital. Thus, it is necessary to distinguish between a corporation's income and capital for tax purposes.

PUC for Canadian tax purposes is analogous to the concept of "stated capital in corporate law": it measures the amount of capital that a corporation can return to shareholders on a tax-free basis. The Act deems payments to shareholders in excess of the PUC of their shares to be income.[1]

One initially determines the PUC of a class of shares under the applicable corporate statute.[2] Hence, the concept of PUC can vary among different corporate jurisdictions. The PUC of a share is a characteristic of and specific to *the share* — it does not attach to the shareholder. Thus, it does not necessarily change when one sells the share. Adjustments to PUC appear on the corporation's books, but do not show on the balance sheet.

In contrast, the adjusted cost base of a share is a feature unique to the shareholder. It does not affect the corporation. An adjustment to the adjusted cost base of a share does not affect the corporation's books or financial statements.

We determine the PUC of shares as at a point in time. The PUC of a share starts off equal to its stated capital for corporate purposes. For example, where a corporation issues shares for $100 per share, both its stated capital and the PUC of the shares is $100. The adjusted cost base of the shares to the initial shareholders is also $100.

The two measures of capital can, however, diverge because of subsequent adjustments for tax purposes that do not affect the corporation's financial records. Thus, a corporation's PUC for tax purposes may differ from its stated capital for financial accounting purposes. It will also vary from the cost base of the shares if one sells the shares. In the example just given, if the shareholder sells his shares for $150, the adjusted cost base of the shares to the purchaser is $150, while their PUC remains $100. Thus, the initial shareholder

---

1   See, eg, *Income Tax Act (Canada)*, s 84 [ITA].
2   *Ibid*, subs 89(1) "paid-up capital."

derives a gain of $50 and the PUC (and stated capital) of the shares remains constant. Hence, in evaluating financial statements for purchase and sale of a business, it is important to bear in mind that PUC and stated capital on the balance sheet may vary. The agreement for purchase and sale should include a covenant on PUC.

Example

Assume: Holdco is a corporation incorporated under the *Canada Business Corporations Act*. Holdco has not issued any shares prior to the transactions described below. Assume also that the shares are issued to, and held by, individual shareholders. Holdco is authorized to issue the following classes of shares:

Class	Rights
Class A	Voting, unlimited participation in dividends and on liquidation ("common shares").
Class B	Voting, no dividend entitlement, preferential participation on liquidation to the extent of $100 per share, redeemable and retractable for $100 per share, convertible into Class D on a 1:1 basis.
Class C	Non-voting, no dividend entitlement, preferential participation on liquidation to the extent of $100 per share, retractable for $100 per share.
Class D	Non-voting, unlimited participation in dividends and on liquidation.

Holdco issues one Class A share for $100.

Then:

Stated capital (Class A shares):

Before issuance	$0
Increase	$100
After issuance	$100

Paid-up capital (Class A shares):

Stated capital	$100
Adjustment	$0
Paid-up capital	$100

Hence, paid-up capital equals stated capital of shares.

Example		

ABC Inc is incorporated with an initial share capital of $10 million. The initial balance sheet would appear as follows:

ABC Inc Balance Sheet as at 1 Jan. 20-1 (in $000,000)

Assets		Liabilities	$0
Cash	$10	Share capital (PUC)	– $10
	$10		– $10

At this stage ABC Inc can return $10 million to its shareholders as a tax-free return of capital.

In 20-9, ABC Inc reorganizes and, as a consequence, its PUC reduces to $1 million. Its stated capital on the balance sheet remains $10 million. If ABC Inc redeems 50 percent of its shares for $5 million, the shareholders will be deemed to receive a taxable dividend of $4,500,000.

C. CLASSES OF SHARES

Corporate statutes presume all shares to be equal and to confer the same rights unless they expressly state otherwise. In order for shares to be considered to belong to different classes, they must, *in substance*, have different rights, conditions, privileges, or restrictions.

One determines the stated capital and paid-up capital of shares of interconvertible classes as if they were combined in one class.[3]

1) Capitalizing Retained Earnings

The amount of retained earnings capitalized affects the stated capital and the PUC of the shares and may also trigger a deemed dividend.[4]

D. STOCK DIVIDENDS

A stock dividend is the payment of a dividend in shares of the corporation. The corporation issues shares to existing shareholders

---

3   CBCA, subs 39(5); OBCA, subs 35(5).
4   ITA, subs 84(1).

without any additional consideration. Typically, stock dividends are prompted by a desire to ostensibly allocate retained earnings to shareholders, but without distributing cash. Subsection 43(2) of the CBCA requires the "declared amount" of a stock dividend to be added to the stated capital of the class of shares on which the corporation pays the dividend.[5] The "declared amount" of a dividend is the amount *declared* by the directors in the corporation's resolutions.

Example

Assume: Holdco declares a stock dividend and capitalizes $50 of its retained earnings to its Class A shares.

Then:

Stated capital (Class A shares):	
Before capitalization	$100
Capitalization	$50
After capitalization	$150

Paid-up capital (Class A shares):	
Stated capital	$150
Adjustment	$0
Paid-up capital	$150

The Act also deems the shareholders of the Class A shares to have received a dividend to the extent that the paid-up capital of the shares is increased without a corresponding increase in Holdco's net assets – in this example, $50. The rationale of the deemed dividend is that the company can now pay out an additional $50 of its PUC tax-free.

E. CONVERSION OF SHARES

Subsection 39(4) of the CBCA requires stated capital adjustments to be made on a conversion of shares from one class into another class.[6] The stated capital of the class from which one converts the shares is reduced by the appropriate percentage. The stated capital

---

5   See also OBCA, subs 38(2).
6   See also OBCA, subs 35(4).

of the class into which the shares are converted is increased by a corresponding amount.

Example

Assume: Holdco's shareholder elects to convert its Class B share into a Class D share.

Stated capital (Class B shares):	
Before conversion	$10
Deduction on conversion	$(10)
After conversion	$0
Paid-up capital (Class B shares):	
Stated capital	$0
Adjustment	$0
Paid-up capital	$0
Stated capital (Class D shares):	
Before conversion	$0
Increase on conversion	$10
After conversion	$10
Paid-up capital (Class B shares):	
Stated capital	$10
Adjustment	$0
Paid-up capital	$10

F. ADJUSTMENTS TO PAID-UP CAPITAL

The PUC of a share starts off equal to its stated capital for corporate purposes. The two measures of capital can, however, diverge because of adjustments that may have to be made for tax purposes. Examples of adjustments under the *Income Tax Act*:

- Subsections 66.3(2) and (4) (flow-through shares);
- Sections 84.1 and 84.2 (non–arm's length sales);
- Section 85 (transfer of property to a corporation);
- Subsections 87(3) and (9) (amalgamation);
- Subsection 192(4.1) (designation by corporation); and

- Section 212.1 (non–arm's length purchase of shares from non-resident).

The difference between PUC and stated capital can be a trap for anyone who relies solely on the corporation's financial statements to determine the PUC of shares. For example, the Act deems that where a corporation redeems its shares, any amount paid over the PUC of the shares is a dividend to the shareholder.[7] Since PUC may be lower than stated capital for accounting purposes, what appears on the financial statements to be a tax-free return of stated capital, may, for tax purposes, be a taxable dividend in the hands of the shareholder.

To avoid the risk of unexpected deemed dividends, it is desirable to reduce a corporation's stated capital for corporate purposes to accord with its PUC for income-tax purposes. This reduces the risk of inadvertently triggering income-tax consequences based on corporate share transactions.

G. SHARE REDEMPTIONS

Where a corporation redeems shares for an amount in excess of their PUC, the excess is deemed to be a dividend.[8] For example, assume that the stated capital and PUC of a share are $100, and the shareholder's adjusted cost base is $150. If the corporation redeems the share for $180, the shareholder is deemed to receive a dividend of $80.

Cash paid on redemption	$180
Paid-up capital	$100
Deemed dividend	$80

At the same time, the Act deems the shareholder to dispose of his or her share and to derive proceeds of disposition, which may trigger a capital gain. In order to prevent double taxation, however,

---

7   ITA, subs 84(3).
8   *Ibid.*

the Act reduces the shareholder's proceeds of disposition by the amount of the deemed dividend — that is, $80.

Cash paid on redemption	$180
Less: deemed dividend	$(80)
Proceeds of disposition	$100
Less: adjusted cost base	$(150)
Capital loss	$(50)

Thus, the shareholder is deemed to receive a dividend of $80 and suffers a capital loss of $50; that is an economic net gain of $30. The treatment of the dividend and capital loss for tax purposes, however, is quite different. The shareholder obtains a tax credit on the dividend if the corporation that redeems the share is a Canadian corporation.[9] Only 50 percent of the capital loss of $50 is deductible for tax purposes, and then only against the shareholder's capital gains. If the shareholder does not have any capital gains, the tax bite can exceed the economic gain.

The Act deems the capital loss of $50 to be nil if the taxpayer is affiliated with the corporation immediately after the redemption. In such a case, we add the amount of the denied loss proportionately (based on relative FMV) to the ACB of any other shares that the shareholder owns. The purpose of this stop-loss rule is to prevent the shareholder from recognizing his loss where he remains a part of an economic group of affiliated persons.[10]

9   *Ibid*, s 121.
10   *Ibid*, subs 40(3.6) and para 53(2)(f.2).

Chapter XI: Law and Accounting

A. GENERAL COMMENTS

Accounting deals with measurement and summarization of financial transactions according to generally accepted accounting principles and concepts. Finance is essentially corporate law that concerns the creation and valuation of financial instruments, such as stocks, bonds, and derivatives. Thus, both accounting and finance become important for lawyers whenever they deal with financial transactions and instruments. Lawyers incorporate accounting and finance concepts in commercial agreements.

B. BUSINESS CONTRACTS

The most common scenario where lawyers encounter accounting and finance issues is in litigation over agreements where the parties interpret them differently. In such cases, lawyers must either negotiate a settlement of the dispute or have a court adjudicate if negotiations are unsuccessful.

Legal disputes involving accounting often centre on basic concepts and terminology, such as "book value," "net profits," and "income." In some cases, the courts defer to GAAP and rely upon the accounting profession's understanding of these terms. In others, however, the courts reject GAAP and insert their own interpretation of the meaning of the words. As the cases that follow show, contractual problems involving interpretation of accounting terminology often arise in corporate agreements involving buyout clauses and in incentive compensation agreements for key employees. Most of the problems can be resolved at the drafting stage by using conventional terminology and defining the meaning of terms in the contract.

An example in the United States, *Piedmont Publishing Company v Rogers*,[1] provides insight into the formulation and resolution of a contractual dispute involving Mary Pickford Rogers (star of silent pictures) and Piedmont. The parties were rival applicants for a licence from the Federal Communications Commission for a television station in Winston-Salem, North Carolina, where Piedmont also owned and published two newspapers and a radio broadcasting station. Piedmont and Ms. Pickford decided to pool their interests and organized a new company, Triangle Broadcasting Corporation (Triangle) in North Carolina to apply for the licence.[2] The parties knew that only one licence would be granted, and that a contest for it might take so long that a television station already licensed in Winston-Salem might capture the television audience. Triangle was awarded the licence and an exclusive local contract with National Broadcasting Company (NBC).

The parties signed an agreement in New York on 25 May 1953 under which Piedmont subscribed for 1,000 shares of Triangle's stock, for $100,000. Ms. Pickford subscribed for 500 shares, for which she paid $50,000. Thus, Piedmont owned two-thirds and Ms. Pickford one-third of Triangle's stock.

The contract contained a buyout clause, which gave Piedmont an option to purchase Ms. Pickford's stock at the end of any of Triangle's fiscal years in 1956, 1957, 1958, and 1959. The formula to be used by Triangle's "regularly employed independent certified public accountants" to determine the purchase price for the stock was as follows:

---

1   193 Cal App 2d 171, 14 Cal Rptr 133 (District Court of Appeal, 2d District, Division 1, California 1961).
2   The facts of the case are outlined in the decision of Justice Drapeau.

An amount per share of stock equal to the *sum* of the two following items, divided by the number of outstanding shares of the corporation:

1. an amount equal to the *total book value* at the beginning of any such period of Triangle's common stock adjusted to reflect an annual depreciation and obsolescence charge of not over 10% against such tangible assets as have been depreciated on the books of Triangle at a higher rate; and

2. an amount determined by multiplying the average net annual profits of Triangle by five.

The multiplier declined over the four years. The multiplier for 1956 was five. If the option had been exercised in 1957, it would have been four; in 1958, three; and in 1959, two.

Piedmont exercised its option on 20 July 1956. The independent public accountants valued Triangle at $1,270,548, which made the Pickfords' one-third interest worth $423,000. The option price was approximately $86,000. The market value of Triangle did not include goodwill in "total book value" in the formula.

Goodwill would be the fair market value of the telecasting licence, the fair market value of the television station, as its listening audience grew in numbers, the value of its advertising contracts, and the fair market value of contracts with National Broadcasting Company. Pickford rejected the offer and the parties ended up in court.

The court concluded that by adding the word "total" to "book value," the parties meant to include the value of Triangle's intangible assets — including the goodwill (licence to telecast, the advertising value of the station and Triangle's contract with NBC). The court interpreted "total book value" to mean "fair value":

> We do not believe that gentlemen in control of Piedmont's policies, with their standing in their community and state, meant to use an accounting method that would cut down the fair value of Ms. Pickford's stock, if they exercise their option. We think, rather, they intended to pay her a fair price for her participation in securing the television license and in making the television station an outstanding success.

Sounder and safer principles of equity and fair dealing dictate the conclusion that when the contract was made everyone intended to include the value of the goodwill of the television station ... in computing the price of the Pickford stock when the time came for Piedmont to exercise its option; or if Piedmont did not exercise its option, the price Ms. Pickford was to pay if she exercised her option.[3]

Accounting principles permit only *purchased* goodwill to be reflected on the balance sheet. Otherwise, goodwill is not included as an asset and does not affect "book value."

However, the court rejected general accounting principles as determining what the parties intended when they entered into the contract, saying that the issue is one of law and fact and is not to be determined solely on principles of accounting.

Of course, the entire dispute could have been avoided if the lawyers had used the accepted accounting terminology, "book value," if that was what they intended. Alternatively, if they intended to deviate from the accounting principle by including goodwill in the formula, the agreement could have been drafted by defining "total book value" in the contract to include such goodwill.

C. EMPLOYMENT CONTRACTS

Executive compensation policies for key employees based upon GAAP can, and usually will, affect management's behaviour. Since the measurement of profit is as much a question of timing as it is of valuation, management has a clear incentive, in most cases, to accelerate the recognition of profit. It is only in rare cases where it is advantageous to delay the recognition of revenues and profits. Ultimately, the incentive effect depends on the wording of the employment contract.

The term "net profit" appears frequently in employment contracts of managers, executives, and chief executive officers of

---

3   *Ibid* at 188–89 (Cal App 2d).

corporations. Net profit is essentially an accounting concept that derives from the principles of bookkeeping applied in the preparation of the income statement.

Net profit of a business refers to amounts that the entity receives, or has receivable, in the form of cash or its equivalent, from completed sales and net of all current expenses. The difference between the cost price and the market price of unsold goods (inventory) is not profit in a going concern. Inventory is an asset or resource that the business will realize in a future fiscal period.

Profits include only realized profits and not potential profits. In *Jennery v Olmstead*,[4] for example, Justice Peckham said:

> The profits are, as I have said, the amount of money received by the bank from its investments, by way of interest, over and above the amount of interest it has to pay its depositors, together with the amount of any money it had received by sale of property over and above its cost to the bank. If such a sale had been made, then a profit had arisen, but if not, then no profit had accrued simply from the fact that the property, if sold, would have resulted in a profit.

"Profit" is a *net* concept, the difference between income and outgoes or expenses. In contrast, "income" means what has come in or been earned as a receivable. Thus, income is a gross concept.

The meaning of "net profits" in a contract derives from the words of the contract and such conduct of the parties as it warranted in interpreting the contract. Without further elaboration, net profits do not include estimated profits, or earnings never received or entered upon the books of the corporation. Thus, without receipt or the equivalent, profits do not legally exist.[5]

The measurement of "net profit" or "net income" involves two components, valuation of the transaction through objective evidence and timing. Thus, we have to answer two questions:

- How much to record? and
- In which fiscal period should we record the transaction?

---

4   36 Hun (NY) 536.
5   *Tooey v CL Percival Co*, 192 Iowa 267 (Supreme Court of Iowa 1921) [*Tooey*].

These questions are particularly important in employment contracts containing bonus or profit-sharing clauses where the employees' employment contract is terminated or comes to an end. In the United States, in *Tooey*,[6] for example, the employee (plaintiff) was employed as the manager of the paper and wooden ware department of the defendant company. His contract provided for a salary of $150 per month "and 25 percent of the net profits of this department up to December 31, 1916 . . . the division of the profits to be made in January 1916 and January 1917." The plaintiff received his normal salary and also the net profits on sales made and delivered to the defendant's customers up to 31 December 1916 when the contract was terminated.

However, the plaintiff claimed additional bonus based upon sales of merchandise prior to 31 December 1916, but which had not been shipped by year-end, and were subject to cancellation. The corporation would record its sales only when it shipped the merchandise to customers. The plaintiff wanted to accelerate revenue recognition prior to shipment of merchandise, which offended the revenue recognition principle.

The Court rejected the plaintiff's claim based both upon accounting principles, which the Court described as "practical bookkeeping," and the legal definition of net profits. The Court also said it is a well-established rule of law that, in all cases in which the terms of the contract or the language employed raises a question of doubtful construction, and it appears that the parties have practically interpreted their contract, the courts will follow that practical construction. The Court reached the same conclusion based on the practical construction that the parties themselves had put upon the terms of their contract.

D. NEGLIGENT MISREPRESENTATION

Negligent misrepresentation of financial statements is an actionable tort. A successful claim for negligent misrepresentation has five requirements:

---

6   *Ibid.*

1) A duty of care based on a "special relationship" between the parties;
2) Misrepresentation of fact;
3) Negligence by the representor in making the misrepresentation;
4) Reasonable reliance by the representee on the misrepresentation; and
5) Damages to the representee by the reliance.[7]

[*Note:* Some Securities Acts have a less stringent statutory civil liability provision for auditors whereby a plaintiff does not have to establish that the auditor owed a duty of care, that there was reliance on the auditor's report, or that the auditor was negligent (although the auditor may have a due diligence defence), but merely that the report contained a misrepresentation.]

Where an auditor issues an unqualified (unmodified) audit opinion on financial statements, the opinion will typically be in a standard form prescribed by the Canadian Institute of Chartered Accountants as follows:[8]

> In our opinion, these financial statements present fairly in all material respects, the financial position of the Company as at . . . and the results of its operations and for the years ended . . . in accordance with Canadian generally accepted accounting principles applied on a consistent basis.

The essential element of this opinion is that the financial statements must "present fairly" and be in accordance with GAAP. Problems arise where the statements are materially misleading, but, nevertheless, in accordance with accounting principles or where GAAPs are evolving.

In *Kripps*,[9] for example, the plaintiffs were investors who purchased debentures from a mortgage corporation that had issued a

---

7   *Queen v Cognos Inc,* [1993] 1 SCR 87 at 110.

8   See Canadian Institute of Chartered Accountants, *CICA Handbook,* loose-leaf (Toronto: Canadian Institute of Chartered Accountants, 2010) section 5400 at para 22.

9   *Kripps et al v Touche Ross* (1997) Court of Appeal for British Columbia, docket CA019919 (1997 0425) [*Kripps*].

prospectus containing financial statements and an audit opinion certified by the defendant accounting firm, Touche Ross. The mortgage corporation disclosed in its notes to the financial statements that it "capitalized" accrued interest on mortgages in default if the company's management believed those amounts to be adequately secured. The uncollected interest was included in the corporation's income and added to the principal of the mortgage. The trial judge found that the company policy with respect to capitalizing unpaid interest was consistent with GAAP during the relevant period. The trial judge also found that the amount of mortgages in default was material information that had not been adequately disclosed and which would have given the investors a better understanding of the risks involved.

However, although capitalizing unpaid interest was part of GAAP at the time Touche prepared its auditor's report, the accounting profession had begun to recognize the inherent failings in this approach. The CICA began to recognize that failing to disclose explicitly the amount of unpaid interest made it difficult for financial statements to fulfil the broad aim of presenting fairly the financial position of the company, and that GAAP had to be changed so as to fulfil the broader aim of fair presentation.

GAAP may be the auditor's guide to forming his or her opinion, but they were retained to form an opinion on the fairness of the financial statements, and not merely on their conformity to GAAP. The Court of Appeal held that the auditor's opinion that "financial statements present fairly the financial position of the company in accordance with general accepted accounting principles" was ambiguous. It was neither a clear statement of opinion by the professional auditor that the financial statements present the position of the company fairly, nor that the financial statements are in accordance with GAAP.

GAAP is only a tool to achieve fair representation and not an end in and of itself: "Given the aim in auditing, the understanding of audits that those who might rely on them have on them, and that auditors know of this understanding, auditors cannot hide behind the qualifications of their reports ('according to GAAP') where the financial statements nevertheless misrepresent the financial position of the company. This does not open the floodgates to liability for auditors" (at 36–37 of *Kripps*).

The test, however, should be applied deferentially to professional practices and standards and only in those circumstances "if a standard practice fails to adopt obvious and reasonable precautions which are readily apparent to the ordinary finder of fact."[10] Ultimately, the selection of the appropriate standard of care is a question of law.[11]

E. INCOME TAX

1) Accounting Period

The *Income Tax Act* prescribes a calendar year for individuals as their reporting period. Corporations are allowed to choose their own fiscal periods.[12] The division of a business into arbitrary segments gives rise to problems of accurate income calculation. A taxpayer's lifetime is similarly segmented into annual periods and this segmentation also gives rise to some special problems.

Businesses carried on in partnership or as a sole proprietorship, do not have a separate legal personality and are not taxpayers as such. The income from such businesses must be reported by the partners or the proprietor in their personal capacity. The business may, however, use a fiscal period that is different from the calendar year. Thus, taxpayers must apply appropriate measurements of net income for each fiscal period.

2) Accounting Methods

a) General Comment

Although employees must report their income according to the cash basis of accounting, businesses are generally required to use the ac-

---

10   *ter Neuzen v Korn* (1995), 11 BCLR (3d) 201 (SCC).
11   *CNR v Vincent*, [1979] 1 SCR 364: see also *Wade v CNR*, [1978] 1 SCR 1064.
12   ITA, subs 249(1) and 249.1.

crual method. The accrual method is considered particularly appropriate for a trading business.[13] There are, however, other methods of accounting that may be more appropriate for some businesses, particularly businesses with peculiar or unique cash flow patterns.

b) Instalment Sales
For tax accounting, sales business may adopt a variation of the accrual method. The instalment method of accounting, for example, is considered appropriate for a taxpayer whose business involves instalment sales that require a small down payment with the balance due over an extended period.[14]

c) Completed Contract
Under the completed contract method, the taxpayer defers recognition of all expenses and all revenues, in respect of long-term contracts, until the contract is complete.[15] The completed contract method of accounting has been rejected for tax purposes although it might be an appropriate accounting method.

d) Cash Method
Income from office or employment is usually reported on a cash basis. This is confirmed by the use of the words "received" and "enjoyed" in sections 5 and 6 of the *Income Tax Act*.

The decision to allow certain taxpayers to use the cash method of accounting is based primarily on a concern for administrative convenience. It would be quite difficult, if not impossible, for millions of employees to prepare their annual income tax returns on an accrual basis of accounting (see the following section). The accrual basis requires at least some rudimentary knowledge of accounting principles (realization, timing, etc.) that is beyond the inclination of most non-accountants.

---

13   *Ken Steeves Sales Ltd v MNR*, [1955] CTC 47 (Ex Ct).

14   *MNR v Publishers Guild of Canada Ltd* (1957), 57 DTC 1017 (Ex Ct) [*Publishers Guild*].

15   *Wilson & Wilson Ltd v MNR*, [1960] CTC 1 (Ex Ct).

Accrual basis statements also require careful auditing by the tax authorities. Since employee income tax returns represent approximately 80 percent of all tax returns filed, mandatory accrual basis returns from all taxpayers would place an intolerable burden on the Canada Revenue Agency's (CRA) resources. The incremental auditing and accounting fees incurred by both taxpayers and the CRA as a result of accrual accounting cannot be justified by the marginal improvement in the accuracy of annual net income calculations.

There is an important exception from the accrual method for farmers and fishers, who are specifically authorized to use the cash basis method of accounting.[16] The theoretical justification for this particular variation is that, in most circumstances, the distortion of net income when using the cash basis method is minimal and, hence, justifiable in that it is easier for these taxpayers to maintain cash basis books of account.

More pragmatically, one recognizes that it would be politically inconvenient to withdraw a tax concession that has been made available to farmers for so long. If anything, the pull is in the opposite direction. Until 1980, only farmers could use the cash basis of accounting; in that year the legislation extended the cash basis of accounting to fishers, a practice that the CRA had administratively tolerated for many years prior.

The requirement of cash accounting for employees does allow for some modest amount of tax planning. Employees can, within limits, reduce their immediate tax liabilities by accelerating payment of their expenses and delaying receipt of their income.

In determining income for tax purposes under the cash method, an individual must include not only the cash that he receives in the year, but also any other payments that the individual constructively receives in the year. Thus, the cash method of accounting includes in income both actual and constructive receipts. The essence of the constructive receipts doctrine is that an individual cannot postpone recognizing income simply by failing to exercise his power to collect it. For example, although an individual can de-

---

16   ITA, s 28.

lay actual payment beyond the year-end, he cannot avoid including an amount in income merely by waiting until the next year to pick up his paycheque.

The distinction between the two situations is subtle but significant. In the first case, the taxpayer does not have the power to cash, or otherwise control, the cheque because he does not receive it until after the year-end. In the second case, the taxpayer constructively possesses the cheque, but chooses not to exercise his power of possession in order to delay including the amount in income.

These distinctions are particularly important in closely held corporations. Where an owner-manager of a corporation performs services for the corporation, she is entitled to payment for services. Although the owner exercises discretion as to the timing of the payment, the salary is not considered to be paid until the owner has the corporation's cheque in her possession. Thus, merely because the owner controls the timing of the cheque does not mean that payment to her is accelerated to a point in time before the corporation actually issues the cheque.

To be sure, this allows owner-managers of corporations considerable flexibility in arranging their annual compensation through salary and bonuses. Depending upon the prevailing rates of tax for a particular year, an owner can elect to accelerate or defer salary payments in order to maximize his or her after-tax returns. This form of tax avoidance is a small price to pay for what would otherwise become an impossibly complex accounting system for employees. Similarly, the owner-manager may choose to forgo some or all of his or her salary in a year. The amount forgone, however, is not imputed to the individual merely because he or she was entitled to the amount. We do not impute taxable salaries to controlling shareholders.

e) Accrual Method

In contrast with the requirement of cash basis accounting for employment income, business and property income is usually required to be reported on an accrual basis. The Act does not specifically stipulate a particular method for calculating business or property income. Section 9 says only that a taxpayer's income from a business or property is her profit therefrom. The term "profit," however, has been judicially interpreted to mean profit calculated in accordance with commercial practice, and commercial practice favours accrual accounting for most businesses. Hence, the accrual method is mandated indirectly through the requirement to adhere to GAAP.

f) Modified Accrual

The "modified accrual method" applicable to professionals is an exception to the accrual basis of accounting. Professionals, like their business counterparts, are required to calculate income on an accrual basis. Professionals can, however, elect to exclude their work-in-progress in calculating net income for tax purposes.[17]

g) Holdbacks

In applying the accrual basis of accounting, the time of sale of goods and services is usually the most convenient time to recognize revenue. The time of sale is not, however, the only time for revenue recognition. Certain businesses may deviate from the norm and recognize revenue at some other time. For example, contractors (persons engaged in the construction of buildings, roads, dams, bridges, and similar structures) can, by administrative grace, defer recognition of their income until such time as "holdback payments" become legally receivable.[18] This rule varies from the usual accrual accounting test, which does not use legal entitlement as the determining criterion for recognizing revenue. Contractors may, however, also accelerate the recognition of profit by bringing into income amounts that may not be legally receivable by virtue of a mechanics' lien or similar statute.

---

17 *Ibid* at para 34(a).
18 See Canada Revenue Agency, Interpretation Bulletin IT-92R2, "Income of Contractors" (1 January 1995).

h) Net Worth Assessments

To this point, we have discussed the more conventional methods of determining income – cash basis, accrual accounting, and modified accrual. There remains one other technique for calculating income, which is particularly painful for taxpayers. This technique is the "net worth" or arbitrary method of calculating income.

The CRA issues a net worth assessment when a taxpayer does not file a return or, in some cases, when it does not accept the taxpayer's figures.[19] The theoretical principle underlying the calculation of income using the net worth basis is simple: income is equal to the difference between a taxpayer's realized wealth at the beginning and at the end of a year, plus any amount consumed by the taxpayer during the year. This principle derives from the Haig-Simons definition of income. Algebraically, the principle is stated as follows:

Income = (WE – WB) + C

where:

WE = Wealth at end of year,
WB = Wealth at beginning of year, and
C = Consumption during the year.

Note, however, that, unlike the Haig-Simons formulation of income, the formula does not take into account any accrued but unrealized gains in the value of property.

For example, assume that a taxpayer started out a year owning $100,000 in property, such as a house, car, clothing, furniture, cash, etc. At the end of the year the CRA estimates that the taxpayer owns $105,000 in property. It also estimates that the taxpayer spent $45,000 during the year on food, clothing, mortgage payments, vacations, children's education, etc. If the taxpayer has not engaged in any borrowing or repayment of loans, her net income for the year is $50,000: that is, ($105,000 – $100,000) + $45,000. If in fact, the taxpayer borrowed $8,000 during the year, her wealth at the end of the year is only $97,000 and her income for the year would be only $42,000.

---

19   ITA, subs 152(7).

Notice the resemblance between the net worth basis of determining income and the Haig-Simons concept of income. The CRA employs this method when a taxpayer does not, or cannot, use conventional accounting records to calculate her income and the CRA does not have any other way of assessing the delinquent taxpayer's income. In these circumstances, the system must rely on fundamental concepts: income is the money value of the net accretion of economic power between two points of time.

3) Generally Accepted Accounting Principles

The Act determines income from business or property by reference to subsection 9(1):

> Subject to this Part, a taxpayer's income for a taxation year from a business or property is the taxpayer's profit from that business or property for that year.

At one time there was a tentative proposal to incorporate in the Act a general statement to the effect that business profits should be calculated according to GAAP. The proposal was never implemented because of the difficulty in establishing just what GAAP means in all cases. The absence of a statutory provision requiring the computation of profits according to GAAP did not, however, inhibit the development of a similar doctrine in case law. Indeed, if anything, we have arrived at virtually the same result through judicial decisions.

a) Section 9

Although there may be disagreement among accountants concerning the best practice in respect of certain matters, it is now well established that section 9 imports into the Act, as a starting point, the standard accounting methods used in the business world. Thorson P dealt with this matter in *Imperial Oil v MNR*,[20] in *Daley v MNR*,[21]

---

20 *Imperial Oil v MNR*, [1947] CTC 353 (Ex Ct).
21 *Daley v MNR*, [1950] CTC 254, 4 DTC 877 (Ex Ct).

and in *Royal Trust Co v MNR*.[22] In this last case, dealing with the deductibility of a claimed expenditure, he said:

> it may be stated categorically that . . . the first matter to be determined . . . is whether it was made or incurred by the taxpayer in accordance with the ordinary principles of commercial trading or well accepted principles of business practice.[23]

The important point, however, is that the determination of net profit is a question of law and not a matter of GAAP.[24] Although a court may look at the treatment of particular items by reference to GAAP, these principles at best only represent some of the guidelines for preparing financial statements. GAAP may influence the calculation of income, but only on a case-by-case basis.[25] GAAP may well be influential in determining what is deductible, but they are not the operative legal criteria. To be sure, subsection 9(1) represents a starting point and normal accounting practices for tax purposes may be overborne by specific statutory provisions, judicial precedent, or commercial practice.[26]

b) Tax Profits

What is the relationship between accounting profit and profit as determined for income tax purposes? For tax purposes, the starting point requires an examination of generally accepted commercial practice. Is a particular expenditure deductible in computing income according to the rules of general commercial and accounting

---

22 *Royal Trust Co v MNR*, [1957] CTC 32, 57 DTC 1055 (Ex Ct) (ordinary principles of commercial trading and business practice are the normal rule for measuring income).

23 *Royal Trust Co v MNR*, *ibid* at 1060 (DTC).

24 *Symes v Canada*, [1993] 4 SCR 695; *Neonex International Ltd v Canada*, [1978] CTC 485 (FCA) [*Neonex*].

25 *Canderel Ltd v Canada*, [1998] 1 SCR 147.

26 See, generally: *Associated Investors of Canada Ltd v MNR*, [1967] CTC 138 (Ex Ct) [*Associated Investors*]; *Neonex*, above note 24; *MHL Holdings Ltd v MNR*, [1988] 2 CTC 42 (FCTD); *Coppley Noyes & Randall Ltd v MNR*, [1991] 1 CTC 541 (FCTD); and *West Kootenay Power & Light Co v MNR* (1991), 92 DTC 6023 (FCA) [*West Kootenay*].

practice? Or is a particular receipt included in computing income according to commercial rules? Once we answer these preliminary questions, other factors may come into play in determining the appropriate tax treatment.

Take depreciation as an example.[27] The general commercial and accounting rule is that, in calculating net income, a reasonable amount of depreciation can be deducted from revenues. Indeed, commercial practice recognizes many different methods of calculating depreciation (for example, straight-line, declining balance, sum of the years, etc.). Provided that the method is acceptable and the amount is reasonable, depreciation expense is a deductible expense in determining net income for financial statement purposes.

The Act, however, *specifically* prohibits a deduction for depreciation[28] and, therefore, such an expense cannot be taken into account in calculating net income for tax purposes. In lieu of depreciation, however, the Act allows a deduction for capital cost allowance (CCA) in an amount that may or may not be related to accounting depreciation. Thus, tax profits and accounting income may be substantially different.

c) Statutory Deviations

The Act deviates from accounting principles in many areas. Three statutory deviations from standard accounting practice are discussed later in this chapter.

d) Reserves and Allowances

Accountants sometimes prefer to anticipate certain contingencies by setting up an allowance that has the effect of reducing income in the current period. The Act seriously inhibits this conservative and quite normal accounting practice by denying, as a deduction, "an amount transferred or credited to a reserve, contingent account or sinking fund except as expressly permitted by this Part."[29] Instead,

---

27 Numerous other examples may be found in Subdivision b of Division B, Part I of the ITA.

28 *Ibid*, para 18(1)(b).

29 *Ibid*, para 18(1)(e).

the Act sets out a specific and rigid regime in respect of accounting for reserves. Thus, there can be a significant difference between accounting reserves and tax reserves.

e) Depreciation

At one time, depreciation expense was recognized as a legitimate deduction for tax purposes, subject to showing a sound accounting basis for the deduction. It is indisputable that many capital assets depreciate with use, but the amount of depreciation and the rate at which it occurs are frequently quite speculative. To control the speculations, and to minimize disputes, the Act details a CCA system, which imposes limits on the amount of depreciation deductible in calculating income for tax purposes.

Although, in general, CCA rates are designed to be reasonably realistic, the system is Procrustean. There is no attempt to guarantee that the rates for tax purposes conform to depreciation recognized for accounting purposes. The rates are the same for all taxpayers although their depreciation experience may differ greatly. Further, the CCA system is also used to achieve other socioeconomic objectives. It may, for example, be used to stimulate economic activity in depressed regions of the country. Thus, income for tax purposes can differ quite significantly from income reported to shareholders or creditors, and there is nothing unusual or improper in this.

f) Inventory

A major component of the expenses of some businesses, and thus a major factor in determining income, is the cost of goods sold. To calculate the cost of goods sold, a business must establish its inventory of goods on hand at the year-end, and determine its value. There are a number of accounting approaches to inventory valuation. One method that is commonly used by accountants for financial statement purposes, the last-in, first-out (LIFO) method, has been judicially rejected for tax purposes as being inappropriate.[30] Here once

---

30 *Minister of National Revenue v Anaconda American Brass Ltd*, [1956] 2 WLR 31 (PC on appeal from SCC) [*Anaconda*].

again, the use of one method for accounting and another for tax purposes can cause a significant difference in the final net income figure.

4) Realization and Recognition of Income

There are many problems relating to realization and the appropriate time to recognize income for tax purposes. Some of these problems are simply difficulties inherent in the nature of the transaction, but others arise from attempts by taxpayers to apply the realization concept to their best advantage.

Stock options are an example of the inherent difficulty in correctly applying the concepts of realization and revenue recognition in tax law. Suppose that ABC Ltd gives employee E an option to buy 1,000 shares of its stock at a price of $10/share, exercisable at any time within three years. The option is given in Year 1 at a time when the stock is trading publicly at $12 per share. E exercises the option in Year 2 when the stock is trading at $15 per share. In Year 3, E sells the stock for $16 per share.

Assuming that the transaction gives rise to income in E's hands, two questions arise: 1) how much income? and 2) in what year? It is arguable that E should be treated as having received $2,000 in Year 1; the company conferred on E, in that year, a benefit in the form of an opportunity to buy for $10,000 what a stranger would pay $12,000 to acquire. It is also arguable, however, that E's benefit is purely potential; if the stock drops below $10 and stays down for three years the option will be worthless.

It could be said that E received the benefit in Year 2 when he actually bought the stock at $5,000 below its market value. Our discussion of the conventional approach to paper gains might suggest, however, as a third alternative, that E should not recognize any income until he sells the shares or otherwise parts with them. If the shares rise or fall in value before E parts with them, the actual benefit to him will be greater or less, accordingly. Using this reasoning, we would tax E in Year 3 on income of $6,000.

The Act provides an arbitrary, but reasonable, solution to the two problems of timing and quantification. Subsection 7(1) generally recognizes E's income in the year in which he exercises the option or disposes of it. The amount of income is either the difference between the option price and the current value of the shares or the amount that the taxpayer receives when he disposes of the option.[31] Thus, in our hypothetical situation, E would recognize $5,000 of income in Year 2. This solution really involves identifying the option as the source of E's gain. It is consistent with our basic discussion of realization to say that E's gain is only a paper gain so long as E holds the option, but it becomes a real gain when he parts with the option by exercising it or disposing of it to someone else.

5) Conformity of Accounting Methods

A taxpayer's income for a taxation year from a business or property is the profit therefrom for the year.[32]

a) Use of GAAP

The term "profit" means net profit. In the absence of any specific proscription, profit is determined according to commercial and generally accepted accounting principles. Hence, absent an express or implicit statutory or judicial proscription against the use of a particular accounting method, a taxpayer may determine income for tax purposes according to any appropriate accounting method. Thorson P explained the rule in *MNR v Publishers Guild of Canada Ltd*:

> If the law does not prohibit the use of a particular system of accounting then the opinion of accountancy experts that it is an accepted system and is appropriate to the taxpayer's business and most nearly accurately reflects his income position should

---

31   Actually, ITA, subs 7(1) is somewhat more complex to provide against artificial dealings through non–arm's length transactions. Further, subs 7(1.1) provides for different treatment in the case of Canadian-controlled private corporations and subs 7(8) addresses shares of publicly listed companies.

32   *Ibid*, subs 9(1).

prevail with the Court if the reasons for the opinion commend themselves to it.[33]

Similarly, in *Silverman v MNR*:

> the statute does not define what is to be taken as the profit from a business, nor does it describe how or by what method such profit is to be computed, though it does contain provisions to which, for income tax purposes, any method is subject . . . the method must be one which accurately reflects the result of the year's operation, and where two different methods, either of which may be acceptable for business purposes, differ in their results, for income tax purposes the appropriate method is that which most accurately shows the profit from the year's operations.[34]

Ultimately, however, the measure of profit is a question of law.

b) Conformity of Methods

A taxpayer can use one generally accepted accounting method for financial statement purposes and another for income tax purposes.

---

33 *Publishers Guild*, above note 14 at 1018; see also *Canada v Nomad Sand and Gravel Ltd* (1990), 91 DTC 5032 at 5034–35 (FCA); *Associated Investors*, above note 26; *Maritime Telegraph & Telephone Co v MNR* (1991), 91 DTC 5038 at 5039 (FCTD), aff'd [1992] 1 CTC 264 (FCA) [*Maritime Telegraph*].

34 *Silverman v MNR* (1960), 60 DTC 1212 at 1214 (Ex Ct); see also *Bank of Nova Scotia v Canada* (1979), 80 DTC 6009 at 6013 (FCTD):

> generally recognized accounting and commercial principles and practices are to be applied to all matters of commercial and taxation accounting unless there is something in the taxing statute which precludes them from coming into play. The legislator when dealing with financial and commercial matters in any enactment, including of course a taxing statute, is to be presumed at law to be aware of the general financial and commercial principles which are relevant to the subject-matter covered by the legislation. The Act pertains to business and financial matters and is addressed to the general public. It follows that where no particular mention is made as to any variation from common ordinary practice or where the attainment of the objects of the legislation does not necessarily require such variation, then common practice and generally recognized accounting and commercial principles and terminology must be deemed to apply.

In the absence of any statutory requirement that a taxpayer use the same method of accounting to calculate income both for tax and financial statement purposes, a taxpayer can select the most appropriate method of accounting for tax purposes.

The purpose for which we calculate income determines the appropriate method of accounting. An accounting method that is suitable for a particular purpose is not necessarily the appropriate measure of income for tax purposes.[35]

What is appropriate for tax purposes? The general rule is to apply that principle or method that provides the proper picture of net income. In MacGuigan J's words:

> it would be undesirable to establish an absolute requirement that there must always be conformity between financial statements and tax returns and I am satisfied that the cases do not do so. *The approved principle* is that whichever method presents the "truer picture" of a taxpayer's revenue, which more fairly and accurately portrays income, and which "matches" revenue and expenditure, if one method does, is the one that must be followed.[36]

c) A "Truer Picture" of Income?

It is not always easy to apply the rule that a taxpayer may adopt whichever accounting method presents the "truer picture" of revenues and expenses. There are cases where a particular accounting principle presents a "truer picture" for income statement purposes at the expense of some accuracy or relevance in the balance sheet. In other cases, the adoption of a particular accounting method more accurately summarizes a taxpayer's closing balances while sacrificing accuracy on the income statement. *West Kootenay Power & Light Co v MNR*[37] rightly emphasized a proper matching of

---

35   *Friedberg v Canada*, [1993] 4 SCR 285.

36   *West Kootenay*, above note 26 at 6028 [emphasis added]. See also *Maritime Telegraph*, above note 33 (FCA) ("earned method" of reporting income for accounting and tax purposes produced "truer picture" of taxpayer's income).

37   *West Kootenay, ibid.*

revenues and expenses and accuracy of the net income figure for tax purposes. Ultimately, however, the computation of profit for tax purposes is a question of law.[38]

A classic example of the conflict between income statement and balance sheet values is seen in accounting for inventory values. Under LIFO method of inventory accounting, the cost of goods most recently purchased or acquired is the cost that is assigned to the cost of goods sold. Hence, the inventory on hand at the end of an accounting period is valued at the cost that was attributed to the inventory at the beginning of the period (first-in, still here). Any increases in quantity during a period are valued at the cost prevailing during the time the accumulations are deemed to have occurred. Any decreases in quantities are considered to have first reduced the most recent accumulations.[39]

Under the FIFO method, the process is reversed: the cost of goods first acquired is assigned to the first goods sold. The closing inventory comprises the cost of the most recent purchases (last-in, still here).

The use of the FIFO method of accounting for the flow of inventory costs tends to overstate net income during inflationary periods and more accurately reflect the current value of closing inventory on the balance sheet. In contrast, the LIFO method more realistically measures "real" net income, while sacrificing some accuracy in year-end balance sheet values.

Most accountants and business people argue that the use of LIFO for inventory accounting during inflationary periods results in a more meaningful and "truer picture" of business income during inflationary periods. The Privy Council in *MNR v Anaconda American Brass Ltd*,[40] however, rejected the use of the LIFO method of inventory valuation for tax purposes. Their Lordships were concerned that the method would permit the creation of hidden reserves:

---

38 *Canderel*, above note 25; *Ikea Ltd v Canada*; *Toronto College Park Ltd v Canada*, [1998] 1 SCR 183.

39 See *CICA Handbook*, section 3030.07.

40 *Anaconda*, above note 30.

the evidence of expert witnesses, that the L.I.F.O. method is generally acceptable, and in this case the most appropriate, method of accountancy, is not conclusive of the question that the Court has to decide. That may be found as a fact by the Exchequer Court and affirmed by the Supreme Court. The question remains whether it conforms to the prescription of the *Income Tax Act*. As already indicated, in their Lordships' opinion it does not.[41]

The accounting principle for selecting the proper method of inventory valuation is clear: the most suitable method for determining cost is that which results in charging against operations those costs that most fairly match the sales revenue for the period. The *CICA Handbook* states the principle as follows:

> The method selected for determining cost should be one which results in the fairest matching of costs against revenues regardless of whether or not the method corresponds to the physical flow of goods.[42]

Anaconda was an unfortunate decision based upon a misunderstanding of accounting methods. The decision rests on two notions: 1) the physical flow of inventory determines values; and 2) the potential for creation of "hidden" reserves. Both premises are fundamentally flawed. The determination of cost does not depend upon the physical flow of goods but on the "fairest" matching of revenues and expenses. The fairest matching of costs against revenues is, presumably, also the method which presents the "truer picture" of income for tax purposes. Thus, the question is: which method of accounting produces the best and fairest picture of annual profits? Equally, the hidden reserve argument ignores the primary purpose that the method serves, namely, the determination of a fair measure of an enterprise's annual income.

---

41   *Ibid* at 1225.
42   See *CICA Handbook*, s 3030 and the virtually identical language of the American Institute of Chartered Public Accountants, Accounting Research Bulletin No 43, ch 4.

d) Non–Arm's Length Transactions

The Act contains stringent anti-avoidance rules to govern transfers of property between persons who do not deal with each other at arm's length. The purpose of these rules is to discourage taxpayers who have close social, family, or economic relationships with each other from artificially avoiding tax through the manipulation of transaction values.

Related persons are deemed not to deal with each other at arm's length.[43]

It is a question of fact whether unrelated persons deal with each other at arm's length. Parties are not considered to be dealing with each other at arm's length if one person dictates the terms of the bargain on both sides of a transaction.[44]

The anti-avoidance rules are as follows:[45]

- Where, in a non–arm's length transaction, a purchaser acquires anything for a price in excess of its fair market value, she is deemed to acquire the property at its fair market value. Consequently, notwithstanding that the purchaser actually paid a price higher than fair market value, the purchaser is deemed to acquire the property at a cost equal to fair market value.

Example

A taxpayer buys land from his mother at a cost of $70,000 when, in fact, the land has a fair market value of $50,000 (this may happen if the mother deliberately wants to trigger a higher capital gain to offset unused capital losses). The Act deems the son to have acquired the land at a cost of $50,000. The mother calculates her gain on the basis of her actual proceeds of $70,000. Hence, the $20,000 difference is taxed twice.

---

43 ITA, s 251.

44 *Swiss Bank Corp v MNR*, [1971] CTC 427 (Ex Ct), aff'd (1972), [1974] SCR 1144 (parties acted in concert, exerting considerable influence together; money transactions merely moved funds from one pocket to another); *Millward v MNR*, [1986] 2 CTC 423 (FCTD) (members of law firm who dealt with each other at less than commercial rates of interest not at arm's length); *Noranda Mines Ltd v MNR*, [1987] 2 CTC 2089 (TCC) (existence of arm's length relationship excluded where one party has *de facto* control over both parties).

45 ITA, s 69.

- Where, in a non–arm's length transaction, a vendor has disposed of anything at less than its fair market value, the vendor is deemed to have received proceeds equal to fair market value. Thus, notwithstanding that she actually received a lower price, the vendor is taxed on the basis of her deemed proceeds.

Example

A taxpayer sells land that has a fair market value of $50,000 to his daughter for $40,000. Paragraph 69(1)(b) deems the father to have received $50,000. His daughter, however, acquires the property for her actual cost of $40,000, leaving her with the potential of a larger gain when she sells the property and the potential of double taxation of the economic difference of $10,000.

The overall effect of these rules is that taxpayers can be liable to double taxation in non–arm's length transactions. Section 69 can have a punitive effect. It is deliberately structured to discourage non–arm's length parties from dealing with each other at prices other than fair market value.

Example

Assume: An individual owns a property to which the following applies:

Cost	$1,000
FMV	$5,000

She sells the property to her son for $4,000.

Then:

Tax consequences to mother:

Deemed proceeds of sale	$5,000
Cost	($1,000)
Gain	$4,000

If the son sells the property at its fair market value of $5,000, he also realizes a gain of $1,000:

Actual proceeds of sale	$5,000
Actual cost of property	($4,000)
Gain	$1,000

Total gain:

Realized by mother	$4,000
Realized by son	$1,000
	$5,000

Thus, an asset with an accrued gain of $4,000 triggers an actual gain of $5,000. The $1,000 that is exposed to double taxation represents the shortfall between the fair market value of the property ($5,000) and the price at which it is sold ($4,000).

6) Timing of Income

Employment income is generally taxed on a cash basis. In contrast, with a few important exceptions, business and property income are normally calculated on an accrual basis. Thus, generally speaking, we recognize income from business and property for tax purposes when services are performed or goods are sold, rather than when payment for the goods or services is actually received. In other words, although a taxpayer may have to wait for some time to receive payment for goods sold or services rendered, he will be taxed on income in the year in which he earns it.

The accrual method of accounting is the appropriate method of determining profit in most circumstances. It warrants emphasis, however, that this is *not* the only acceptable method for tax purposes. Since subsection 9(1) is silent on the method of accounting that one can use to calculate "profit," a taxpayer is free to use generally accepted accounting principles appropriate to his circumstances if the method is not prohibited by the Act or by judicial precedent.[46]

a) Payments in Advance
The accrual method is modified by the Act for certain payments. For example, payments received in advance of rendering a service or sale of goods are included in income even though the payments represent unearned amounts that would usually be excluded from

---

46 *Oxford Shopping Centres Ltd v Canada*, [1980] CTC 7 (FCTD), aff'd [1981] CTC 128 (FCA).

income for accounting purposes. Under accounting principles, un-earned revenue is considered a liability. For tax purposes, unearned revenue is included in income in the year that the taxpayer receives the payment, rather than when he earns the revenue. A taxpayer may, however, claim a reserve for goods and services to be delivered in the future.[47]

b) Receivables

A taxpayer is to include in income all amounts receivable by the taxpayer in respect of property sold or services rendered in the course of business carried out during the year.[48] "Receivable" means that the taxpayer has a clearly established legal right to enforce payment at the particular time under consideration:

> In the absence of a statutory definition to the contrary, I think it
> is not enough that the so-called recipient have a precarious right
> to receive the amount in question, but he must have a clearly
> legal, though not necessarily immediate, right to receive it.[49]

For example, in the construction industry, it is usual practice, when work is performed under a contract extending over a lengthy period of time, for interim payments to be made to the contractor. These payments, which are based on progress reports, are usually subject to a percentage holdback to ensure satisfactory completion of the project. In these circumstances, holdbacks need not be brought into income as receivables until such time as the architect or engineer has issued a final certificate approving the completion of the project.[50]

An amount is deemed to be receivable on the earlier of the day the account is actually rendered and the day on which it would have been rendered had there been "no undue delay" in rendering the account.

---

47   ITA, paras 12(1)(a) and 20(1)(m).

48   *Ibid*, para 12(1)(b).

49   *MNR v John Colford Contracting Co* (1960), 60 DTC 1131 at 1135 (Ex Ct), aff'd without written reasons [1962] SCR viii.

50   *Ibid*.

7) Professionals

a) Modified Accrual

The rules in respect of the computation of income of certain professionals (accountants, dentists, lawyers, medical doctors, veterinarians, and chiropractors) vary somewhat from the normal accrual basis of accounting. These professional businesses may report income on a so-called modified accrual basis by electing to exclude work in progress in the computation of income.[51] On the sale of the professional business, any work in progress previously excluded is brought into the income of the vendor.[52]

b) Work in Progress

Generally, if a professional elects to exclude work in progress in the computation of income, her income is computed on the basis of fees billed, subject to any adjustment for undue delay in billing. The election is binding on the taxpayer for subsequent years unless it is revoked with the consent of the minister.[53]

c) Advance Payments

Amounts received in advance of performance of services are included in income unless the funds are deposited in a segregated trust account.[54] For example, a lawyer who obtains a retainer that must be returned to the client in the event of non-performance of services may exclude the retainer from income if the funds are deposited in a trust account.[55] The taxpayer may, however, claim a

---

51   ITA, para 34(a).

52   *Ibid*, para 10(5)(a) and s 23.

53   *Ibid*, para 34(b); see Canada Revenue Agency, Interpretation Bulletin IT-457R, "Election by Professionals to Exclude Work-In-Progress from Income" (15 July 1988), online: www.cra-arc.gc.ca/E/pub/tp/it457r/it457r-e. txt.

54   ITA, *ibid*, para 12(1)(a).

55   Canada Revenue Agency, Interpretation Bulletin IT-129R, "Lawyers' Trust Accounts and Disbursements" (7 November 1986), online: www.cra-arc. gc.ca/E/pub/tp/it129r/it129r-e.txt.

deduction in respect of services that will have to be rendered after the end of the year.[56]

d) Farmers and Fishers

Income from a farming or fishing business may be calculated on a cash basis. Thus, the income of a taxpayer from a farming or fishing business is computed by aggregating amounts received in the year and deducting therefrom amounts paid in the year. Accounts receivable are included in income only when they are collected by the taxpayer.[57]

F. DRAFTING AGREEMENTS

Many business agreements contain financial clauses and refer to financial statements. The following are the more commonly used legal agreements:

- Buy-sell agreements;
- Partnership agreements;
- Purchase–sale of assets;
- Purchase–sale of sales;
- Joint ventures;
- Supply contracts;
- Minutes of settlement in litigation; and
- Marriage contracts.

Despite the variety of legal contracts, there is substantial commonality in the principles that apply to them. We discuss some of these principles following.

1) Mutuality

Equality is not always fair. It is said that the "law applies equally to rich as well as the poor from sleeping under the bridges of Paris";

---

56   ITA, para 20(1)(m).
57   *Ibid*, s 28.

an elegant phrase, to be sure, but one that has not been tested with empirical evidence. There are no cases reported on the rich sleeping under the bridges of Paris.

For the lawyer, the first question is whether he or she is representing the richer or poorer client. Assume, that A and B own 30 percent and 70 percent of the shares of a company, respectively. If they have an agreement — such as a buy–sell contract — that provides for a right of first refusal on the sale of shares, are the parties in equal circumstances to respond? Does A have the financial assets to take advantage of his right? If he does not, the right of first refusal is an apparition.

2) Past Agreements

Lawyers like precedents. They save time and reduce costs. They can be very productive and increase the gross margin on billings.

Precedents may, however, have embedded flaws. The executed agreement is the final product of past negotiations and concessions between the parties. Do the concessions in the negotiated document apply equally to the new situation for which the lawyer is considering using the precedent? With a "negotiated" precedent, your adversary can do no worse than his predecessor in the negotiations.

3) Form Documents

Form documents can be very useful and save time (and costs) and are even faster than custom-drafted precedents. The essential question is whether the form document has an inherent bias towards one party or the other. For example, a form lease is typically drafted for the benefit of the landlord and not the tenant. A partnership agreement is usually drafted for the benefit of the controlling partner and not for a benefit of a minority partnership interest. A sale of shares form document is usually drafted for the benefit of the vendor and not the purchaser. Hence, it is important to understand the inherent bias of the form.

4) Length of Documents

Power lies in the control over events. Is a long document better than a short document? The answer depends upon whether you are acting for the majority (controlling) or minority partner or shareholder. A shorter document is usually better for the majority partner in any venture. The majority partner has control unless inhibited by contract. Control allows one to pick the accounting principles, for example, that the business will apply under IFRS or GAAP in a particular situation. A longer agreement will generally be better for the non-controlling partner (shareholder) because it can contain provisions that circumscribe and curtail the power of the majority partner or shareholder.

5) Revenues or Net Income

The top line refers to the top of the income statement — revenues. The bottom line refers to the bottom of the income statement — net income. Should one focus on the top or bottom line in a contract that links performance to the financial statements?

The answer to whether one should link payment or compensation or reward to the top or bottom line depends, once again, upon the size of the ownership interest. A person with the majority interest has control. A person with the minority interest has no control.

A bottom line agreement will usually favour the majority interests. For example, the majority interest can determine accounting principles under IFRS or GAAP in respect of depreciation, accounts receivable write-downs, inventory obsolescence adjustments, amortization policies, and accrual of liabilities, such as deferred income taxes. The greater the opportunity to make decisions about accounting principles, the greater the opportunity for "creative accounting." To summarize, a majority interest owner will typically prefer a short agreement, and a bottom-line approach.

A minority-interest owner will prefer a long agreement so that he or she can stipulate as much as possible in the agreement to circumscribe the majority power. Thus, a minority-interest owner will prefer a top-line approach because there is less "creative accounting" in the top line. There is even less discretion in cash flow statements, but they are not always useful for legal agreements.

Actors, producers, and writers frequently work for royalties as a percentage of earnings, referred to as percentage points. Skilful accounting can convert winners into losers. Art Buckwald, for example, wrote the movie *Coming to America*, starring Eddie Murphy. The movie reputedly generated $100 million in sales, but showed a net loss on the bottom line for royalty purposes. Thus, the percentage points became "monkey points."

6) Life of the Agreement

Accounting is concerned with the allocation of expenditures between assets and expenses. The longer the life of the agreement, the less important is the accounting for allocations, provided that the business applies IFRS or GAAP consistently. This is because financial statements typically involve allocations between time periods. The importance of allocations diminishes over time. The longer the life of the agreement, the less critical the role of allocation over the life of the agreement.

Here too, the majority holder controls allocation decisions and royalty.

7) Terminology

It is best not to be too creative in drafting legal agreements involving financial terms. Instead, one should stick with words and phrases that have an accepted business meaning, history and jurisprudential support. The following words, and acronyms, have established legal meaning.

- IFRS
- GAAP
- GAAS
- Audit

- Review
- Compilation
- Net book value
- Opinion

8) Full and Proper Disclosure

The purpose of financial statements is to provide proper disclosure so that users of the statements can make proper decisions. Governments must make decisions on the appropriateness of taxes that the taxpayer declares; shareholders are entitled to a report of proper stewardship of their company; and investors need financial information to make investment decisions.

Regulators must ensure full and proper disclosure in a timely manner to ensure a smooth functioning of the Markets.

There is a difference, however, between disclosing information and having investors use it wisely. As Herbert Simon (Nobel Prize–winning economist) said,

> Information consumes the attention of its recipients. Hence a wealth of information creates a poverty of attention.[58]

The disclosure of information by itself is not enough. Users of financial statements, such as investors and analysts, must be savvy enough to decipher the information and analyze it in meaningful terms. Indeed, there is evidence to suggest that the greater the disclosure, the less likely it is to influence rational decisions.

G. IFRS AND GAAP

IFRS is concerned with principles that are relatively new in Canada and still being developed. The United States has not adopted IFRS.

---

58 Herbert A Simon, "Designing Organizations for an Information-Rich World" in Martin Greenberger, *Computers, Communication, and the Public Interest* (Baltimore, MD: The Johns Hopkins Press, 1971) at 40–41.

GAAP is well accepted in financial circles for use in financial statements. To be sure, GAAP is generally understood (at least by professional accountants). However, GAAP tends to be conservative and backward-looking, and it understates income and assets. GAAP is a good place to begin, but not necessarily to end for analytical purposes.

In legal agreements, particularly in cross-border contracts, one must determine whether IFRS or GAAP should apply. GAAPs evolve and change over time. Thus, one must ask:

- Should one apply the principle at the time of agreement?
- Should one apply the concept in effect from time to time (the ambulatory approach)?
- Should one apply GAAP at the time of invoking the agreement, but with some time adjustment?
- Which GAAP or IFRS should one apply — Canadian, American, or international?

H. BALANCE SHEET AGREEMENTS

Legal agreements often refer to balance sheet items. For example, a termination of a commercial agreement might refer to "insolvency," a term usually defined by reference to financial status. The purchase price of a business might be based on book value, net worth, or total assets. Similarly, restrictive covenants may be tied to working capital, tangible assets, or net worth. Credit lines are often linked to receivables, inventory, and fixed assets.

Each of the balance sheet agreement concepts uses terminology that needs to be clearly understood or defined in the agreement to ensure that all parties to the agreement are of the same mind.

I. INCOME STATEMENT AGREEMENTS

Many agreements rely on income statement measurements for their substance. For example, the following agreements would all contain items that appear regularly on the income statement:

1) Employment contracts;
2) Labour contracts;
3) Acquisition agreements;
4) Purchase price on future income;
5) Licence, royalty, and franchise amounts;
6) Partnerships and joint ventures;
7) Preferred share provisions; and
8) Pension benefits.

Hence, income statement terms, such as, gross income, operating profit, income taxes, and net income, should be considered and, if necessary, defined in the agreement.

Index

About the Author

Vern Krishna, CM, QC, FRSC, FCGA, MCIArb, earned a B Comm (Manchester), MBA, LLB (Alberta), DCL (Cambridge) and LLM (Harvard). He is a professor at the University of Ottawa Faculty of Law. He is also of Counsel, Borden Ladner Gervais LLP and Executive Director of the Tax Research Centre at the University of Ottawa. Professor Krishna is a member of the Order of Canada, an honourary Doctor of Laws from the Law Society of Ontario, and a Fellow of the Royal Society. He has been a Bencher of the Law Society of Upper Canada since 1991 and served as its Treasurer from 2001–03.

Professor Krishna is the author of *The Fundamentals of Canadian Income Tax*, now in its 9th edition, *Income Tax Law* (2012), three volumes on general taxation, corporate taxation, and international taxation in *Halsbury's Laws of Canada*, and the Editor of *Canada's Tax Treaties*. He is listed in *Who's Who* and *Lexpert* has recognized him in Best Lawyers in Canada in Trusts & Estates and Tax Law.